A Vanished World

A

ILLUSTRATIONS BY NANCY B. PERKINS

Vanished World

BY ANNE GERTRUDE SNELLER

SYRACUSE UNIVERSITY PRESS · 1964

Library of Congress Catalog Card No. 64-16923

First printing, June 1964
Second printing, October 1964

Manufactured in the United States of America by Vail-Ballou Press, Inc.

TO MY SISTER

Ethel

WHO SHARED THE AFFECTIONS AND
EXPERIENCES HERE SET DOWN

Foreword

THIS IS THE STORY not only of a vanished childhood, but also of a vanished world. The speechways we grew up with are gone, the habits and customs changed, the standards of conduct have been replaced by others quite different. The background of trees and meadows and orchards, of white houses and red barns, of stump fences and stone walls has disappeared and is as irrecoverable as though it had never been. The laurels are cut down.

But in age the land of lost content can be revisited. The trees of that far country still stand; the hills are clear and blue as on a winter day; the farms and the spires of the white churches remain untroubled and untouched by time.

Whether everything was as I have written about it I do not know—only that this is how the photography of time pictures it. The colors may be too dark or too bright.

The story here has to be told through the lives of those I watched and listened to—men and women working, talking, planning, loving, and dying. As they come and go, time moves backward and forward with them. That too is the way all that we remember comes and goes.

ANNE G. SNELLER

Brewerton, New York
November, 1963

Contents

ix

Contents

A Vanished World

Grandfather and Grandmother Moulton

MY GRANDFATHER was so old when I first remember him that I hardly realized we were in the same world. He was an ancestor, still walking around or sitting in his rush-bottomed chair reading by the kitchen fire. His bent figure, his thick grizzled hair, and his sharp black eyes were a little frightening. Sometimes he asked me to play checkers with him. He must have thought it would amuse me, for it could not have amused him to play checkers with a child who did it so badly. I did not enjoy checkers, and I did not wholly enjoy my grandfather.

Yet grandfather was our link to the first Moultons who came from England to America in 1637. Through his father, his long life touched the Revolutionary War and covered the building of the United States as it unfolded across a continent in the nineteenth century. It was from this Revolutionary great-grandfather, William Moulton, that the family tree took root in my mind. He had served in the war as a soldier for six months, not too strenuous a term for a country boy, but every little bit helped—and his grateful country rewarded him with a grant of land on Grantham Mountain in New Hampshire. It was chiefly rocks and forest, but there great-grandfather brought up his family. He had three wives, six sons, and three daughters, a very modest contribution to the census of that time. There was a tale handed down in the family that some unnamed, remote great-grandfather had taken an Indian girl as a blanket wife. Like most Americans the Moultons enjoyed believing that they had a little touch of Pocahontas in their veins, and the black eyes and hair that appeared every now and then among them bolstered the tradition. At least great-grandfather Moulton reared his children in an Indian love of the land and a Revolutionary attitude toward love of country and personal independence. "No one in those days," said my grandfather, "felt that he had to do or think what everybody else did," and grandfather himself thoroughly absorbed the nonconformist tradition of New England.

Grandfather's mother was the third wife, a pretty Irish girl who bequeathed her curling red hair to some lucky descendants. Of her sons only Joseph Myrick, my grandfather, succeeded in getting a book education. That was partly because he was the youngest and partly because he had the kind of mind to which education is a necessity. The academy at nearby Meriden offered Latin and algebra and astronomy, together with a thorough grounding in the common branches. There grandfather studied, and he told us that he sometimes went to school in winter with his feet and legs wrapped in rags to keep out the cold on the long walk down Grantham Mountain.

For the rest of his life grandfather was an avid reader of everything that fell in his way. His copy of the Koran with his penciled name in it is on my bookshelf now. Why did he buy the Koran? Perhaps it was because religion—all sorts and conditions of religion—was pondered and discussed in the nineteenth century as intensely as Communism is today. Grandfather was a freethinker, a name that by no means conveys the horror that conservative people then felt on hearing the word. For a freethinker was an atheist: he regarded the Bible as uninspired and the problem of a burning hell or a harpful heaven as purely unrealistic.

No one in his family would have minded grandfather's freethought if he could have been persuaded to keep it to himself. But his strong, shrewd, well-stocked mind and a somewhat dictatorial nature made argument irresistible to him. When the minister in his regular rounds came to tea, my grandmother was accustomed to plead with grandfather: "Now, Myrick, don't—don't get into an argument with the minister!"

Grandfather may have intended to keep the peace, but his doubts would not permit it. To his triumphant question: "How can a finite being commit an infinite sin?" the minister was forced to answer as well as he could.

But grandfather's religious debates belong to a later period. After his schooling was over, he worked on the farm and found picking up stones from the endless supply in the fields more and more distasteful. At nineteen he went to live as a teacher at Shaker Hill, and for two years taught the Shaker children, observed their curious religion, meditated on their beliefs, and learned the Shaker songs which he in turn taught to his own children. My mother's tenacious memory kept them in her mind, and she used to say and half-chant one of them to my sister Ethel and me.

> Come, Life, Shaker Life,
> Come, Life eternal,
> Shake, shake out of me
> All that is carnal.
> I'll take nimble steps
> I'll be a David
> I'll show Michel
> How he twice be-havèd.

The words meant nothing understandable to us, but the swaying rhythm was a delight.

Grandfather did not wish to stay any longer with the Shakers when the two years were up. Life with them was interesting, but had no future, and there were still more stones left on the Grantham farm than had ever been picked up. He thought he would hunt for a place where there were no stones, or at least a manageable number. His brother Emery had early given up the struggle and moved to New York State. Now he wrote glowingly of the smooth level land in northern Onondaga. Thither would grandfather go and never pick up another stone if he could help it. Much later, his sons found it necessary to do that work, but there was general agreement in the family that grandfather never engaged in it.

So in 1832 he left the hills and stones of New Hampshire behind him and started west on horseback. He was twenty-one years old. He must have been an impressive figure, too, riding along. He was well over six feet in height and very erect. His jet black hair and eyes and his high-bridged nose testified to the family legend of the Indian blanket wife. But

6

he was Yankee to the bone in speech and outlook, with a stern dignity not to be trifled with.

Almost at the end of his long ride he stopped in Pompey. Pompey is the highest part of Onondaga County, and though the hills around the village are not like Grantham Mountain, they are pleasant hills and overlook a lovely countryside. On the village green in Pompey there stood then a pillared white church that might have been transported from Lexington or Concord and not too far away was a tavern. Grandfather Moulton put up for the night at the tavern and, like all riders in ballads, he fell in love with the tavernkeeper's daughter and later married her.

But let no one think that my grandfather intended to settle among the hills of Pompey and repeat the experience he had fled from. His brother Emery's farm was at Cicero, ten miles north of Syracuse and not far away from Oneida Lake and River, with not a hill to get a plow over; and to a farm near his brother's, grandfather decided to take his bride. Everybody in Pompey felt very sorry for Eliza Moulton, going to live in Cicero, that was more than half swamp, filled with wild things and rattlesnakes and breathing out malaria on all who came near it. Nor was everybody so mistaken as grandmother hoped. The swamp is still there, some three thousand acres of it, and the rattlesnakes are there and sometimes venture into meadows neighboring on the swamp and get caught up by hay loaders or even impaled on rakes and carried into the barns.

About the time of the First World War, someone in authority, needing a project, thought of having the swamp drained and the muck soil beneath it set to growing vegetables. The attempt was made and the swamp torn up on the edges, but it refused to be conquered by time, money, labor, and dynamite. So the idea was abandoned, the swamp reclaimed its losses, and the wild creatures, the snakes, and the frogs have had their Eden to themselves ever since. But a wife in the 1830's, whatever her fears, followed her Adam, and happily grandfather's living space was at least ten miles from the swamp.

I do not know how much land grandfather was able to purchase at first, but little by little he acquired some fourteen nearby parcels, irregular in shape and with the boundary lines vaguely indicated on the deeds by such phrases as "as far as the ash tree on the Lawrence corner." The deeds cover a period of many years, for grandfather would sell off a piece when he could get another more to his liking. One hundred and twenty years later, when the farm passed into the hands of strangers, there was great difficulty in getting a legal search that checked with the old deeds, for certainly grandfather had never reflected that ash trees are finite.

In the beginning there was the house, large enough for life as it was lived then and colored by the weather the silver grey of all unpainted wood houses. There was an orchard at one side and great trees around the front, pine and maple and one huge tamarack. And there was a long barn and a lane leading into the fields and ending in a grove of mighty chestnut trees.

But the woods came up close to the barn, and there were seven creeks to cross on dubious little bridges in planting or harvesting time. In summer the creeks sometimes dried away, but in a rainy season they could get up surprising little floods of their own when the water rose to the bellies of the horses. Grandfather must have learned very early that farming was not much more profitable to him in New York State than in New Hampshire, or it may have been that his Yankee mind suggested a diversified economy. So his farm, rather more than most, came to resemble a manor courtyard in the Middle Ages. The buildings were set about so as to form a wide circle—the barn, the long sheepfold, the great gate, the well, the cheesehouse, the cooper shop, the lane gates, the pigpen, the henhouse, and back to the barn again. All the buildings were of the same silver grey color as the house.

My own memories of my grandmother are shadowy, for she died when I was three and a half. Her funeral was on a dark December afternoon. I was called to the kitchen window to watch the funeral procession go by and had to be lifted up to see it, and what I saw was a long black line against the white snow, moving slowly along the road. At that time funeral processions always went as slowly as the horses could walk. No one was hurried to his grave. The picture of the funeral train is clear in my mind still, although it had no meaning then. What I really know of Grandmother Moulton is what others told me.

Eliza Hibbard Moulton was very little and of extreme delicacy of feature and of very fair complexion. Her eyes were deep blue and her fine thin hair was the shade of brown that attracts no attention. She had the education of her time; she spun and wove and sewed beautifully; she cooked excellently and transmitted her skill to her daughters; and she bore ten children to my grandfather, two sets of twins among them. She was gentle and hard working, so that grandfather's choice of her offered no reason for repentance on his part.

One trait of hers that all my aunts spoke of was my grand-

9

mother's superstitions. She was often under the shadow of signs and portents and threatening old sayings. Fortunately, only one of her children inherited her faith in them—Aunt Elvie, the youngest child. While Aunt Elvie often quoted the signs, when she was seriously questioned about them, she took refuge in, "Well, that's what folks used to say." In general, the Moultons were, as "folks used to say," too hardheaded to believe easily.

Uncle Charles, the oldest of the ten children, was nineteen when the youngest was born. The names of the ten were all family names except one: Charles and Jane and Sophia; then the first set of twins, William and Wealthy; next Alfred and the second twins, Ann and Ellen; then Sarah. All these names look out over and over from the pages of Moulton history. But like the Vicar of Wakefield's wife, who read novels during her pregnancy and in consequence gave her daughters romantic names, grandmother had been reading a story in the *New York Ledger* before her tenth arrived, and the heroine's name was given to the baby. "Elvie the Foundling" became Elvie Ermina Moulton.

Grandmother had not wanted this tenth child, so the older aunts told me, and yet this particular child grew to be the best loved by the whole family. Her loving heart, her overflowing kindness, her eager generosity, her willingness to do all that would help or give pleasure to the others made Elvie the special joy and blessing that grandmother had not foreseen.

In the early years of her married life, poverty pressed hard and grandmother had to exercise the utmost prudence in every household matter. Comfort was possible only if children learned early that thrift must be practiced even in the smallest details. It was natural that she quoted wise old sayings handed down for many generations to strengthen her own opinions on economy and extravagance. "Waste not; want not" was often on her tongue, along with "If you don't take care of poor things, you will never have good ones to take care of," and "You will never miss the water till the well runs dry." In an age of faucets, the last proverb has no significance for the young. Looking at one's self in the mirror was not exactly forbidden; there were too few looking glasses for steady practice, but "Handsome is as handsome does" was ready to check any rising vanity.

These sayings in turn were passed on to Ethel and me as rules for conduct, and we understood that "Where there's a will, there's a way" and "If at first you don't succeed, try, try again" meant that you couldn't give up just because you felt like it. They were stern sayings with no loophole to escape duty and effort.

Probably grandmother was not less happy than other women in the neighborhood. Her children loved her dearly, though they were completely undemonstrative. They showed their affection by works rather than words. In 1857, my uncle Charles gave his mother a tiny shining gold quarter-eagle, as it was called, worth two dollars and a half. It was newly minted with the 1857 date on it. Grandmother never spent it except perhaps in imagination; it was too precious for anything but cherishing. In the end she gave it to Aunt Elvie, born in 1857, and the cherishing process has gone on ever since. Nor was grandmother shut away from society. The neighbors came with their knitting of an afternoon, relatives arrived to spend the winter, and homeless old folks found grandmother's house a refuge for an indefinite stay, during which washing dishes, bringing the water, or filling the woodbox were regarded as adequate return for their keep.

Grandfather continued to have activities of his own. Besides the profits from the farm, the salt industry offered further opportunities. It was salt which by 1840 had brought the first prosperity to the area. The village of Salina on the northern side of Syracuse was then rather more important than the city which later absorbed it. Salina was named from the salt springs on the edge of Onondaga Lake. These salt springs had been known for generations to the Iroquois Indians, Mohawks, Oneidas, Onondagas, Cayugas, and Senecas. The deer knew them well too and all the other wild creatures that love salt.

Little by little, from 1825 on, the salt industry flourished, though it was at first primitive enough. The salt water was pumped into huge iron kettles and the water boiled away. But this method was slow and expensive, for wood had to be cut and fires stoked. It occurred to someone that the sun could do the work cheaper and faster. Wells were drilled over the springs, water forced down them to absorb the salt, then forced up and carried in log pipe lines to the salt sheds and left there to the mercy of the sun. It was astonishing how quickly evaporation took place. The box-like wooden sheds were spread over a considerable space and had covers. In the midst of them was a bell mounted on a high standard. When it rained or threatened to rain, the bell was rung and all the women nearby rushed out to cover the boxes and keep the salt dry. For this service they lived rent free in the wretched little houses near the salt works.

The salt industry caught the first big wave of Irish immigration. The Irish bog boys or "salt boiler boys," as they were called, were feared by sober citizens. They were young and poor and tough, spoiling for a fight and almost universally unable to read and write. The Liverpool Academy near the salt springs suffered at their hands. During the summer term only little girls and boys too young to work went to school. The winter term gave the older boys their chance to learn readin'-and-'ritin'-and-'rithmetic, and the salt boiler boys with nothing to do in winter came to school en masse. Apparently they had no wish to master the three difficult arts, but they had a grand opportunity to rush the teacher, throw him out, and prove that muscle conquers brains.

For the trustees of the Liverpool Academy the matter was serious. During one winter term about 1840, various teachers had been thrown out and none had any wish to return to the combat either to pluck the shamrock or plant the seed of etiquette. And here comes grandfather.

How the trustees heard of him I never knew, but they did ride out to the farm and offer grandfather the job on any terms. This, they recognized, was not a position—it was an invitation to front-line warfare. Grandfather thought he could manage.

His only preparation on the morning of the first day of school was to take with him his ox goad, weighted with lead in the butt end, and with this in hand he entered the schoolroom. The boys were waiting and ready. He called them to order, and according to pattern they started to rush him. Grandfather backed up against the wall, and as they came on he laid about him with the heavy end of the ox goad. He was very strong and accustomed to flail grain, and the Irish skulls cracked under the blows. The boys fled and grandfather turned to the business of the day. He had established law and order and he taught successfully all winter.

More valuable to grandfather than his schoolteacher's

13

wages was the effect of salt making on his cooper shop. Coopering had been profitable from the beginning. Salt created a new demand, for it was shipped in barrels all over the country. Wood of the right sort was at hand, and grandfather, with relatives and helpers, was busy in the shop all day long. It was pleasant work in good company, but it demanded skill and strength.

In 1847 the first plank road in the United States was built between Syracuse and Central Square, some twenty miles to the north, and it went past grandfather's farm. Over this road went four stages a day, two each way, carrying passengers, mail, and light freight—and over this road went grandfather's clean white barrels for the clean white salt. The new plank road made the problem of transportation easy. It was the finest kind of road until concrete came. Men worked all the year round replacing worn plank and mending any spot that threatened danger to the heavy stages and lumber wagons or light carriages.

Since it had been built by a chartered private company, the plank road was expected to pay its way and reward the builders. There were three toll gates, spaced six or seven miles apart and all built similarly: on one side of the road a house for the gatekeeper to live in, and on the other side a high board wall, built parallel to the road and attached to the house by a long sloping roof. A heavy bar went across the road from the gatekeeper's house to the wall side. The bar was pushed back out of the way by day and closed late at night so that farmers driving to market at three o'clock in the morning could not escape the toll. The toll was five cents a horse each way. If a man drove a team from Central Square to Syracuse, he paid a sixty cent toll.

Much of the profit for the company depended on the honesty of the gatekeepers. A strict oversight was kept by the directors. A very old gentleman once told me that at a meeting of the directors where he was present, one of them

demanded that a certain gatekeeper be dismissed. He knew for a fact, he said, that the gatekeeper's family had had *oysters* twice that winter, and he couldn't have bought oysters out of his wages without cheating.

Grandfather had been eager to have the plank road built, and he had contributed land for the third toll gate house and garden. The land he gave was on the north side of his house just beyond the orchard. His teams therefore had only two toll gates to go through and only two tolls to pay when he sent loads of barrels to Salina. This was important, for he was sending three loads every week. Each load consisted of a hundred and one barrels. The odd barrel paid the toll and left the profit from the hundred others for grandfather. It was the cooper shop that put grandfather and his sons on their financial feet.

Uncle Charles told me all about coopering, salt, and the hundred and one barrels and I turned it into rhyme:

> The springs are trapped—
> Trapped in iron kettles, twenty in a block.
>   Bubbling, frothing, up comes the water,
>   Caught in prison kettles as it bursts from the rock.
> The coopers are busy—
>   (Twenty—thirty kettles!)
> Clean white barrels for the clean white salt;
>   Hark how the kettle sings!
>   Thirty—forty salt springs!
> But the railroad and steamboat
>   See how they have changed things!
>   Springs are not immortal,
>   Time may call a halt—
> Time may have a word to say about our making salt.

It was true. Salt making and coopering gradually ceased. The Irish found work for their restless brains and entered politics; the West was calling and the Civil War already cast its shadow ahead. The plank road, however, continued for many years, though the section from Cicero to Central

Square was given up about 1870. That part of the road was succeeded by a hard gravel highway on which toll was still paid. Eventually, when the charter for the road expired, the toll gates ceased to function; the land grandfather had given to the company was bought back by Uncle Alfred and the circle was complete.

Grandfather might be busy, but he often had to take time out for his migraine headaches. He lay in a darkened room while grandmother applied remedies that did no good. When the pain finally subsided he would call out, "Marm, make me some buttermilk pop." Then grandmother knew the worst was over and hurried to make the pop. I wish I knew how buttermilk pop was made or what it looked like and how it tasted. Mother said that as well as she could remember, the buttermilk was heated and a sort of dumpling stirred in it. It sounds like a migraine in itself, but for some reason the heat and sourness settled the sick head and the sympathetic stomach.

Sick or well, discipline went on in the household with or without tears. Usually grandfather's sternness was sufficient to enforce obedience and repentance. Sometimes the threat of punishment seemed quite as bad as the reality might have been. Mother got herself in trouble through her love of words. A new word heard meant that she would use it at the first opportunity. Somewhere, somehow, from someone, she heard the word "bully." It was used evidently in the later Theodore Roosevelt sense, for mother understood it to mean pleasant, nice, just to one's liking or approval. A chance to show it off came at school, and mother promptly said, "Oh, that's bully!"

Her two older sisters heard her and went into shock. On

the way home from school they decided that they must in duty report the awful word to Pa. They reported. Grandfather called mother aside, looked at her long enough to establish the atmosphere of a court room, and said: "Sarah, you have used an indecent word. If you ever use that word again, I shall whip you hard." Mother did not understand why the word was wrong nor dare to ask, but she felt deeply disgraced and she knew that the nice new word was an outcast from her vocabulary forever.

Of his grandchildren, grandfather was fondest of Ethel and it was Ethel to whom he told family stories. But he had no mind to let her grow up in ignorance. One spring afternoon when she was not more than six or seven, she was staying at grandfather's for supper to eat the first maple syrup of the year on Aunt Elvie's hot biscuits. Aunt Elvie's biscuits were never long for this world. They were huge puffy affairs, cork-light with golden-brown tops and golden butter to spread on them and golden syrup for their perfect companion. Every one at the table did well by the biscuits and Ethel's superlative efforts fixed grandfather's attention. He eyed her for a few minutes and finally laid down his knife.

He said, "E-thel, you're eating a lot of biscuit. You're old enough to learn how to spell two useful words. You can't have another biscuit till you learn to spell it, and you must learn to spell victuals too and that will cover the butter and syrup."

Ethel was willing. She had a quick, retentive memory and mastered "biscuit" and "victuals" in no time. (There were still biscuits waiting to be eaten.) But why should a harmless word like "vittles" turn out to be spelled "victuals"?

She never forgot grandfather's spelling lesson and "victuals" was a useful word. It was constantly on the tongues of country folks then, taking the place of words like meals or food. A man got his vittles where he worked and at grandfather's table he got good vittles. As between "eats" as a noun and "victuals," I'm all for vittles.

But the life of my grandparents was not without variations. They took a trip to New Hampshire in 1851 and saw all grandfather's brothers and sisters and cousins. It was an undertaking to pay a three weeks' visit and leave behind a big household to be fed and looked after. And who was left in charge as housekeeper? Who but their oldest daughter Jane, aged eleven, already able to bake excellent bread and pie, and wash and iron and sew. She could be depended upon to do what was right in any emergency. Sophy, at nine, was an active second and Charles, at thirteen, could be trusted to look after things in general. But the real burden rested on Jane's young shoulders and she carried it nobly. It became a family legend that Jane at eleven was equal to anything.

But if the relatives on one side were visited, those on the other side must not be neglected. So not long afterwards a journey westward was made, to Lockport, where grandmother's brothers and sisters were living. Lockport is about twenty-five miles north of Buffalo, and the locks on the Erie Canal were there. Grandmother would not have ventured anywhere alone, but with grandfather along all would be well—if only grandfather didn't get to arguing religion with someone on the boat! For they were traveling in that most delightful and leisurely way—by packet boat on the canal, through a green countryside that must then have been unbelievably lovely. Grandmother had a two-handled wicker traveling basket, a pretty and commodious affair so well made that it is still in existence. She wore her second-best dress on the boat and had her best dress and a dark calico in the basket. The calico would serve when grandmother helped out with the work, as a visitor should. When she came home, grandmother said it was the happiest journey she had ever made. Not only was the packet boat wonderful, but grandfather hadn't mentioned religion once on the whole trip. She thought, though, he had had a hard struggle with himself once or twice when the cousins got to going about hell.

As my mother grew older, grandfather came to enjoy her mind and her interest in reading, so like his own. When he lay dying at eighty-five and mother was sitting by him, he said, "Sarah, I'm dying. You tell them I wasn't afraid." That was his final firm rejection of the consolations of religion.

His funeral was on the wildest of March days. The long black coffin was placed in the back parlor and on it a sheaf of golden wheat, always used then for the death of the old, symbol of the length of days and the gathered harvest. I am not sure but that I like it better than the meaningless masses of gladioli that sometimes seem to take away the dignity of the dead by claiming attention for themselves. Death with a single sheaf did not pretend to be an affair of flowers.

The War Remembered

THE WIDE SHADOW of the Civil War stretched across my late Victorian childhood so that it is sometimes hard to remember that I did not actually live through the war. Although it had ended eighteen years before I was born, the talk of it went on over and over; the old soldiers were everywhere, and it governed our politics and selected our candidates. The Republican party was still young, and the town of Cicero so completely Republican that it was difficult to find a Democrat willing to run for any office, even for that of the humble pathmaster or poormaster. Of late years as these offices have been ennobled to Highway Superintendent and Welfare Commissioner, and as the Democratic party has steadily encroached upon its rival, there is no trouble at all in persuading someone to try his luck. Yet the town today is still reckoned bedrock Republican.

In our district school the history books devoted at least a third of their contents to the Civil War and every battle was set down in detail, often with a map beside it. I suppose no generation after ours was required to learn and know the battles, generals, plans, armies, and achievements of both sides as we were. The events were recited without bitterness and with a breath-catching thankfulness that in the end the Union had been saved. There remained in our minds forever the rollcall of battle names: Shiloh and Shenandoah, Malvern Hill and Cold Harbor, the Wilderness and Island Number Ten. If the words were not beautiful in themselves, they became so to us by the splendor of association.

If I felt I had a part in the war, my mother had strengthened the idea by the stories that she told us. She was nine years old when the war broke out—a child of strong imagination and with a memory that preserved the events of the four years so vividly that we saw the war and lived it.

Grandfather was a Lincoln man from the beginning. The battle of Bull Run was fought on his fiftieth birthday. As if his anxiety over the outcome of the war were not enough, it so happened that, scarce as Democrats were, his neighbors on both sides were Copperhead Democrats; that is, Democrats who sympathized with the South, thought the Southern states had a right to secede, and publicly rejoiced when they won a victory. In the early years of the war they appeared to be winning all the victories. When the newspaper reported their successes, Mr. Wright and Mr. Wicks would come shaking their papers triumphantly under grandfather's very nose as if they had led the Confederate armies themselves.

Grandfather relied on the *New York Tribune* for news of the war, and Horace Greeley's opinions determined his. The paper was brought out from Syracuse by the stage that ran between the city and Central Square, and was thrown off at the tollgate which one of the Copperhead neighbors kept.

Mother was always sent down to get it and would run as fast as she could to learn the news. After supper, holding a candle in one hand slanted across the paper in the other, grandfather read aloud to the family—news of battles, changes in generals, and sometimes Mr. Greeley's severe criticisms of Mr. Lincoln, which seriously disturbed grandfather and almost shook his faith in what his Yankee tongue called "Mr. Grilley's paper."

When the news of Gettysburg came, grandmother stopped him in the middle of the reading. "Don't! Don't!" she said. "I can't bear it."

Though the enlistment from the village and countryside had been heavy, no son of grandmother's was in the Army —Uncle Charles was a cripple, Uncle Bill was needed on the farm, and Uncle Alfred was thought too young to go. But from grandfather's cooper shop went the Warner boys, Henry and Charley, Irving Coonley, and George Welch. There was a special sadness in their going, for Aunt Wealthy was engaged to Henry Warner and Aunt Jane to George Welch. George and Irving came safely home, but Henry and Charley Warner died of wounds and camp fever. The chaplain of their company wrote to grandfather telling him what good and steadfast soldiers they had been and how much loved and lamented by their comrades. When the news of Henry's death came, mother remembered, Aunt Welt threw her apron over her head and went out to the garden alone. After a time mother followed her, eager to offer comfort if she could. She found Aunt Welt staring into distance, and when mother spoke to her Aunt Welt cried out, "Oh, Sarah, as long as I live I shall never have another grief like this!"

Lincoln's first call for troops had been eagerly answered. Of the men who had gone from the town there were good soldiers and poor ones, the simple and the shrewd, the sensible and the short-minded, the brave and the cowardly. Stories about them drifted back home and the folks there had a fairly clear idea of which ones had measured up to their good opinion of them and which ones had confirmed their former judgment. Everyone heard without surprise that Doc Davey had pulled Danny Freer out from behind a stump and threatened to shoot him if he didn't come on with the rest of them. But only a few, and those not until long afterward, knew that Abel Cooper had deserted and then, stricken in conscience, had re-enlisted under another name and fought till the war was over. It was under the assumed name that he drew his pension. Those who knew the story considered that Abel had squared accounts and was entitled to the pension. He was loved and respected all his life, and the G.A.R. held its meetings in the big room over his store.

One day when I was quite a little girl on an errand to the candy counter in Abel Cooper's store, he and I discussed the war as equals. He said there was a picture up in the G.A.R. room that I might like to see. Upstairs the picture was hung high on the wall, and Mr. Cooper lifted me up on a table so that I would miss nothing. It was a picture of the Andersonville stockade—a terrible picture: the skeleton faces, the dead, the dying, the open graves, the brutal-faced guards with guns and clubs, trees without leaves, men being beaten away from a tiny stream—no savage detail was missing.

Mr. Cooper explained to me all the torments that the men went through there. He had heard it at first hand from one of his comrades, Jim Crampton, who had been a prisoner in Andersonville and had lived to come home and tell the awful story.

Mr. Crampton went to our church, and after I had seen the picture I understood why he looked like a creature that had gone through death. So Lazarus returning to life must have looked, I thought. His head was a bare skull, the skin like yellow wax, the eyes settled far back in the head, and the mouth a toothless, gaping wound. Once in church when he passed the collection basket I had a glimpse of his hands—claws with strange, ridged fingernails. In recent years, novels and plays and histories have been written about Andersonville. But Mr. Cooper's picture told its story to me, and those who saw Jim Crampton needed nothing more.

As the war went on and defeat followed defeat and victory seemed more and more doubtful, enlistments slackened and the government resorted to bounties and the draft. It may be that as the knowledge of what war was like reached communities that had had no conception of it, men felt more reluctant to face its horrors. The first bounties, mother said, were one hundred dollars, but gradually they rose to one thousand dollars, and a man if drafted could hire a substitute for three hundred dollars. Uncle Tim Wright found a substitute. He had a sick wife and young children on a poor farm and probably felt justified in staying at home. A modern draft board would doubtless have exempted him. But hiring a substitute was not the only method of escaping the war. Two of the prominent men of the town, Mr. Adam Meriwether and Mr. William Harter, both members of the Universalist Church, had all their teeth pulled so that they could plead inability to chew hardtack and be declared unfit for service. At least rumor said their teeth would have lasted longer if peace had suddenly come about.

To men on farms who remained at home, the years of the war often brought increasing prosperity. There was plenty of help for hire in the large families growing up in the neighborhood; prices for farm products were high; and without any lack of patriotism, my grandfather found himself well-to-do. But the things the womenfolks needed and wanted were high-priced too. Calico took on the airs of linen and was almost too costly for everyday wear. One of the stories we loved to hear mother tell was about Aunt Elvie and the pink calico.

However grandmother managed it, and only she knew how, in the midst of wartime shortages and worries she bought calico to make dresses for her two youngest daughters, mother and Aunt Elvie. Probably she made the effort because she was tired of seeing them in the long succession of hand-me-downs from their five older sisters. Pink calico. At seven years old, little Elvie's heart was thrilled. Above all colors she loved pink to the end of her ninety-sixth year, and she was to have a new pink calico dress!

The material had been laid on a shelf in the closet to be safe from dust till the day of making it up came. Elvie, considering that her eyes had seen the glory once, did not think she could sleep that night without a second look for reassurance that the pink calico existed and was waiting in the closet. The others were too busy to pay attention to this youngest child, and she lit her candle unobserved and went softly with it into the closet and shut the door.

Nobody knew how it happened, least of all Elvie. In her eagerness she may have held the candle too close, but the next thing was the scream of a frightened child. The wonderful calico was burning up. She was rescued without injury, the fire was put out, and the holes burned straight down through the folded goods were all that remained to break a little girl's heart. But the dresses were made up with piecing and patching and undoubtedly were thoroughly worn out.

Mother was thirteen when the war ended. She was living that spring with her older sister Sophia on a ninety-acre farm that grandfather had recently bought. It was a good two miles across lots and over creeks from this farm to the home place—far too long a distance for the hired men to waste time going back and forth for meals. Grandfather decided that Aunt Sophia, twenty-three years old, should live on the farm to cook and wash for the men and that mother should stay with her for company.

Early one April morning, they saw grandfather hurrying toward the house and ran to meet him. Something terrible must have happened, they knew, for the tears were streaming down his face and he could hardly speak.

"I came over to tell you. Lincoln—Lincoln is dead. He's been shot." They stared at him and grandfather went on, "And now with Lincoln gone, prob'ly the South will start up the war again."

That was the way the news was told, mother said, and everywhere it spread grief and the same foreboding—the South would start up the war again.

Then Lincoln's body was borne across the country on its way to Springfield and rested briefly in many cities. When the train halted in Syracuse, grandfather and my uncles were among the crowd gathered to pay their last respects to one whose purposes they understood. It was thought proper by

the family that all the menfolks should go out to meet the train, and no one thought of proposing that they should take with them the young sister who would have remembered it longest of all.

The strange thing about this story, as mother told it to us, was that beyond our knowing that the name of the assassin was John Wilkes Booth and that he was an actor, nothing much was ever said of him. The greatness of his victim obscured him completely. Only Booth's name bore witness to the sad history that linked them together.

A month after Lincoln's death, Jefferson Davis was captured and put in prison. The next news was that Horace Greeley had signed the bail bond to free him. Mother said that grandfather was shocked and angered by Mr. Greeley's action. Horace Greeley was helping Jefferson Davis! A traitor going free through the efforts of one of Lincoln's friends! What would Lincoln have said to that?

As a whole, the soldiers who fought in the Civil War were not writers. There was no spate of books by the ordinary soldier such as followed the World Wars. But to most of the men who came back from the South, the war was the greatest experience of their lives. They never traveled so far again; the peace and safety of the home country were enough. But if they did not write, they talked. They told stories of things seen, done, or imagined. They argued strategy and had good and bad words to say for the generals, and on every occasion some of them were ready to deliver orations. No one begrudged them the pride and comfort they found in doing so.

Uncle Alfred always regretted that he had been too young to fight in the war. Fifty years after the battle of Gettysburg, he had at least the happiness of going to the battlefield. In

July, 1913, the government was sending trains to carry all old soldiers, Union and Confederate, to Gettysburg for the commemoration of the battle; and Uncle Alfred determined to go with them if I would go along to look after him. Three hundred men had once marched away from our part of the countryside. Now those that were left would go South again.

It was a very hot morning when we joined the blue-dressed soldiers on the train in Syracuse. On the journey the old men talked steadily of things they had done and seen in the war—worn stories with the edges blurred by fifty years. A surprising number of them had fought at Gettysburg, for the New York regiments were heavily engaged. What I heard them say of the battle then and at other times, I thought of as the speech of one man, though it was in reality the gathered speech of many men, halting as they tried to remember or failed to find the words for their experience. I have written it down, one speaking for all.

"It was weather just about like this—awful hot, you know. We could hardly stand it. But we had been heading north and that kept us going. Gettysburg was a pretty village, nice shade trees, and a lot of white houses. Not painted like ours at home, but whitewashed, and everything neat and clean. The wheat was ripe—as good wheat as I ever saw—and there were peach orchards. We didn't have much idee what we were getting into, but we judged it was going to be bad. The first two days were the worst any of us had ever lived through, if we did live through 'em, and the third seemed there wouldn't be anybody alive by the end of it. . . .

"I was with the gunners on Cemetery Ridge, they called it. It had got to be afternoon and the shelling had let up some and it was almost quiet. All of a sudden we see the rebels coming across the valley right straight at us. We were high enough up so we got the whole length and breadth of 'em—fifteen thousand we heard afterwards. They didn't make a sound hardly with every man moving forward together. I remember my breath kinda stopped, knowing what was going to happen to 'em, as if I wanted to warn 'em and send 'em back. But we just watched and waited. It was the handsomest sight I ever saw, those men marching, if it hadn't been war. . . .

"I've thought a good many times I've wished I could have heard Lincoln make his speech about the battle. The place where he stood wasn't so far from where we were, I guess. I've heard the speech read often, read it myself, but that isn't the same as hearing him say it, and I wanted to see him. I never did get to. He was a homely man, they always said, but he knew the right thing to say. I liked what he said about the men who fought there having dedicated the place without the need of anything more. Better than a lot of talk."

The next day the old soldiers, uncle, and I saw the spot where the words were spoken that we hold as prophecy— *that this nation, under God, shall have a new birth of freedom and that government of the people . . . shall not perish from the earth.*

We went on to the Devil's Den. Men in blue and grey were pointing out where the deadly sharpshooters had been posted, and a Union soldier was telling how he had gone at night to Spangler's Spring for a drink and had found the water mixed with blood. Close by, two Confederate soldiers listened. One of them drawled, "Fifty years ago we'uns didn't expect to meet you'uns here today." Lincoln had said: *Suppose you go to war. You cannot fight always.*

Mother taught us songs of the war very early in our child-hood. The Union armies were singing armies, and their songs were brought home and sung for many years after-wards. In the beginning a spirit of elation breathed through them and they were eager and joyous. You felt that quality in

> We are coming, Father Abraham,
> A hundred thousand strong

and in

> Yes, we'll rally round the flag, boys,
> We'll rally once again—
> Shouting the battle cry of freedom.

And no army ever had a better marching song than "John Brown's Body."

But as the war went on, there was a change in the songs. The tunes grew plaintive and the words were melancholy, rising out of the deep longings of homesick, tired men. They were not unlike sad old ballads. Mother never forgot them, and sang them to us. There was "The Vacant Chair":

> We shall meet but we shall miss him,
> There will be a vacant chair,

and "Tenting on the Old Camp Ground":

> Give us a song to cheer
> Our weary hearts, a song of home.

One song was bitterly reminiscent of McClellan's constant report of "All quiet along the Potomac":

> 'Tis nothing—a private or two, now and then . . .
> Not an officer lost—only one of the men.

The War Remembered

I loved "The Faded Coat of Blue" for its refrain

> No more the bugle calls the weary one.

Another began

> Heavily falls the rain

and had a sorrowful repetition

> And yet, and yet, we cannot forget
> That many brave boys must fall.

The soldiers also picked up songs of the woes of slavery. Some were in the speech of the slaves, but most of them I think were written by others who knew of and sympathized with their suffering. "My Darling Nellie Gray," which told the story of a slave sold to toil in the cotton and the cane, was not of slave origin. But there was a song that was the cry of a slave's rebellious spirit:

> Oh, freedom! Freedom over me!
> And before I'd be a slave I'd be carried to my grave
> And go home to my Master and be free.

Another brought a picture of swamps and bloodhounds.

> And at night when all was dark
> We could hear the watchdogs bark
> And we'd listen to the murmuring of the waves
> Oh, they seemed to say to me
> "All ye people shall be free"
> In those agonizing cruel slavery days.

One song that may have sprung up among the Negroes themselves told the story of Nicodemus, who was bought for a bag full of gold.

33

'Twas his last sad request
Ere we laid him to rest
In the shadow of the old gum tree
"Wake me up for the Great Jubilee."

And when the Day of Jubilee, the Day of Freedom, arrived, there was a rousing chorus:

Run tell 'Lijah to wake up Pomp
Meet us by the gum tree down in the swamp
For we're gwine to wake Nicodemus today!

Since mother never saw the words printed and learned the tune only by hearing it sung, it is likely that both words and music underwent a change, but the wild joy over freedom in one or two of the songs was not lost.

The songs of the Confederate soldiers also reached our community. Some soldiers returning from the war brought with them a Negro boy. He worked on a neighborhood farm and went with the other children to school, where his presence created no resentment, only interest. Mother's memory of him was that he had a beautiful singing voice and taught them Southern war songs, particularly "The Bonnie Blue Flag that Bears the Single Star."

The Grand Army of the Republic—the G.A.R., our first alphabetical abbreviation—was highly important from 1865 to the end of the century. Not much was heard in our town of attempts to get pensions raised. From the point of view of self-interest the G.A.R. concentrated on electing to office candidates who would give minor or even major jobs to veterans. The pensions were small, twelve dollars a month, and around 1900, when age was really beginning to creep up on the soldiers, the amount was raised to twenty dollars.

The average G.A.R. enjoyed his position in the community. In winter came the annual Campfire, which everyone attended. It was held in the Parker House hall, decorated for the occasion with flags and evergreen. The hotel was unduly large for the size of the village, and that added to the grandeur of any meeting held there. First came the speech of the evening. Sometimes an outside speaker was brought in, but the audience preferred home talent and was willing to listen to the same thing every year. They were delighted to hear Danny Freer describe how he had fit, bled, and died for the Union, and they did not hold his retreat behind a stump against him. Danny wasn't much of a soldier, they knew, but war was scary business and maybe they would have acted like that themselves.

The veterans as hosts appeared in dark blue uniforms with the G.A.R. badge pinned to their coats, and their black slouch hats had a little laurel wreath in front made of *real gold*. Refreshments too were the same each year, supposedly what the soldiers had eaten. Very black coffee was served in tin cups such as the soldiers had used; baked beans and hardtack went with the coffee, and sometimes there was ham as a concession to nonmilitary appetites. The rest of the evening was spent in dancing the Lancers, Virginia Reel, Portland Fancy, a waltz or two, and square dances of intricate variety. The leader of the three-piece orchestra called off in the voice of a major general, and commanded the dancers to swing and circle and join hands.

Hardtack was a magic word to me. No one explained what it was, but it was a part of the Campfire and I longed to taste it. One year when Ethel and I were still too small to be taken along and were left at home for safekeeping with the hired girl, mother promised to bring us some hardtack. The next morning I got up early, unwilling to put off the delicious experience another minute. I went to the sitting room where a bright coal fire made the room light. Mother had left her best black plush coat lying on a chair, and I ran to look in the pocket for the hardtack. It was there. *And hardtack was only a dry square cracker.*

The Campfire I remember best was one when Ethel spoke a very long piece beginning, "Boys in blue, once more we greet you." It went on with a flowery tribute to the Boys. Ethel stood up on the little platform where the orchestra sat and she looked so pretty and knew her piece so well that she received great applause. One of the G.A.R.'s, Mr. Thomas Scott, rushed over to my father and whispered that it was the finest thing of the evening; in fact, it was possibly the finest thing Mr. Scott had ever heard. Mr. Scott was an Englishman, so his opinion was valuable and father admired him from that time forward.

About three years later, when I had arrived at speakerhood, I recited a piece at the Campfire. It told of a soldier escaping from prison, and the signal for him to make the attempt was the whistling from outside of a bar from "Annie Laurie." I couldn't whistle and didn't want to perform, but father said he would stand in the back of the hall and at the right moment would whistle "I'd lay me down and die." So it was arranged, and father whistled and the soldier escaped and I lived through it. I was not the success that Ethel had been: Mr. Scott, though polite, was not overcome.

The black coffee and baked beans of the Campfire were suited to wintertime. But in spring came a solemn ceremony.

On the Sunday in May before Decoration Day (it was not called Memorial Day then), there was a union church service in the village. Methodists, Presbyterians, and Universalists forgot their three-sided distrust of one another's doctrines and remembered that they had a common country even if there was no likelihood that they would occupy a common heaven. The service was held in turn, first in one church, then in another.

Did the sun always shine in harmony with the union service? It seems to me that it did. The service was always in the afternoon and the church was always crowded. The Universalist Church had great plain glass windows reaching from the high ceiling to within a few feet of the floor. Through these windows the sun flooded everything with light, and while they waited children could watch the wind blowing the young leaves of the trees or listen to the birds. People were prompt in coming and were well settled in the straight pews with expectancy in the air when the slow beat of a drum was heard. Everyone rose and turned a little to see the men of the Grand Army march in and take their places in the front pews. The sun brightened the flags, the old men stood in silence, and the congregation sang a hymn of praise and thanksgiving.

Of the sermons I remember nothing. But once when I was very little I read in mother's scrapbook the text of a sermon preached on a similar occasion by a famous minister and it puzzled me: "I will say unto the North, give up, and to the South, keep not back." I had no idea that the text applied to giving up anger and not keeping back from friendship. Instead I thought it meant that the North was to give

37

up fighting and the South was to invade the North. It was a strange idea, I thought, since it was by then too late to change things.

A few days after Union Sunday came Decoration Day. On the day before, when school was over, Ethel and I would be busy gathering flowers. In May flowers were everywhere —violets along the roadsides, honeysuckle in the fence corners, and under their pale green umbrellas the perfect waxen-white, golden-centered mandrake blossoms. There were lilac trees in bloom by empty old houses, and in the garden at grandfather's, tulips and pansies and fragrant flowering currant. We made bouquets and wreaths and sometimes small crosses. We liked to make the crosses best, for it was easy to nail two pieces of lath together, wind them with string, and then stick the short-stemmed mandrake blossoms in the twine and finish with wild ferns at the ends of the cross.

All these were for the graves of the family—our grand-mothers and Aunt Ann who had died young and was only a name to us and Uncle Martin, who had been killed in the Seven Days Battle before Richmond and always had a flag on his grave. The graveyard was on a little hill half a mile from the village, and everyone gathered there on Decoration Day morning. There were the flowers to be admired and the familiar inscriptions on the gravestones to be read and old neighbors to meet, since this was a day of returning to the past.

Then faintly at first came the drumbeat and slowly the column of men in blue came down the road, the steady tramp of their feet matching the drum. They paused at the gate, the flags were furled, and the drumbeat softened before they marched up the hill and formed a square. The officer of the

day read the service, a prayer was said, the bugle played Taps
—and then it was over. No one who grew up seeing all this
from year to year ever lost the knowledge of the price men
had paid to preserve us a nation.

The House

IN 1868 GRANDFATHER decided to build a new house. The old one was bursting at the seams with ten children, now fairly or completely grown up, with hired men who were part of the family, and with relatives or unfortunate old folks who came to pay indefinite visits and helped indoors or out according to their strength and ability.

Grandfather's brother Emery had already built a square white house with ceilings fourteen feet high. His nephew John had done likewise, and his nephew Emery had purchased a fine brick mansion only a scant mile away. Who was grandfather to fall behind his relatives in Progress?

The new house was to be white, of course, and grandfather intended to build it unto all generations. He made a contract with the lumber company by which he was permitted to inspect and choose all the timber for his twenty-room house. He paid extra for the privilege, but his New England eye missed no flaw or imperfection. The company, so it was said, regretted the bargain, as grandfather rejected every piece of timber that did not meet the standard he had set. The One-Hoss Shay that ran a hundred years to a day was the forerunner of grandfather's house. It has stood four-square, solid, and sound to this day.

In style it combined New York and New England. The "upright" was the roomy, comfortable New York type; the wing attached at the rear was New England, and was always called the "gable." There were long porches to north, west, and south; there was a bay window off the back parlor; it lacked only the cupola that topped such houses in that period. Finest of all were the front staircases. The first one led from the main hall to the upper hall. It had a beautiful walnut balustrade and low, easy treads. The second rose just above it in the upper hall and was exactly like the first except that the stairs were painted pure white, while the lower ones were carpeted. The second staircase led to the attic and was never used, since the attic was unlighted and unfinished. When it was necessary to dispose of things downstairs too poor to keep and too good to throw away, they were deposited in the rear attic, reached through a trap door in the back hall. The ceilings in the two big parlors were a mere twelve feet high, and the woodwork throughout the house was painted white. What it meant to keep the whiteness of porches and doors and windows, cornices and corbels in a state of unblemished purity cannot be described, but it was so kept.

To carry out his inspection plan and meet the cost of building, grandfather had to borrow $6,000 at six per cent from Squire Benjamin Sweet in the village. Squire Sweet was so satisfied with the arrangement that he was reluctant to have the debt paid off, but it was paid within four years. Thinking perhaps of the cupola that he had wanted to add but could not afford, grandfather made a sad entry in his account book: "It cost too much."

The family moved into the new home on December 3, 1869, Aunt Wealthy's and Uncle William's twenty-fifth birthday. It stood nearer the road than the old house, now relegated to use as a woodhouse and washhouse. The new house was only fourteen years old when I was born, yet it seemed always to have been there—and it was unthinkable to me that there had ever been a time without grandfather's big white house.

The furniture belonged to the middle Victorian period. It had been selected by Uncle Charles. Among the pieces were a walnut sofa covered with black horsehair and suitable for skiing, a matching rocker, and a marble-topped center table. I asked the aunts once if none of the women went along to help choose the furniture. They said no, Charles had good judgment and they knew that what he picked out would be right. I guess it was, for more than eighty years later the furniture was still youthful, with the kind of youthfulness that in women is called "well-preserved."

The parlors were prim, the lace curtains hung stiffly, but cleanliness, order, and sunlight gave a beauty of their own. The big double doors that separated the parlors could be folded back into squares that made splendid little playhouses furnished with numerous stools. Stools were easy to get if a child worked quietly, for carpet-covered footstools stood near every chair ready to comfort aching feet. It was only when a large company came that the double doors were opened and playhouses possible, very decorous playhouses that had to be managed in silence.

The carpets were pure wool ingrain in simple patterns.

Tiny branches of cedar were kept under them, on the theory that cedar kept away moths. At least it gave a heavenly smell to the parlors. I loved to go along on cedar expeditions. They came every year; on a fall Sunday old John would be harnessed to the equally old democrat wagon, and Uncle Alfred and the aunts and I would go down the lane to the west lot. It was goldenrod and wild aster time in the lane, a mountain ash tree gleamed with red berries, and everlasting flowers starred the west lot. While the aunts cut the cedar, Uncle Alfred went in the woods to look for ginseng. He believed that if he found the plants he could make a fortune. He never found any, but he was happy in the hope that, given time, he would be lucky and discover a luxuriant stand of ginseng as good as China offered. On such Sundays when I was part of the cedar and ginseng business, I was close to perfect happiness. The high fall skies, the sense of rest and peace away from daily tasks, the earth smells, and the kindness wrapped around me became, as Lorenzo said of the music of the spheres, the touches of sweet harmony.

The carpets thus secure against moths, there were the rooms above the parlors to consider. They were always called the chambers. I never heard them referred to as bedrooms. Except for "chamber" music, that English word has disappeared altogether. Only Hamlet and Mother Goose, the two extremes, preserve "my lady's chamber." "Bedrooms" meant the sleeping rooms upstairs in the gable. There was a huge room over the kitchen that was not used for sleeping but was always known as the kitchen chamber. It had bright blue painted walls and there stood Aunt Welt's spinning wheel and there I watched her spinning skill. At the south window in winter she had her house plants, geraniums and fuschias and oxalis and foliage plants. Her tiny white and yellow chrysanthemums were brought in early from the garden for their Thanksgiving flowering in the back parlor. Ethel and I were regularly marched upstairs or into the parlor to see each pot as it came to bloom. Aunt Welt wanted us to share her admiration for a pansy geranium or a pink and white fuschia, and we did, only without very much idea of the work that lay behind the bright display. When, long after, Ethel became a gardener herself, she kept from year to year some of Aunt Welt's "artemishys," as she usually called her small chrysanthemums. If she used the longer word it was always contracted to "chrysanth'ums." We grew up saying "chrysanth'um" and I still think it much prettier in sound with the harsh extra syllable omitted. The old English names of flowers had not yet been given heavy and unmusical Latin ones, which show botanical knowledge, but have no effect upon the imagination. When we spoke of morning glories, larkspur, marigold, four o'clocks, bleeding hearts, honeysuckle, forget-me-not, and all the other lovely ones, we knew their opening and closing time and their shape and color from their names.

The important everyday part of the house consisted of the dining room, the kitchen, and the buttery, shortened to "butt'ry" for common use. The dining room was the first room in the gable and very large. It could and often did seat Christmas or church companies of thirty or forty at one time. From it opened eight doors. There was the front door to the south porch where visitors came, for no one within memory ever knocked at the great hall doors to the west. Next were the doors to the parlor, the hall, grandmother's bedroom, and the north entry, which led to the north porch and served for hanging up shawls and Sunday coats. The buttery door finished the north side of the room, and around the corner from it was the door that after a little space led to the kitchen. Last of all was the door to the back staircase. Eight doors and three windows—and yet the room was so large there was still a good deal of wall space for furniture. My earliest memory of it was that on one wall hung a map of the United States with most of the Far West marked as the Great American Desert and with many states still labeled territories. Below the map was a sort a daybed, its frame of walnut and its narrow husk mattress a comfortable place when sleep overtook you from the warmth of the wood fire.

There were no fireplaces. The house was built when they were being displaced by stoves and before they returned to favor. Wood was burned from kitchen to parlor. Warm and bright or fiercely hot, maple and appletree crackled in the stoves, and of a wintry evening big red and yellow Northern Spy apples and dark red Kings were brought up from the cellar, cold to the teeth and delicious in the fire glow. And there were platters of Aunt Elvie's popcorn balls made especially for us children and set outside to cool on the porch so that the molasses syrup that bound the popcorn tight would snap when we bit into them.

Built into the dining room wall in the far west corner was an oak cupboard where the best dishes were kept. How sorry I feel for children who live in homes where there are no "best" things, even if the everyday ones are handsome. For the dishes used only for Thanksgiving and Christmas and on important occasions take on a special enchantment. We did not see the best dishes often enough to be on familiar terms with them, and so there was always the surprise of seeing how splendid they were, accompanied by the best knives and forks and teaspoons and the silver caster and the silver cake basket and the special plates for bread and pie. Ordinarily in summer the dining room table held a vase of Aunt Welt's nasturtiums or sweet peas. In winter you did not pick off geranium blossoms for the table. Instead of flowers, the green and pink majolica compote held apples, or, particularly on New Year's, oranges in their natural color.

The neighbor womenfolks sat and "visited" in the dining room. More impressive and less intimate callers were guided to the back parlor. The menfolks and the farmers who came to see them did their talking in the kitchen, and there the family ordinarily ate. One of my permanent troubles at grandfather's was that nobody ever sat through a meal at the same time. There were those who started eating before the others, those who jumped up to get something forgotten, and those who tended something on the stove till the last minute in order that the rest might have it piping hot.

On social occasions there was likely to be a sharp separation of men and women guests during the conversation period, but husbands and wives were always seated next to each other at table. It was considered highly improper or even dangerous to put either partner beside some attractive outsider. For if they should, oh, what would come of it!

The buttery was another large room. A glass cupboard that held the everyday dishes had the north side of the room to itself, and long shelves ran along both east and west sides to hold the pans of milk set for cream to rise. There were windows north and east, a spice cupboard, bins for flour and sugar, and in the center of the room a long table to receive what cupboards and shelves had no room for. The buttery

The House

was cool on the hottest day of summer and bone-chilling in winter. Pie was always served cold and to secure complete frigidity was placed in front of the north window till dinner time.

The buttery with its stocks and supplies was intermediate in use between kitchen and storeroom. The storeroom had been carefully planned for the farthest northwest corner of the house at the end of the long front hall. My aunts, of course, had to travel the entire length of the house to reach it. This storeroom I believed to be the coldest place on earth, but its contents were a dream of feasting. It sometimes seems incredible to me, when I reflect on foodstuffs purchased for a few days at the supermarkets, that there was ever a storeroom like the one in grandfather's house. The temptation to catalogue what was there is irresistible. Perhaps Homer loved ships and that accounts for his careful list of them. I love the memory of storeroom wonders. Great barrels of sugar and flour, pans of sausage, baskets of grapes and pears, a table loaded with caps of honey, a cheese or two, hams waiting to be sliced, graham meal and cornmeal, jars of butter—a kind of sprawling plenty such as is not likely to return to American life.

The cellar—it had not yet become the rumpus room or the basement—ran underneath the whole house and was what was called "grouted," that is, it had a floor of concrete or cement, but not quite as smooth as we know it today. It was unusual in 1868 to have anything but a dirt floor in the cellar; grandfather may have bargained for the mortar. The contents of the cellar went on where those of the storeroom left off. The dark bins held apples and potatoes and root vegetables, and the barrels were full of cider or vinegar. An

47

enormous cistern had been built in at the east end of the cellar and the supply of soft rain water never gave out. The size of the cistern was a little terrifying to a child—as if it were a kind of dungeon that might hide all sorts of evils. The water for drinking and cooking came from the well by the cheesehouse—a limestone well deep and cold. The cold of limestone water did not grow warm with the rapidity of melting ice cubes. Lemonade made with it was shivery to the last drop.

The setting of the house was suited to it. Besides the circling trees a Michigan rose grew on a lattice near the south door; a bed of myrtle stretched beside the wall of the bay window; a very large, practical, circular clothesline owned the part of the yard by the kitchen door. The heavy post in the center was a grey tree trunk, with supports radiating from it; the wires rested on the supports and crossed one another like a spider's web. These wires at a push moved obediently round and round so that the Monday morning washwomen could carry out the basketfuls of clothes, turn the wires as they needed room, and never stir till the baskets were emptied and the clothes flapping on the lines.

At the end of the walk from the front door was the horseblock. It had two steps leading to the platform from which you stepped carefully into carriage, phaeton, or democrat, long skirts gathered up so as not to catch in the wheel. If the horse stood quiet, you landed safely. Farm horses taking a day off as carriage horses were seldom rarin' to go, but accidents could happen. If the horse was young and lighthearted, someone, usually Aunt Elvie, would stand at his head and hold him tightly by the bridle till the rest of the family were seated in the wagon. When the horseblock was not serving what would be called today its functional purpose, it was a charming place to play house, with an upstairs and down.

Directly across from the horseblock on the other side of the driveway was the gate into the garden. The gate and the picket fence were entwined with honeysuckle and all summer the honeysuckle scented the air. There were other fragrances in season. A flowering currant bush sweetened every breeze; at the foot of a tall pear tree bergamot grew close to the ground to be picked and crushed in the fingers till it gave out a melodious smell, at least if the harmony of all the senses is like music. Rarest of all and dearest to us were the dark purple double English violets that grew in no other garden we knew and were the unfailing sign of spring.

This then was the house and its surroundings that through many years was our second home. Our friends were welcomed and loved because we loved them, and the married daughters who went away from the house called it home to their last breath. In time there were changes; a furnace was put in, electricity took the place of lamps. Yet with all the changes the house remained the same. It may be that memory triumphs over reality to help us endure loss.

Aunts and Uncles

THROUGH LOVING association and letters and visits and through the stories the aunts close at hand told us of the brothers and sisters, Ethel and I had an idea of their characters fixed in our minds as well as if they had all been living still in grandfather's house. But so far as we could remember, only Aunt Welt, Aunt Ellen, and Aunt Elvie, spinsters all, lived with grandfather and took care of the house, while Uncle Bill and Uncle Alfred looked after the farms.

Grandfather's children, either as a result of his attitude toward religion or by the law of their own natures, were distinctly not religious. They went to church and supported it generously; they worked hard at church suppers and church cleaning and church building repairs, but in the deep sense they were without religion. They were honest and decent and moral, but of faith in the old-fashioned sense they had little and of doubts they had a multitude. That was why the doctrine of Universalism made a strong appeal to them. If the Universalist heaven was not too bright, hell at least was not too glaring. No creed or dogma was required and worldly pleasures were not frowned upon. Universalists they became and unlike grandfather they never felt it necessary to discuss what principles of religion lay beneath their whole-hearted undertakings in church affairs.

Of all my uncles, Uncle Charles was the most remarkable in intellect and force of character. From his father he had inherited a certain sternness and dignity, and from his Irish grandmother his curling russet hair and deep blue eyes and the twinkling humor that had skipped grandfather, but helped Uncle Charles to bear his tragic handicap. He was born, as every firstborn should be, a very beautiful and healthy child. But when he was two years old a blow fell utterly mysterious to his parents and to the community.

Suddenly one day he was seized with a high fever, and little as they knew of illness, they knew he was a very sick child. The nearest doctor they could get was a doctor only by assuming the title, and Doctor Genung had no more idea than they what the trouble was. His standing remedy for all strange diseases was calomel, a preparation of mercury and a violent purgative. With this he dosed the little boy heavily. The child lived, but with recovery came the fearful knowledge that his feet were twisted and he would never walk normally again.

There is little doubt from the account of his symptoms and the pitiful result that Uncle Charles was a polio victim. The name and the disease were equally unknown to the countryside then. His father and mother could do nothing except year by year to have queer looking shoes and boots made for him by the village shoemaker, as the feet turned

51

inward more and more until they were almost at right angles to the legs that bent to adjust his weight. Grandmother believed to the end of her life that the calomel Dr. Genung had given the sick child had made him a cripple—a heartbreaking thing for a mother to believe.

Uncle Charles's mind was untouched. He grew tall even with the crippled feet shortening his height, and his body above the waist was powerful. He had broad shoulders and strong arms that, as he said, "evened up" for his feet. His head was impressive. Many years after his death I saw Raphael's famous portrait of Pope Julian II, and in the set of the head and the steady gaze of the eyes I saw Uncle Charles again.

He was so young when he was stricken that his adjustment was made unconsciously. He took his share of the farmwork with the others. He could drive the teams, work in the garden on his hands and knees, and was invaluable in the cooper shop, where his great strength could be put to service with the type of tools used in barrel making. In all his long life no one ever heard a word of self-pity from him or any suggestion that he was entitled to something easier than the rest. He thought laziness the most astonishing of all sins. How any man with two good feet to move about on could choose to do nothing was beyond his comprehension and he judged him accordingly.

It was his special quality of judgment that the family relied on. He seemed instinctively to know values in land, in animals, and in the minds and characters of men. The quality is rare and because of it people trusted his opinions. The keenness and sometimes the severity of his judgments were modified in expression by his humor, but not, I suspect, with any interior change in his feeling on the subject. There was a sunniness along with the severity, and I never heard of any outward display of temper from him.

He liked school and learned quickly, but he suffered often at the hands of boys older than himself. They were sometimes a rough lot, and the aunts told me that on the playground they would run up to Uncle Charles and step on his feet, knowing that he could not run after them. It was like being "It" all the time. This was not the idyllic country school of early American poetry.

Uncle Charles was almost forty before he was married— to a woman who had the good sense to look at his head instead of his feet. He bought a farm of his own in Brewerton, built a comfortable large white house, and spent the rest of his life there.

For many years Uncle Charles was elected justice of the peace by his fellow townsmen. As a young man he had wished very much to study law, but grandfather could not get along without him. The office of justice suited him exactly. He read law, thought of law, and judged according to law. By custom he was called Squire. The title held over from old English days when the squire, as representative of the gentry, was the natural judge of the village. In the United States it was a social title rather than a professional one. Today in New York State, justices of the peace are universally called Judge, never Squire. Is that a rise in status or a fall?

As justice, he was often called on to marry couples who had no church association. He was very doubtful about the outlook for one couple. Some months after the ceremony he met the wife on the street and asked her how things were going.

She said, "Well, Mr. Moulton, you know you told me I was taking Jim for better or for worse. I kinda hoped it would be for better, but it's turned out to be for worse."

At least once Uncle Charles's judgment gave serious dissatisfaction. He had sentenced or fined a man in a quarrel between neighbors and the man vowed he would pay him back. Just how he would manage it no one guessed. Uncle Charles had a good team of horses such as every farmer needed and had if he could afford it. One morning when he went to the barn he found the horses dead—poisoned, as it developed. There was no proof as to the guilty person nor was there any doubt in the village as to who had done it. Uncle Charles accepted the loss philosophically: some folks were like that.

A visit from Uncle Charles meant a chance to hear him tell stories or invent new ways of saying an obvious thing. Once he said of a stupid man that we shouldn't find fault with him; he'd always been a little underminded. Once too, when we said a certain woman in town was very homely, Uncle Charles shook his head at us and said, "Come, now, she's just as pretty as she can be." Ethel and I said, "Oh, Uncle! You know she isn't!" The twinkle came into his eyes. "Now, girls, I said she was as pretty as she could be. If she could be prettier, of course she would be."

Uncle Charles had a strong belief that a just debt must be paid, no matter how long delayed. When the First World War came and France was in desperate danger, all Americans were arguing the question of our entering the war. Uncle Charles did not argue; he stated the case:

"I look at it this way. Lafayette came over here and helped us when we needed it. It's no more than right that we should go over there and help France."

Grandfather's family had felt that half the house went away when Uncle Charles married. Something solid and dependable and formidable against mistakes went with him. In his later years, after Aunt Marietta's death, he often came back for a long visit, and was to them what he had always been—a very rock of comfort and support.

Aunt Jane's head was the model of a Puritan—dark-eyed, straight-haired, and angular. There was rather more severity in her expression than in the faces of the other aunts. Perhaps this sprang from the deep seriousness of knowing from her earliest days that life was earnest, duty was demanding, and work, though spoken of as a blessing, was a stretched-out blessing from dawn till dark. She must have been a great comfort to grandmother. As the oldest girl, her responsibilities were heavy. One could not readily associate her with a carefree, happy childhood. If she was without a sense of humor, she had a sense of justice that made her a wise guide for the younger brothers and sisters.

Grandfather rewarded her diligence in a way not granted to his other children. He sent her back to New Hampshire for a year to go to school at the Meriden Academy. Aunt Jane was as conscientious in schoolwork as in housework. She learned thoroughly and mastered easily the complications of mental arithmetic and natural philosophy. Her handwriting was beautiful; not quite so excellent a thing in a woman as a soft voice, but very agreeable for those who read what she wrote.

She fell in love at an early age with young George Welch, who was working in grandfather's cooper shop. George was English and had arrived in the country with his parents at the age of fourteen. His seriousness and high principles matched Jane's. One afternoon she had been popping corn and carried a dish of it out to the cooper shop to George. They both agreed that this was the beginning of their romance. Jane with a big dish of snowy white corn touched with melting butter was suddenly revealed to George as the one maiden to share his future. He used to say that he didn't pop the question to Jane; she popped it with the corn.

George enlisted in 1861 "for the duration," and he fought through all the four years in the Army of the West. While Aunt Jane was busy stitching, starching, and ironing shirts for the family she had time to think about him. She wrote regularly to her soldier, and as she thought only perfection was suitable for George, she was careful to have no mistakes or errors in her letters. She wrote them out first on a slate, corrected them, and then carefully copied them in ink on paper. I cannot help thinking that any words of too warm endearment must have cooled off in the creative process.

After the war was over, Uncle George made a home ready for his bride on the prairie acres he had purchased in northern Indiana. It was treeless country then and lonely, but he set out trees tirelessly, planted crops in the rich soil, and prospered. For many years, however, the fruit that had been so plentiful in New York State could not be obtained in the prairie country, and a barrel of apples from the home orchard was sent every fall to Indiana to help out. The three sons born to Uncle George and Aunt Jane grew up in an old-fashioned Christian household. Uncle George remained a Universalist, but since there was no Universalist church anywhere near their home, Aunt Jane at length entrusted her salvation to the Methodists. To her nature the positive rewards and positive punishments of the Methodist doctrine, in contrast to the Universalists' relaxed optimism, seemed just and fitting.

When I was about seven or eight, Uncle George and Aunt Jane came "down from Indiana," as the family always said, to pay a long visit to all the relatives. This was the only time I ever saw Aunt Jane, and her precision of speech impressed me and made me a little afraid of her, though she was very affectionate and kind to "Sarah's girls." But she was genuinely shocked to find that neither Ethel nor I at our advanced ages had been taught to knit and had never pieced a quilt. Mother was a gifted seamstress and knitter; unfortunately heredity had not passed on these arts to us. Aunt Jane resolved that she would do what she could; she would at least teach me to knit. Since I seemed docile and loved dolls, she decided to begin the lessons with stockings for my doll. Poor Aunt Jane! Those tiny stockings offered cruel problems for a child who had never learned even the simple garter stitch. It must have been trying for her. My mistakes needed to be unraveled every few minutes, I was clumsy and awkward and didn't remember what I was told. I would have loved to know how to knit beautifully if the accomplishment could have descended on me with no effort on my part. As it was, I lacked patience and interest in the learning process. When Aunt Jane went back to Indiana, she had finished one stocking for me and urged me to work on the other. The other remained stationary on the needles until mother wanted to use them and cast the part-stocking aside.

Aunt Jane found time all her life to write long letters to Aunt Sophy, Aunt Welt, and mother, although knitting and sewing for her three little boys must have kept even her rest periods occupied. After her death, Uncle George wrote to mother as long as he lived. He and Aunt Jane had a good life together. They shared the same integrity of character and were bound by the tie of early association and by the tie of enduring love. Of all the Moulton marriages, this was the happiest.

In April of 1842, a clock was bought for the dining room. It was tall, though by no means in the grandfather class, for it fitted comfortably on its broad shelf. This was the period when, thanks to Connecticut ingenuity, clocks had multiplied at a reasonable price, and most families could afford one. The face of the clock had plain Roman numerals on the top half, and below that a picture of a large weeping willow tree spreading its branches over a house painted red, green, and white. The clock arrived the April before Aunt Sophy's birth, in June, so it was always easy to remember how old the clock was. It is now, in November, 1963, one hundred and twenty-one years old and ticks off time as quickly as ever, punctuating each hour with a loud, unmelodious strike as if it were anxious to get the matter over with as soon as possible. The clock was used by the family for fifty years, until an ugly, squat rival in a marbleized case succeeded to the shelf and old Eighteen Forty-Two was banished to the attic. Although the new clock looked more fashionable, it was a poor timekeeper and was always being taken somewhere to be adjusted. Up in the attic Eighteen Forty-Two, which had never needed anything done to it, may have brooded over the injustice of life till it was rescued in 1940 and came to enjoy the prestige of an antique. This was the clock that from her birth counted time for Aunt Sophy and watched her improve each shining hour as Dr. Watts urged.

At home Aunt Sophy was always called Goody because of her amiability and kindness. She was the sister who particularly looked after and brought up the little ones, loving them devotedly and loved by them in return as their favorite sister. She was one of the four children out of the ten who had grandfather's dark eyes, only hers were smiling eyes. She had all of the household skills and was probably the best cook among the sisters, for even when in her married life she had very little to do with, she always produced appetizing meals.

I never quite understood why Aunt Sophy did not marry earlier, unless it was that the presence of a large family of brothers and sisters often intimidates a would-be suitor. Besides, there was so much to do that she could hardly have had time to entertain a wooer. When a candidate at length came forward, grandfather's opposition to the marriage was extreme. There really was good reason for it. To make that clear, I must go back a generation.

Grandfather's sister Jane, my grandaunt, was very dear to him, and he had named his oldest daughter for her. Grandaunt Jane was a spinster who earned her living, as so many New England women did, by braiding straw hats. A scanty living at best, and with no prospect of improvement. By careful saving and scrimping, she put aside enough money to come to New York State and pay a visit for the winter to grandfather and grandmother. She was welcomed with warm affection by the whole family. The picture we have of her shows a plain, pleasant face; and she wore plain dark grey or brown dresses, reserving black for best.

Nearby at this time lived John Wright, a sound Republican and a not too successful farmer. At the time Grandaunt Jane came visiting, he was a widower with three sons almost grown up and three undisciplined and disagreeable daughters. John Wright was casting his eye about for relief from his burdens and it fell upon Jane. He proposed to make her his wife, his housekeeper, and the overseer of his family. It was an uninviting assignment, as grandfather did not fail to point out. The Wrights, he said, were a selfish lot who always took more than they gave. John was considerably older than Jane, and grandfather felt that what he offered was not prompted by affection but by his own convenience, and meant only a hard life for Jane. She must have thought over her brother's objections and probably realized their truth. On the other hand, a return to New England meant braiding hats for the rest of her life, while marrying John would give her a home of her own near her brothers and all the nephews and nieces she loved. There was also the prospect of having, if not children of her own, stepchildren whom she could do for and love if they would let her.

So she became Grandaunt Jane Wright, and grandfather's prophecies proved all too true. There could not have been many bright spots along the way, though two of her stepsons, Tim and Dolph, valued her and appreciated what she did for them. But there was no end to the ceaseless round of heavy work. Her stepdaughters were a trial in manners and conduct, and she fell back on her nieces, particularly Sophy, for comfort and help. The family believed that she died from overwork. By that time Uncle John, as they called him, had grown too old and feeble to live alone. He divided his big farm among his sons and went to live with Tim.

Tim Wright's share of the land included the most undesirable portion, offset by a large, pleasant white house and good orchards. He had married a pretty, delicate girl who bore him three sons and a daughter and died of consumption, leaving him in the same plight that his father had faced, or worse, for Tim's youngest boy was only two years old and there was Uncle John added to the household, a difficult old man who had to be watched and tended like a child. What could have been more natural than that, after looking about and considering, Tim's choice fell on Sophy Moulton. If grandfather had been displeased by his sister's marriage, he was outraged at the thought that his daughter would repeat her aunt's experience.

But Aunt Sophy was thirty years old; Tim was respectable and a devoted Universalist, and so, sadly enough, grandfather yielded. In their hearts the family was never reconciled to losing their dear Sophy to the Wrights. Her brothers, like grandfather, thought all the Wrights lazy and selfish. Uncle Alfred expressed their view by saying that if the Wright boys had a bottle of hair oil and a stickpin they would winter well. They did what they could in various ways to ease their sister's lot, but Uncle Tim remained an outsider to the end.

Aunt Sophy and Uncle Tim were married early on a Monday morning. Only the relatives on both sides were present, each one doubtless reserving his opinion of the occasion until it could be expressed freely later on. The time of the wedding was fixed by someone else than the bride; the choice of Monday morning depended on the minister. At that time the Universalist minister came every Saturday from his home in Auburn, some thirty-five miles away, to preach in Cicero on Sunday. He drove back on Monday morning and could not be expected to delay his return. I wonder if Aunt Sophy felt happy that morning. I hope she did. She was going only a quarter of a mile from the home she loved so much, but remembering her Aunt Jane and her father's prediction, there must have been a little uneasiness thrust away at the back of her mind.

Her wedding dress was quite lovely. Whatever they thought, the family permitted no slackness in appearances. The material was what was called silk alpaca, a combination of silk and very fine, soft wool. The color was ashes of roses, that is, pearl grey with rose overtones. It was made with an overskirt and many furbelows and a handsome lace tucker. A very nice dress indeed.

For the wedding feast—in this case almost a wedding breakfast—grandmother had cooked a turkey with the proper accompaniments, and grandfather gave as a wedding present a set of silver teaspoons marked—with reluctance—SW. Not much, one thinks, in return for all Aunt Sophy's years of work at home. But money was in the hands of the menfolks among farmers, and women were not expected to receive anything for their labors for the family. And so Aunt Sophy was started on her new life, and the spoons were treasured and used only for best. Their plainness is their beauty.

After I was old enough to think about it and to ponder family remarks on the subject, I wondered a good deal about Aunt Sophy's marriage. I am not sure but that she was happier than she would have been living on at home. Uncle Tim had countless relatives who visited them for long periods and brought work for their burdened hostess. But if they brought work, they brought pleasure and interest too. They

truly loved Aunt Sophy, and in her old age they were faithfully kind. So far as he was able, Uncle Tim was "a good
provider" and always hospitable. Although the house lacked
even the humblest conveniences—to the end of their lives
it was without electricity or a furnace or a decent kitchen
stove—it was a big house, and we children loved to run
across the road from school to eat dinner there if the contents
of our dinner pails were unsatisfactory. Uncle Tim always
welcomed us warmly, and Aunt Sophy seemed always to
have something specially good for us to eat. There were
many treasures to admire in Aunt Sophy's sitting room: the
three-tiered workbasket that stood by the south window
fascinated me, and the red and green oval pieces of glass set
in the brass frame of the hanging lamp. The shining crystals
that swung from the lamp added diamonds to the emeralds
and rubies—fairy tale jewels. Then there was a colored picture with the title printed beneath it: "Simply to Thy Cross
I Cling." It showed a young lady in her nightgown—or so I
interpreted it—clinging to an enormous cross while the
breaking waves dashed high around her. How could she be
saved!

Best of all were the flowers—damask roses, pink and
white, by the porch, circular beds of daffodils in the front
yard, and a magnificent yellow rosebush that turned to
dazzling gold in early June. When we, two of us always,
came over from school to get a pail of water from the well
up Uncle Tim's lane, we took our time, forgetful of the other
children back at school, dying of thirst, and waiting for us
to bring them a drink. We would call out, "Aunt 'Fy, can
we have a daffodil?" or maybe it was a yellow rose or a
hundred-leaf rose we wanted. We called the damask roses by

that name because each one had such a crowd of tiny petals there *must* have been a hundred. Sometimes we increased the number and asked for a thousand-leaf rose. Aunt Sophy never refused us.

Among her other talents, Aunt Sophy had the lovely one of choosing for us at Christmas time exactly the kind of present we would like. I remember the Christmas when she brought me a little round flat glass bottle filled with cologne. A paper watch front was pasted on one side of the bottle and a brass chain was attached to the stopper, just like a real watch, only sweet-smelling.

Thanksgiving was held to be Aunt Sophy's special holiday for entertaining the whole family, and little roast pig and scalloped oysters were the special food to be served. Outside, at the end of November, there would be light snow on the hard-frozen, ringing earth; inside by late afternoon the fire had burned down to a ruddy mass of coals, and then it was time to beg Uncle Tim to play for us on his jew's-harp. He was always ready to perform for us and would take the tiny harp down from its peg in the dining room and begin a tuneful sound like the crickets on a fall night. We listened with a rapture akin to Maggie Tulliver's over Uncle Pullet's music box. Uncle Tim could play the bones too, and they had a rattling rhythm in his hands, but they did not reach my heart as the jew's-harp did.

Uncle Tim and Aunt Sophy were alike in their fondness for children, and all the children in the neighborhood knew it and claimed a share of their time and affection. It was sad that Uncle Tim's sons were such a disappointment to him. All that the Moultons said of them was well founded: they were lazy, selfish, and ill-behaved. Their father clung to them because they were his own, but he had much sorrow because of them and in his old age much unkindness from them.

As a part of Aunt Sophy's life, Uncle Tim's children were a part of our lives too. However, Nina, the daughter, was the only one of Aunt Sophy's stepchildren that engaged the attention and affection of the Moultons. She married unwisely at sixteen and went to live in a sod house out in Wyoming. We always put the "out" in because that made Wyoming much farther away and more adventurous. It was still a territory then and equally full of Indians and buffalo. Nina wrote home long detailed letters that were always read to us, and through her eyes we saw the Old West. Her experiences were exciting and to the homefolks appalling. She wrote of rattlesnakes that crawled near the sod house; of a buffalo stampede coming so close that she shook with terror until, almost at the last minute, the herd veered in another direction; of Indian visitors demanding food when she had nothing but cornmeal and potatoes to give them or her three boys. Sometimes she recorded sorrowfully that her husband had been away weeks at a time "prospecting," and then finally that the long absences had grown into permanent desertion. Uncle Tim sent her a little money when he could, and by a great effort was once or twice able to spare enough to pay the railroad fare for Nina and the boys to come back home for the winter.

From hardships and dangers Nina developed courage and character and built for herself a satisfying life. From her own trials, she realized in maturity what her stepmother had endured and done for the family and showed her love and gratitude. In later life, she often returned for the winter to help out at home, and we all enjoyed her tales of adventure in the West.

All the Wrights became deaf at an early age. I cannot recall Uncle Tim as otherwise than very deaf, and Aunt Sophy through most of her married life was shouting to him fragments of news, scraps of conversation, or her opinion on some household matter. He was patient under the affliction, never complained or asked to have something repeated to him. His great comfort was in reading the *Universalist Leader,* the chief periodical of the church. In it he found sermons that made up for the fact that he heard not a word in church, though he sat in the front pew every Sunday with his hand cupped behind his ear, still hopeful of getting the message. He always discovered a particular piece in each number that delighted him and he wanted me to share his enthusiasm. So I read the piece aloud to him and the second reading was as satisfying to him as the first.

Aunt Sophy did not care much to read, except a good love story now and then. She said it was all right for Sarah to like hearty reading, but it wasn't interesting to her. In some way she had acquired several of the Elsie Dinsmore series and the Horatio Alger books. It was from her stock of these that I made the interminable acquaintance of Elsie and Phil the Fiddler and Tom the Bootblack. Aunt Sophy enjoyed these unreal heroines and heroes, but did not rate them very high when we talked them over.

If she did not wish for books, all her life she had longed for a more worldly possession, a string of gold beads. Gold beads were much worn in her youth, but quite beyond her reach. When at length she realized that she would never own the necklace she coveted, she transferred her desire for it to

Ethel and me. She would have loved to be able to buy the beads for us. Since that was not possible, she encouraged us to buy them for ourselves. Solid gold beads were a good investment, she argued, and would be so becoming to us. Now by the law of contraries that operates between generations, both Ethel and I thoroughly disliked gold beads. It was hard to explain to Aunt Sophy that we didn't want them either by gift or purchase.

Ethel and I were almost grown up before we knew that Uncle Tim's real name was Warren, and Tim merely a nickname which he disliked. Ethel at once took to calling him Uncle Warren, much to his pleasure. When Warren Harding was elected president, Uncle Tim was greatly excited. The name proved that Harding was undoubtedly an extraordinary man, and Uncle Tim put up a large campaign picture of him over the dining room mantel. He constantly called the attention of visitors to the handsome bland face of the president so fortunately named. Well, the name was as good a reason as any other for voting for Harding. Uncle Tim was certain that Warren Harding would go down in history as one of our greatest presidents. He did not live to be disillusioned by history.

When Aunt Sophy was eighty-five and Uncle Tim ninety-two, they met with an accident. They were driving to the village in an old carriage drawn by a slow-moving horse. While automobiles were not omnipresent on the roads in 1926 as now, they were numerous enough and the carriage was struck by one. Aunt Sophy was thrown forward and severely hurt across the breast. The injury revealed cancer. Her sisters provided a nurse who cared for her tenderly and eased the pain as much as she could. But Aunt Sophy's wish in her wandering thoughts was only to go home to grand-father's house again. She pleaded pitifully to be taken back, saying over and over, "I'd be willing to ride on a stoneboat if you will just take me down home."

Life for her had been riding on a stoneboat for many a long year. Uncle Charles and Uncle Alfred and Aunt Jane and Aunt Wealthy had gone before her, and with them had gone the old days when they had all been together "down home."

Mother had the sad task of laying out clothes for the burial and found only such patched and darned undercloth-ing and stockings that she cried over the poor things that were all Aunt Sophy had to wear. No one in the family had quite realized how poor they were at the last.

At first after the accident Uncle Tim had seemed un-injured, but it was all too much for him. He had been mar-ried to Aunt Sophy over fifty years and he did not know how to go on without her. Three weeks later he too was dead.

The first twins were born on December 3, 1844, and were named William and Wealthy, though always called Bill and Welt. Both were blond and blue-eyed and each possessed a lifelong iron industriousness, and there all resemblance ceased.

In manhood Uncle Bill was nearly six feet four inches in height, of scantling proportions, and with sandy-reddish hair and long sandy-reddish mustachios and very long arms—like Rob Roy. Indeed he could have passed for a Scotchman with no trouble at all. He might have been regarded as good looking but for a slight cast in one eye that gave him an unpleasant sidewise glance that seemed, and perhaps was, evasive. The expression of his face by the time I remember it was sullen and morose, and his most marked characteristic, after his industry, was an invincible obstinacy, almost as if there were some sort of impediment in his mind that made it impossible ever to change an opinion or purpose.

His childhood was stormy, for his temper was violent and its outbursts were followed by long resentful grudges against whomever or whatever called them forth. His older sisters remembered that when he was a small boy he had thrown his piece of bread and butter on the floor in a fit of anger. Grandfather ordered him to pick it up. He refused, and grandfather had to spank him three times before Uncle Bill yielded and picked up the bread and put it on his plate. Whether or not he ate it the story doesn't say; probably not.

The incident ought to have shown the family that here was a disposition that could be dangerous to happiness and that needed guidance and patient firmness. Yet, as happens again and again in such cases, instead of attempting to correct and soften his natural traits, the family applied its energy to pacifying and placating Bill and to trying to prevent Bill's getting mad. If that happened he would not speak to any of them for weeks and sometimes would sleep in the barn on the hay and ignore his sisters' pleadings to come back to the house.

It was not only the family that stirred his wrath. There was in him a streak of cruelty that vented itself on the horses and cows. He passed from under grandfather's control as soon as he became too strong to be punished, and while grandfather would remonstrate against his brutality it had no effect whatever on Uncle Bill. Once when grandfather told him that he expected a horse to know more than himself, Uncle Bill answered that there would be horses after he was dead. "None that you ever owned," said grandfather.

I was always relieved if Uncle Bill was away or not deigning to be present when I went down to grandfather's for dinner or supper. I cannot recall that he ever said anything in particular to me at any time. He ate in silence and spread a dark cloud over everything.

Considering his unwillingness to be balked in any direction, his humiliation must have been painful when two different young ladies declined his attentions. The family would have been delighted to have either girl marry Bill, but the young ladies decided against him. And so Uncle Bill arrived at forty-nine, still a bachelor, and the neighbors judged that it was too late for him ever to think of marrying.

Aunt Welt once said to me that she thought life had not been very generous to her, considering what it had required of her. Her keen blue eyes were not strong and needed glasses very early; her hair was thin; her teeth so poor that false ones were an improvement. Hardest of all, her nerves wore out from unremitting work and from wrestling with others less shrewd and sensible than herself. She had been denied the schooling she had wanted as a girl, for she could not then—or ever—be spared from the farm economy.

But in her estimate of her appearance, Aunt Welt was mistaken. In any group of women she stood out. She did not sink her identity in a crowd, but was distinguished and remembered from the rest. She carried her head high and her body erect. She sat like any Victorian without ever touching the back of the chair. Her simple wardrobe always seemed becoming and suitable. Such women are ageless. They can be trusted to behave with dignity and propriety in all circumstances. Aunt Welt's opinions were asked and listened to, and people liked to have her approval. As Kent said of Lear, she had that in her countenance by which men are mastered —authority. When I remarked on the way others consulted her, she told me the secret: she never talked on subjects of which she knew nothing. That suggests both her intelligence and her honesty. It is, unhappily, the fate of such characters to be admired and respected more than they are loved.

Once I was at grandfather's when a gypsy knocked at the door. Aunt Welt opened it.

"Lady, let me tell your fortune," the gypsy wheedled.

Aunt Welt said, "I have known my fortune for a good many years. I don't want to hear anything more about it."

The woman looked at her a second and shook her head, then turned away. At the time I thought maybe the gypsy was cross at being dismissed like that. Now I wonder if the headshake did not mean that she recognized in Aunt Welt someone who had experienced the kind of fortune a gypsy does not foretell.

There is no question that Aunt Welt dominated the family. Perhaps it is inevitable that the one who is the cleverest and has a driving will and authority and disciplined nature will always dominate. But underneath Aunt Welt's domination went a great love for the family she directed and, in a sense, governed.

She could turn her hand to any sort of work successfully, and she had the insights and knowledge that kept her busy from morning to night in planning, guiding, overseeing, and executing. There are pictures of her that I recall out of the past as beautifully clear as if she stood before me: Aunt Welt dyeing rags for a new carpet and hanging on the fence skeins of brilliant blue, strong green, rosy red, and golden yellow, like a fallen rainbow; Aunt Welt training her nasturtiums into a waterfall of brightness over the sides of a big barrel filled with dirt. I have spoken of her spinning and sewing, but she was also the best pie maker in town, her doughnuts were prize takers, her sugar cookies were marvels of deliciousness, and who could ever equal her salt-rising bread—an art lost forever. The name survives commercially, but the product is no more like the true article than Hamlet felt akin to Hercules.

When "Saratoga potatoes" first appeared in the American diet and were added to the menu of church banquets, Aunt Welt was one of three women in our church who could be trusted to make them. There were no commercial Saratoga potatoes (not yet "chips"), so Mrs. Loomis, Mrs. Klosheim, and Aunt Welt were appointed to provide them for the feast. Mrs. Loomis had been away visiting in Syracuse and had brought back the recipe. I watched Aunt Welt the first time she ever made them. There was a large kettle of fresh fine lard boiling away over the wood fire; clean white towels covered the kitchen table; and, standing like a priestess before it, Aunt Welt cut the pared potatoes so thin they were transparent. Next she laid the slices in rows on the white cloths to absorb any bit of moisture, and, when all was ready, she dropped the slices into the boiling fat, leaving them only long enough to reach the right shade of golden brown. Then out they came crisp and delectable and were spread again on the cloths. A few less perfectly perfect ones were put aside to taste for salt and flavor, and I was allowed to sample these and report. The report was always favorable.

But her most splendid creation was undoubtedly the enormous fruit cake she made for great occasions, such as weddings and Christmas and choice company. One summer morning when I was nine years old, I went down to grand-father's and found Aunt Welt in the kitchen surrounded by flour and sugar and eggs, butter and molasses and every kind of spice, alongside lemon peel, orange peel, currants and raisins and citron—all giving out a heavenly smell. Since it was a long time before Christmas and I hadn't heard of an Occasion, I inquired what this cake was for. Aunt Welt hesitated a little and finally said, "This fruit cake is for your cousin Anna's wedding. She's going to be married in September. A fruit cake has to season through to be good." Wonder-ful news! For Ethel and I would be present at the wedding with the fruit cake.

Aunt Welt's dearest friend, Miss Angelia Douglas, had gone South after the Civil War to teach in a freedmen's school established by the Presbyterian Board of Missions. For all the time that Miss Angelia lived and worked in the South, a barrel went each year from grandfather's farm, care-fully packed by Aunt Welt. It contained clothing and towels and sheets and quilts, some new, some repaired, all good, along with many little things such as children love and value. This barrel-sending lasted on into my own childhood and it was exciting to watch the things going into the barrel, sometimes bits of ribbons and lace that I coveted for my dolls, but which the barrel always swallowed. In return, Miss Angelia wrote long letters about her work, the progress of her pupils, and the discouragements and failures and hardships she had to face. Our church did not send missionary barrels, but Aunt Welt's barrel was the next thing to it.

If Aunt Welt had moved in court circles, she would undoubtedly have been appointed Mistress of the King's Thresholds. Every room at grandfather's was connected with the other rooms or with the outdoors by broad raised thresholds over which the doors closed snugly. The thresholds were usually painted a light color. Dust color was the favorite because the aunts believed it did not show the dust so quickly as a dark color. No one was ever supposed to put a careless foot on any threshold. If anyone—say, a visitor—did, the marks of his shoe or boot were removed with a damp cloth as soon as he had left, probably stepping on the threshold again on his way out. Aunt Welt taught us from our earliest days always *to step over the threshold*. It became so automatic with us that even today if I encounter a threshold (not many survive) I step *over* it with extreme care and with all deliberate speed.

Next to thresholds, chair rungs were the objects of respect. You did not twine your legs around chairs or twist your feet through the rungs. Your feet belonged on the floor, your legs parallel to the chair legs, and well-brought-up children left no trace of their occupancy on the chairs.

When I look around in a restaurant at the shoes slipped off and lying on the floor and at the chair legs in the tight embrace of beautiful modern legs, I know what Aunt Welt would think: *Who* brought them up?

Uncle Alfred was, to me, the dearest of my uncles. That was partly because of his affection for me, and partly because in a way he lived in a child's world. He was interested in the things a child cares about; he had the same wonder that trees and plants and animals were so unfailingly surprising, and he had a child's innocent trust in the goodness and honesty of men—a trust often betrayed, though never reducing him to a state of suspicion. If he had ever heard of Timon of Athens, he would have been as much amazed at Timon's behavior as at the treachery of his friends.

Uncle Alfred had kind brown eyes and dark hair and the narrow figure of a tall farmer early made stoop-shouldered by hard work. His hands were patterned, I used to think, after the projecting roots of an old tree, brown and gnarled, with broken nails, and in winter with deep, painful cracks on thumbs and fingers that resisted all efforts at a cure till spring came.

He started a high proportion of his sentences with "Well" and "guessed" his way through them. His vocabulary was plain and the pauses gave the effect of considered judgment. He liked to talk and he liked to listen.

It is difficult to think of my childhood without thinking of Uncle Alfred. When he took the grist to mill he always stopped to take me along for company, for going to mill and waiting for the grist to be ground lasted most of the day. The grist was for all sorts of purposes: graham flour for Aunt Elvie's muffins (she called them "graham gems"), buckwheat for the winter pancakes, wheat for the fine white flour from which Aunt Welt's salt-rising bread was made, and so straight down the list to middlings for the pigs. Graham muffins were a lovely yellowish color and had a dark brown crust, halfway between whole wheat and ordinary flour. They were supposed to be good for us. It was no hardship to eat half a dozen muffins just out of the oven, and we were willing to be done good at any time.

It was eight miles west to the Baldwinsville mill and eight miles east to the Bridgeport mill. The choice depended on the kind of grinding Uncle Alfred wanted done. Both roads were a journey into enchantment. We would stop at a grocery store and Uncle would buy dead ripe bananas to eat as we rode along. A dead ripe banana lends savor to any landscape.

On certain Sundays in summer, old Doll and Fan were harnessed to the double carriage to take Uncle Alfred and the aunts for a visit to old Mr. and Mrs. Welch. I was included in the party. The Welches lived ten miles away in country unfamiliar to me. Aunt Elvie rode on the front seat as a possible substitute driver, and I was wedged between Aunt Welt and Aunt Ellen on the back seat. They always took a picnic basket so that the old folks would not be inconvenienced by our noontime arrival. The quiet fields kept the Sabbath day holy. In some of them shone the whiteness of daisies or blossoming buckwheat. The maple-shaded road wandered between stone walls. And all this built up in the heart of a child an image of Sunday peace and beauty. Uncle Alfred amazed me by saying that this part of the country was called Stone Araby. The geography had put Arabia in another part of the world, and here we were riding through it! Uncle Alfred said he guessed they called it that because there were so many stone walls. Our progress through Araby felix was not majestic. Doll and Fan had lived too long not to know that a plowing gait was as suitable for Sundays as for weekdays. The rate of travel lengthened the delight. At the end of the road we came to the little stone house where the Welches lived. I listened to their soft English voices as they talked to my elders. England, like Araby, could be very near.

Valentines were much in my thoughts one year when I was eight or nine. No valentine parties were held at school, and no valentines given to one another among the children. The teacher occasionally found an ugly anonymous one on her desk, but the kind I wanted never appeared. I yearned for a *real* valentine. I think I must have talked about it a good deal, since it was so heavily on my mind. The likelihood of my getting one was scant. February was a shut-in month, and on Valentine's Day the snow was deep and the wind tore at doors and windows. The dark set in early.

It was almost supper time when there was a great rattling at the little stormhouse door and a stamping of feet shaking the snow off boots. Then the front door opened and Uncle Alfred thrust his head and shoulders inside the room. His hat and the old tan scarf he always wore were covered with snow, and a blast of cold air came in with him. In his hands was a big envelope. "Here's a valentine for you," he said, and held it out to me.

He had been peddling apples and potatoes all day long in the storm and cold and had taken time to stop at a store and buy a valentine for me. It was handsome beyond my dreams. Lace paper edged it, and pale yellow ribbons crisscrossed it. In the center, in old lettering printed against gilt, was a verse of poetry and that was best of all. I learned it once and forever.

> Pack, clouds, away
> And welcome, day.
> With night we banish sorrow.

Sweet air, blow soft,
Mount, lark, aloft
To give my Love good morrow.
Wings from the wind to please her mind,
Notes from the lark I'll borrow—
Bird, prune thy wing,
Nightingale, sing,
To give my Love good morrow!

I loved the flowing song and years later found it in the *Oxford Book of English Verse*. It had been written by Thomas Heywood in the sixteenth century. By strange and happy fortune, Uncle Alfred's valentine contained a treasure that has lasted all my life.

Uncle Alfred's peddling was one of his greatest pleasures. It meant loading the wagon the night before with potatoes, apples, sweet corn, butter—whatever was in season. At four o'clock in the morning he started for the city and reached there by breakfast time. He went from house to house offering what he called "good prod*uce*," accent on the second syllable. The customers year by year became his valued friends.

I heard of only one startling adventure. He had been asked to stop at a new place. The potatoes were satisfactory to the lady of the house, and Uncle Alfred carried them down cellar and returned to the kitchen for his pay. Then, as nearly as his sisters could extract the story, the lady made advances to him and suggested other means of her paying for the potatoes than cold cash. Uncle Alfred told her he guessed he'd take his potatoes and fled with them back to the safety of the prod*uce* wagon.

Recounting his narrow escape, Uncle Alfred said dreamily, "I guess she was what they call a trumpet."

"Alfred," said Aunt Welt, "you mean a strumpet!"

"Well, mebbe," said Uncle Alfred.

His customers must sometimes have been put to it to translate his terms for money into their own. Uncle Alfred was a shillings man by straight New England inheritance. To the end of his life he figured in shillings—four shillings, ten shillings, twelve shillings. It was very puzzling to Ethel and me. After we got beyond two shillings, which we knew was the wealth represented by twenty-five cents or a quarter, we were wholly lost. But Uncle Alfred thought in shillings. A dollar was eight shillings to him and it was nothing more.

Another habit of his amused the neighbors, but for some reason annoyed my father. In a world where the driver of a horse or team always sat on the right-hand side of the seat with an eye on ditches and the edge of the road, Uncle Alfred regularly sat on the left side. He said he could keep better watch there of other wagons. He would have enjoyed a little private triumph if he had lived to see automobiles all driven from the left side for the same reason as his—a better watch on other vehicles.

Every year the Masonic Society arranged an excursion, either to Niagara Falls or the Thousand Islands. I had heard the names, but the places were as remote as the stars from my experience. The price for the excursion was cheap, and a special train carried the passengers, mostly our neighbors and friends. One year when I was about eleven, Uncle Alfred and Aunt Elvie decided to go on the Islands trip, and I was told, to my astonishment and joy, that they were going to take me along.

The night before The Day I stayed at grandfather's. Aunt Elvie waked me up about half-past three to get ready for the train that went from Brewerton at four-thirty. It was already daylight on a summer morning. We ate a hurried breakfast, gathered up coats, rubbers, and umbrellas (it might rain), and the picnic basket, climbed into the democrat wagon and were off. We were in plenty of time for a long wait before the train came. These waits went on at intervals all the morning, for the special train had to be shunted into sidings while regular trains whistled by us. By ten o'clock all the picnic baskets had been opened and serious inroads made on the contents. Aunt Elvie's basket was planned to withstand any emergency of famine, and she was able to pass around triangles of blackberry pie to neighbors whose food supplies were reduced. The blackberry pie oozed deliciously over pieces of newspaper made to serve as napkins, and all was well.

After long hours, though they did not seem too long, the train shuffled into the station at Clayton and we rushed from it to the waiting excursion steamer. How terrible if it should go without us! It was the largest boat in the world, and, as it is difficult for any boat to be ugly, this was white and beautiful. On it, sitting by the railing with nothing but the sky over our heads, and the river moving in silver and green and purple below us, we moved forward with it among the islands. They rose out of the water, each in a frame of pines and spruce, and above the trees a stone castle or a white mansion looked loftily down on us as we sailed by. How in the world were those fairy castles built? How could anything so beautiful take possession of islands so far from land and builders? It was part of the magic of the day to look and wonder.

Later the boat turned from the islands and we were told we were going to Kingston—Kingston in Canada. We were to enter a foreign country. When we passed the fort outside the city we were close enough to see the red-coated soldiers on guard and parading. My cup ran over. This was Lexington and Bunker Hill and "Don't fire till you see the whites of their eyes." It was really the last chance for a child to see the Revolutionary War before the scarlet uniforms yielded to khaki.

Of Kingston I remember only one thing. It was a hot afternoon, and as we walked about I saw a sign in a drugstore window that said, "Sodas 5¢." On our infrequent visits to

Syracuse I had met sodas, and I felt very knowledgeable when I explained to Uncle Alfred how delicious and refreshing they were. Uncle Alfred thought they sounded all right, and maybe we ought to have one before we went back to the boat. He'd never tasted any, but he guessed he could try one. We went into the store and sat down on stools. Uncle Alfred ordered vanilla because it was a familiar flavoring, and I chose chocolate, a relatively new taste to me. Aunt Elvie had followed us in, but stood afar off while we sipped luxuriously. Not for worlds would she have risked her life on a soda. Who knew whether the glasses had been rinsed in boiling water or the spoons washed on both sides? At the end of the soda, Uncle Alfred said, "Well, that was pretty good. We might as well have another." This time he experimented with chocolate and pronounced it equal to vanilla.

We reached grandfather's about four o'clock the next morning, in time for Uncle Alfred to change his clothes and help with the milking. He had learned to milk when he was eight years old and, except on the few occasions when he traveled away from home, he never missed a milking. One of the hired men told me a story about him that I hope is true. Uncle Alfred wore rubber knee boots that were wide and flopping at the top. The cow he was milking, in an effort to be cooperative or perhaps more comfortable, lifted one foot and slid it down inside Uncle Alfred's boot. According to the hired man, Uncle Alfred looked at the cow in surprise and said, "Well, either you or me has got to get out of this boot."

In the course of his seventy-eight years, there were stretches of time between the journeys Uncle took. He did not regard excursions as travel. First and perhaps happiest was the memorable occasion when "Me and Bert" went to New York. Bert was Aunt Jane's son. He had come down from Indiana to visit the relatives and had persuaded Uncle Alfred to go with him to New York. Two more innocent travelers never set forth. Bert had a modest jewelry business and wanted to visit Tiffany's to pick up, as he said, some ideas. After all, what did one go to New York for if not to learn? So Bert and Uncle Alfred entered the Tiffany portals, and a haughty gentleman came forward to ask what they wanted. He saw Indiana and upstate New York written all over them. Bert said he would like to see some of their best plated ware. His Haughtiness said magnificently, "Tiffany's does not deal in plated ware." Uncle Alfred and Bert nodded and left.

Today, in the light of the study of customer psychology, they would have been treated politely, and it is entirely possible that Uncle would have bought something *not* plated to take back to the aunts, as he always did when he returned from a journey. He and Bert thought the Tiffany man was funny and relished telling the story. It never occurred to Uncle Alfred to be embarrassed because he was a farmer and unaccustomed to city ways.

He and Aunt Elvie went to the Chicago World's Fair in 1892, along with father and mother, Uncle John and Aunt Alice, the Hamiltons and the Loomises, about half the neighborhood. They felt better traveling in groups when they went out West. In 1904, Uncle Alfred tried the St. Louis Exposition, rode on a Mississippi river boat and saw gamblers hard at work. He stood watching them so intently that one of them asked him to sit down and take a hand—Uncle must have looked a bird ripe for plucking. Uncle Alfred said no, he wasn't much on cards. The man turned on him roughly and said, "If you don't want to play, get out of here." Uncle Alfred got out with his money safe in his inside pocket.

In his old age, Uncle Alfred determined to go to Florida. He had some idea of picking up one of the wonderful real estate bargains of which the papers were full. The aunts announced that I must go with him or he would come home in possession of five hundred acres of swamp. This was the winter of 1919. We sailed from New York on a blustering February day and almost from the moment he stepped on board the boat Uncle Alfred was seasick. The trip to Jacksonville was acutely miserable for him and Florida a continuous disappointment. He had pictured warm sunshine, orange groves blooming and sweet as a northern orchard in spring, and soil so fertile that enormous vegetables almost leaped out of it. Instead it was one of the coldest and most unpromising winters that ever belied a real estate man's oratory. We shivered outdoors and went back to shiver inside hotels ill-equipped for genuine cold weather. Uncle Alfred trudged stoically on one sight-seeing expedition after another. He looked drearily at crocodiles and palm trees and was very unhappy. After a month I suggested that we go home by train. The plan involved getting from the west coast of Florida back to Jacksonville, and included an all-day trip along the twisting Oklawaha River, a 'gator on every log —and then another day along the St. Johns River, surely as lovely as any river could be.

Uncle looked out the window as the train moved north and the dreary landscape slipped by. He confided to me that he felt about the way old Uncle George Thomas did once when he went from Syracuse to Rochester and was asked to tell what he saw. Uncle George Thomas's travelogue must have been the briefest on record. He said, yes, he'd been from Syracuse to Rochester and back and the land was more or less alike. So much for Florida.

The Florida adventure was not wholly a loss. At least he had seen the state and could talk about it as other folks did, maybe with more reservations. Anyway, Florida was a finished job. When spring came he would plant some apple trees.

All his life Uncle Alfred was a planter of fruit trees, apple, cherry, pear, plum, like a later Johnny Appleseed. He pored over catalogues and meditated on the virtues of new varieties. When a tree-planting friend came to see him, they conferred at length on the improvements offered over the tried and true kinds they had known from boyhood. His cherry orchard flourished and so did his plums, but the new species of apples he set often disappointed him. The banana apple in particular was a failure. The tree bore profusely, to be sure, only the catalogue had promised Uncle Alfred that the apples would look and taste like bananas. The only resemblance was that their color was a pale, unhealthy yellow. The flavor was flat. The banana apple had to be written off as unworthy of its name.

Uncle's real pleasure was in setting the trees and anticipating the time when they would come into bearing. Age did not subdue his enthusiasm. His relatives and neighbors never neglected to point out to him that he was too old a man to be setting so many trees. He would never live to eat apples from them. Uncle had not read Cicero's wise reflection that there is no man so old he does not hope to live a year. Instead he gave his own wise answer. He said he had eaten apples all his life from trees that other men had planted. It was only fair that some day someone should eat apples from his trees.

I like to think of him in the orchard. He was for the most part a happy man, and happiest perhaps when he was doing work that sent his thoughts forward picturing how the tree full grown would blossom and the blossom become fruit and the cycle would repeat itself year after year. Planting a fruit tree is a creative act performed in faith, hope, and love. Uncle Alfred did not think of it in those terms. Nonetheless, he knew it for what it was.

In 1925, Uncle Alfred said he guessed they'd better have a party on his birthday, the twenty-first of January. He'd get some oysters and oranges and the girls could make some ice cream and he'd invite a few people in to eat supper. Probably this was the only party he ever initiated. But Aunt Wealthy was gone, and Aunt Elvie and Aunt Ellen were unequal to preparing the supper Uncle Alfred had in mind. Ethel volunteered to help with the cooking—roast beef, scalloped oysters and all the rest, working up steadily to the ice cream and oranges. Uncle Alfred's part of the preparations was to invite the guests. For a week or so, he went to the village every day, and when he came home would announce that he had met so-and-so and had invited him and his wife to the party. As the days went on, he saw many more so-and-so's who might just as well be asked. We thought he hunted them up. Most of those of his own age were gone, but he had never stopped making friends or enjoying being hospitable. Finally Ethel sat down with him and they counted up the guests: there were forty or more who expected to come, allowing for those Uncle Alfred didn't mention.

The dining room was large enough; the problem was

the cooking. It looked mountainous. Ethel decided it would ease things if they didn't have potatoes. Potatoes were almost a requirement at country meals, but they were then at a low ebb of fashion, and their absence would do away with the necessity of making gravy. That was a job Ethel hated, for it was one of the few things in cookery that she did badly. Aunt Elvie thought it would look queer not to have potatoes and gravy with their meat. Ethel pointed out that the beef and oysters and squash and cabbage salad and celery and baked apples and currant and raspberry jelly and pickled peaches and cucumber pickles and hot biscuit and brown bread and three kinds of cake, and pie for those who preferred it, and ice cream and oranges and the tea and coffee were enough, and there were limits to the stove and the oven. She prevailed. I think, though, that Uncle Alfred would have liked potatoes.

This was what our town still called "a cooked supper." The word "dinner" for a night meal had reached us, but people felt a little awkward about using it freely. Dinner was for most folks the noon meal. If you had a roast and hot vegetables at night, it was automatically "a cooked supper" as distinguished from an ordinary supper, where usually leftovers were warmed up and cold pie and applesauce added.

The night of the birthday party was perfect. January moonlight streamed down on snow and icicles and on the big white house, lighted from top to bottom. The forty-or-more arrived, the party began, supper was served. But where were the potatoes? The men looked about for them to make their appearance and slowed down their assault on the beef and oysters. Finally a neighbor stopped Ethel, busily passing sundries, and said, "Ethel, some way the potatoes missed me," an understatement for telling her that he some way missed the potatoes. In considerable embarrassment, Ethel explained that there were no potatoes. An incredulous look went round. *No potatoes!* They were too polite to say so, but the missing potatoes were undoubtedly a conversation piece at a good many breakfast tables next morning. Aside from the potatoes, the supper was a great success and the party a night to remember.

A year after the party, Uncle Alfred died on his birthday. There had been a gradual wearing out of the strong body that had served him so well. He knew that the end was near, and his thoughts were not for himself but for his sisters. As I sat beside him he said, "You and Ethel will have to look after the girls." I promised him that we would.

Only his name and the date are carved on the stone in the family burial lot. His epitaph is the memory he left in our hearts.

The complete names of the second twins were Laura Ann and Laura Ellen, but except on their gravestones the *Laura* disappeared and the twins went forward with the family standbys, Ann and Ellen. Ann without the final *e*. Ann and Anne may sound the same to the indifferent ear; they do not look the same in print or feel the same in the mind.

These twins were not identical. The unlikeness in their appearance extended to everything about them. Aunt Ann was the beauty of the family. Her hair was curling auburn, her eyes deep blue, and her lily-and-rose skin all that the Victorians desired. But her gifts of fortune did not end there. She had an eager, studious mind that could learn anything and wished to learn everything. Her youth was much easier than that of her older sisters or of her twin. Why she was spared the hardships so plentifully distributed among the others, no one ever said. She was always spoken of with peculiar tenderness, and her little possessions cherished in her memory. It is over ninety years since she died, and she was already a legend in my childhood.

Aunt Ann began teaching school at an early age. After a year or two, she wished very much to go away to school herself. The opportunity came in 1868 when her dear friend Clara Wright was sent to spend the winter at the home of an aunt who lived in Syracuse. Clara had a persistent cough and her father thought the open country too severe for her. She would get better in the sheltered city. Grandfather evidently believed that Ann should have her chance too. Her good mind deserved more training. It was arranged that she should board with the aunt and share Clara's room. The advantages of a city education were to be hers.

At first, the two girls must have had a happy time together. All their experiences were new and exciting. Aunt Ann went to the Unitarian Church, and its pastor, the Reverend Samuel May, was her idol. He was worthy of a young girl's adoration. His fame had begun before the Civil War. He was the uncle of Louisa May Alcott and—I almost wrote *therefore*—a New England Abolitionist.

When the Fugitive Slave Law was passed in 1850, it was a matter of conscience with him to disobey it. There was living in Syracuse at that time a Negro named Jerry who had escaped from bondage some years before and was earning a respectable living as a carpenter. After the law went into effect, men known as "slave catchers" appeared from the

South with writs to seize any and every Negro alleged to be a runaway slave. These Negroes were taken South for sale if no master claimed them. A profitable enterprise. Jerry was captured and helpless.

That night a mob gathered in front of the building where Jerry was known to be confined. The Reverend Samuel May rallied the crowd to action. They broke into the building and spirited Jerry away to safety under the very eyes of his captors. For this act of civil disobedience, Dr. May became a hero to the town and the countryside. A tablet commemorating the event is on the walls of the May Memorial Unitarian Church, named for him. No wonder Aunt Ann admired a Christian who had not been content with preaching the Word, but was a doer of it also.

The winter that began so happily for Ann and Clara turned slowly into anxiety and then into sorrow. Clara's cough grew worse, hemorrhages followed, and she died in the spring. At that time no one knew that consumption was infectious. Through the months of Clara's illness, Ann had continued to share Clara's room and sleep with her.

After Clara's death, Aunt Ann's days as a student ended. Grandfather, that Great Arranger, had bespoken the Pine Grove School in Cicero for her. Before term time she received the offer of a school near Syracuse at much better wages and accepted it. She too had a cough, but it was disregarded. The school went successfully all the next winter until suddenly one day she was taken with the fatal "bleeding at the lungs." She closed the school and came home, never to leave again.

The treatment of "galloping consumption" as practiced then was carried out with devotion by the family. Not a breath of fresh air was allowed to reach the patient. She was dosed with hot drinks and strong medicines, and she was watched carefully to see that the heavy blankets were not thrown off when she was burning with fever. She died on May 25, 1870, the eve of my mother's eighteenth birthday. This was the first death in the family, and there was not to be another among the brothers and sisters for almost fifty years.

Outside was the May world at its most beautiful with flowers and fragrances. Inside the new house, lived in only for a scant half year, the flower of the family was dead at twenty-one. Mother told me that among the flowers sent in from the neighbors' gardens were some tuberoses. She had never seen tuberoses before, and always afterward whenever she saw them, the heavy scent brought back the sharp memory of Aunt Ann's funeral.

Grandmother did not forget that bees leave their hives and go away when death enters a house unless they are carefully told what has happened. So Aunt Elvie was sent out to the garden where the hives stood among honeysuckle and pear blossom in the sweet May twilight. She laid strips of black cloth on the hives and told the bees that Ann had gone away forever. In what words did she tell them?

Ethel and I were occasionally allowed to look at some of Aunt Ann's possessions while we were growing up. There were the little books that she had won as Sunday school prizes, and the fine pillowcases, made perhaps for an imagined hope chest. And there was her Bible. It had gilt clasps and gilt corners in a grape pattern. It was printed in Oxford in 1864 and the gilt is still untarnished and shining. I used to believe it was solid gold. Aunt Ann had received the book as a prize for knowing perfectly so many Bible verses. The print, however, is so minute that the youngest eyes would be tried by it. The pages are unsoiled. I think Aunt Ann must have read the big family Bible instead.

My favorite among Aunt Ann's books was not the Bible. It was a book she had bought for the use of her pupils in school and bore the terrifying title *Slate Pictures for the Useful Self-Employment of Young Children*. The leaves of the book were black and the pictures in white lines, such as a slate pencil would mark on a slate. The pictures were more remote in subject even than the world of 1870. They were English pictures of dovecotes and soldiers in uniforms like Wellington's men and all the odd tools and furnishings of an ancient English kitchen. By laying a piece of silk paper over the page you could copy the picture and be your own artist. Silk paper is now called tissue paper—not so rich sounding. My hours of tracing the pictures were as happy as those of Aunt Ann's pupils in their useful self-employment, but the book was always put back on a high shelf.

Aunt Ann's short life does not seem too sad to look back upon at a distance of three generations. It had the quality of a nineteenth-century idyll, shadowy and touching, like a poem where death inevitably awaited the young and beautiful. Yet in its way it was complete: she was lovely, she was beloved, and she was spared the pain and grief that her sisters endured. I do not believe they ever spoke of her as beautiful; that was a word outside daily use. Instead they said always that Ann was very fair, and fair has been chosen to picture the king's daughter since English began.

In thinking about my other aunts and all that happened

to them during their long lives, the wide gulf between what they wanted and what life gave them, I reach always the same painful conclusion: Aunt Ellen's was saddest of all. Saddest because of its emptiness. It was not enough that her twin sister had all the charm of mind and body, but nature had dealt unfairly with Aunt Ellen in other ways. She was very little; her hair, like Aunt Ann's, was red, of a pale color redeemed from carrot by flecks of gold, but thin, straight, and unmanageable. Her very dark blue eyes, pansy or violet a poet would have said, were her prettiest feature, but they did not shine with the light that comes from happiness or understanding. A sort of blankness enveloped her so that no one noticed whether she was there or not.

She was slow in school. She could write her name, but I never knew of her writing a letter, and her reading was always carried on by pointing to the word and saying it half aloud just as she must have done in district school. Beyond darning her stockings or sewing on a button, she had no hand skills whatever.

A different kind of treatment by the family might have developed latent possibilities in her. Unfortunately, once it was decided that Ellen was slow-witted, she was given no opportunity to do anything responsible about the house. She washed mountains of dishes and heavy iron pots and kettles; she was never allowed to wash the best dishes which might have been a pleasure to handle. She carried innumerable pails of water the long distance from the well to the house and brought in staggering armfuls of wood and mopped the big kitchen floor and scrubbed the back steps and pared potatoes, all useful and all deadly as year followed year.

No one was actively unkind to her, though she was sometimes scolded or rebuked for forgetting something or doing it awkwardly. They meant to be just to her. She had plenty of clothes, cloaks, and shawls for summer and winter, a black silk dress and a fine wool one, but she never chose them. The older sisters decided for her. If she was sick—she seldom was—every care was taken of her and she lived to be eighty-three years old.

One of the things she liked to do was to scrape apples for Ethel and me. Almost as many theories were held about the digestibility of raw apples as Mr. Woodhouse set forth when he tried to keep his guests from eating their baked apples. A scraped apple was thought to be perfect for children, whereas a Northern Spy swallowed in big gulps would doubtless have kept the child's mother up half the night tending him.

Aunt Ellen sat in a little rush-bottomed chair by the kitchen fire. She had armed herself with a big apple and an old steel case knife grown sharp with use. We stood at her knee. She pared and scraped and held out the result for us to swallow from the blunt end of the knife blade. I *hated* scraped apple. The flavor of the steel knife combined with the mushy apple was repulsive to me, and Ethel felt the same way. Yet I am sure neither of us said so, and Aunt Ellen scraped happily to give us pleasure.

In the morning in summer, Aunt Ellen baked potatoes for breakfast, and Aunt Elvie made cream codfish to go with them—using real cream, real butter, and real codfish cut off in a chunk at the grocery store from an original undiminished fish. At suppertime from the baked potatoes left at breakfast, Aunt Ellen produced her one and only cooking triumph, the best warmed-up potato anyone ever ate. To the potato foundation she added all the cream the potatoes could hold and topped them with all the butter that would stick. Calories and cholesterol had not yet appeared on the dietary horizon, and the potatoes suited the appetites of tired men after a long day's work.

However slow Aunt Ellen's mind, there was much that must have hurt her. When the family as a whole was invited for holidays or church affairs, Aunt Ellen went along and beyond a remark on the weather sat in silence unregarded. But in afternoon companies of women, when Aunt Jane and Aunt Sophy and mother were married and gone, only Aunt Welt and Aunt Elvie were mentioned and expected at the party. The hardest thing to bear must have been that it was taken for granted that Aunt Ellen did not mind being the one left at home. The others went to the Chicago World's Fair and to visit Aunt Jane in Indiana and to my college commencement. Aunt Ellen stayed behind. It was not intentional unkindness—far from it. It was not thought about at all. Perhaps Aunt Ellen *was* happier at home away from the sharp contrasts and the consciousness of being ignored or neglected.

It is comforting to remember that her old age was happier than her earlier life. When all the rest, one by one, had gone, Aunt Elvie and Aunt Ellen developed something like real companionship. They were the only ones left who could say to each other, "Do you remember?" Astonishingly too, Aunt Ellen in her last years often displayed more insight into people's motives and acts than anyone would ever have thought possible. She was invited out with Aunt Elvie and enjoyed it. Her clothes, which I chose for her with her approval, were becoming, the red hair took on blondness, the blue eyes remained very blue, and the fair skin unwrinkled as in youth. Age did not seem to touch her for the worse. Her death was unexpected and swift, without warning or pain. Because she had always been at home, the house suddenly lacked something when the busy little trotting figure was not there. We missed the voice that had been silent through most of her life.

Aunt Elvie, safely named and rescued from the candle-started fire, was not expected to grow up. This expectation was based by the family on the long weakness that followed her attack of scarlet fever and diphtheria as a little child, and it was often voiced in her hearing. It created in her mind a fear of illness and death never to leave her. As a matter of fact, she lived longest of all the family—to the great age of ninety-six.

How does a child come to understand what death is and

to be seized with terror at the thought of it? It may have been that Aunt Elvie saw the death of animals on the farm, or perhaps she heard talk of the death of friends as the end with nothing to follow. Every night when she was put to bed she would ask grandmother, "Ma, do you think I'll die before morning?" Grandmother's reassurances never soothed or satisfied her.

Actually, in womanhood she was tall and wiry and distinctly tough in her powers of endurance and her vitality. Her supposed delicacy did not hinder her working. She scrubbed and cleaned, and took care of the chickens from the hatching process to chicken as it appeared on the dinner table; she washed and ironed ceaselessly, helped out occasionally with milking, picked berries in the hottest sun, canned and preserved and pickled, and always was ready to do something extra when needed. Her only sewing was to make superior buttonholes on the shirts and dresses and nightgowns Aunt Welt handed over to her. She was proud of her accomplishment in this field, which she had all to herself. Though she liked to work outdoors, her flower-raising was limited to beds of pansies and hyacinths in the spring.

I cannot imagine our childhood without Aunt Elvie. It was she who gave tea parties for my dolls, and when fascinators were fashionable she knitted a lovely little scarlet one for Queenie, my best doll. Fascinators were triangular in shape, knitted of soft wool and worn either as complete headgear or tied over cap or bonnet. Pretty young women found fascinators as becoming as Spanish mantillas, and old ladies and children had their ears kept warm by them. They were made in all colors. Naturally the Moultons preferred their fascinators to be of black or sober dark brown or grey. Since

Queenie was a doll, it was quite all right for her to wear scarlet. Aunt Elvie loved gay colors, but she would not have ventured to appear at church in a scarlet fascinator.

One of my earliest memories of Aunt Elvie is of a chestnutting expedition. She and Ethel were about to start for the chestnut grove at the end of the lane, and I wept loudly because nobody considered me old enough to go along. Aunt Elvie could not bear to see me cry, so she said she would carry me, and she got a pint tin pail from the pantry for me to put nuts in, provided I picked up any. The grove was a good half mile away, and there were fences to climb, but Aunt Elvie managed. The pint pail shines in my remembrance of things past.

In spite of forebodings of early death, Aunt Elvie's nature was sunny. She shared with Uncle Charles the gift of humor. It was not wit, such as Uncle Charles had, but rather the blessed power of seeing that everyday things had their funny side. Her unexpected combinations of thought and words amused everybody, and they said Elvie was good company. Above all, she had the loving heart that is instantly felt by others to be the foundation of kindness and sympathy.

Yet a sort of continuous sadness existed beneath the fun. The bright hopes with which she began something or looked forward to something were only too likely to disappoint her or fail altogether, until as she grew older she prefaced every statement of a plan or intention with the words, "if nothing happens." Like an ancient Greek she tried to conciliate the gods of destiny. But something almost always did happen. She would buy the cloth for a new dress to wear on an important occasion and it would be spoiled in the making. She would work so hard to get house and food prepared for a church party that when the day came she would have a prostrating sick headache. The family believed these headaches descended from grandfather's migraine; it is more probable they were due to exhaustion.

This happened not once, but over and over again. Life simply did not keep its promises to her. At sixteen she became engaged to Charley Lawrence, a neighbor's son, a blue-eyed, rosy lad of English stock, only a year or two older than she. Both families thought well of the engagement. Charley gave her a heavy plain gold ring that could serve later as the wedding ring. Engraved inside it were their initials and the curious motto *United We Stand*. Aunt Elvie did not think the motto odd. She wore the ring till she died and kept Charley's picture, framed in red velvet, first on the parlor mantel shelf and later in her top bureau drawer.

For Charley did not live to fulfill the motto. On a stormy day in February he and Uncle Alfred started with a sleigh-load of teasels for Skaneateles. Teasels were then used to card and unsnarl flax and brought a good price. Skaneateles was thirty miles away on icy roads and over steep hills. The boys were all day reaching there and delivering their load. The storm had not lessened and they did not want to face it in darkness for thirty miles. They decided to spend the night in the village, where Charley had cousins. They were kindly welcomed and given the spare bedroom. Any bedroom any-where was likely to be unheated in winter, and this spare room was freezing cold. The boys shivered and shuddered in the icy bed and resolved to start for home as early as they could. By morning Charley was coughing and burning with fever, and the cousins begged him not to attempt to go back. But he would not listen. He huddled down under the blan-kets of the sleigh while Uncle Alfred drove. When home was reached, Charley was put to bed, pneumonia set in, and he died in a few days.

Aunt Elvie's grief was sharp, yet not, I think, so heart-breaking as Aunt Welt's over her young soldier. Aunt Elvie loved less intensely than Aunt Welt, whose loves were fewer and went very deep.

Some years afterward Aunt Elvie had another romance and an even briefer engagement. This time grandfather was in opposition. He pronounced the young man a worthless good-for-nothing and forbade the marriage. The great weakness of Aunt Elvie's character was that she could not stand out against pressure from others or endure being at variance with those she loved. She always feared it would cost her their affection. She lacked Aunt Sophy's will to resist grandfather and gave up the young man. His broken heart healed rapidly: he married a girl in the village who died in childbirth, and he departed to live in Syracuse, where he married again.

Forty years later, when Ethel was buying a coat in a department store in Syracuse, she gave the clerk her address in Cicero. The woman looked at her strangely and said, "If you live in Cicero do you happen to know a Miss Elvie Moulton —if she is still alive?"

Ethel said yes—Miss Moulton was her aunt. "Well," the woman said, "she was engaged once to my husband. I always wanted to tell her how lucky she was that she didn't marry him and have to lead such a life as I've had with him." Grandfather should have been living!

Ethel and I decided that we had better not pass on the word of Aunt Elvie's luck to her. She never spoke to us of either of her lost loves. Yet was it luck that she was neither wife nor mother as nature intended her to be? I am afraid she minded being unmarried, though she met the situation head on by referring to herself frequently as an old maid. There was alleviation in some degree since Uncle Alfred did not marry, and a man's presence in the house kept it from narrowing into a spinster's world. Uncle Alfred was always available to take his sisters to church doings or wherever other women went with their husbands. Aunt Elvie made up for the lack of children of her own by lavishing her love on many children. No child of hers would ever have been subject to discipline. She could not have compelled obedience nor would she have had the resolution to resist their demands, however extraordinary. But if those children had had Aunt Elvie's nature they would have been nice to have around.

Aunt Elvie's brief career as a teacher ended in her fleeing the schoolroom forever. It must have been grandfather who thrust her into the lion's den. He could not credit that a daughter of his would be unequal to coping (it was not called coping then) with any child that walked. For one awful term the children in district fourteen ruled unchecked. Then Aunt Elvie resigned and told grandfather she would rather take in moppings than go on teaching.

She had no more love for books than the children had. In the paper she read the Woman's Page, chiefly recipes and Useful Home Hints, and she liked stories that turned out happily. Books with a problem that bore on wide issues she did not open; books that dealt with the young who had no problems except those that centered in the home and in the course of true love she thoroughly enjoyed. From *Little Women* to *Heidi,* she found peace and pleasure in heroines safe from the slings and arrows of outrageous fortune.

In her old age she told me that what she had really wanted to do was to work in a store where everybody came in to buy groceries and boots and thread and ribbon and sundries. She said it would have been a chance to get acquainted with a lot of people and talk over what was going on. Aunt Elvie had never heard that the reward of travel is to meet such nice people; she would have been wholly content to meet the nice customers who came to the store. Modest as her wish was, it was unobtainable. There was too much work at home for her to leave, and money enough so that there was no need for her to go away to earn wages. Nor was there any lack of visitors at home for Aunt Elvie to meet and welcome and wait on. She regarded the house as empty when there were no more than three or four people in it. Poor company, Aunt Elvie said, was better than none. She could not understand my own willingness to be by myself and would shake her head and say, "You are a queer child." To her Ethel and I remained perpetual children. When she spoke to one of us, she always addressed us as "dear child." No words were ever more faithfully tender. After she had gone from us we knew with an aching sense of loss that no one would ever again call us "dear child."

Aunt Elvie's love for people showed itself in many ways, most often by food. It was a subject for smiles in the village that wherever Elvie went she brought a basket. It might contain freshly picked strawberries or blackberries, a loaf of graham bread or a can of pickled peaches—whatever was at hand that would help the hostess the day after the party. We often had parties of school friends, to which Aunt Elvie always came to help mother with the supper and the dishes. If we were sick, she would trudge up the road carrying a pail with a bowl of ice cream inside to cheer us up. When I was in college, a box from Aunt Elvie regularly arrived during the February finals. This was intended—unconsciously I hope—to lessen the pain should I fail to pass the examinations. The box held fricasseed chicken, strawberry preserves, and angel food cake made with a dozen eggs. Aunt Elvie's cakes seldom suited her and she was in the habit of mourning, "This one isn't as good as the last one I baked." We would set up an answering chorus: "No, it isn't as good as the last one you baked, but it's plenty good enough for us." Aunt Elvie never made sugar cookies, fruit cake, or pie. They belonged in Aunt Welt's province. All other cakes and confections she produced in profusion and perfection.

The sad feature of her cooking was that she was not a consumer. Almost as far back as I can remember, Aunt Elvie began adopting quirks in food. Coffee was first to be pushed off her diet list. She loved coffee smothered in cream. Unfortunately, articles appearing on the Woman's Page pointed out how dangerously caffein affected the nerves and the high probability that it acted as a slow poison on the digestive tract. The ladies at church agreed that coffee-drinking was deplorable, but only Aunt Elvie dropped it. She pinned her faith to green tea for sick headaches. The year before she died she restored coffee in a faint measure to its place in her regard. She put one teaspoonful of coffee in a cup of hot milk and was, as far as she could tell, none the worse for it.

Meat was banished next after coffee: beef, pork, veal, and fowl. To the family protests Aunt Elvie replied that she didn't think meat was good for her. So the delicious chicken pies, the browned spareribs, the ham and sausage, and steaks and roasts were cooked for others and untouched by her. She made one or two exceptions. Lamb was eaten by people in the Bible, and a small, a very *small* piece of tender lamb could be trusted to do no mischief. And fish was different from meat and strengthening, and so was bacon, if cooked till the fat was all out; and creamed dried beef wasn't hurtful if you didn't eat the beef.

Candy and sweets were discarded; she sometimes permitted herself to eat the *inside* of a piece of pie, custard or fruit, but never touched the crust contaminated by lard. Her pie eating was confined strictly to home, for she would not have hurt the feelings of any hostess by leaving the crust on her plate. "Elvie couldn't eat my piecrust" would have been the conclusion drawn from the evidence. Piecrust was a touchy point in our town. You swallowed it if it killed you; otherwise you implied that it was too tough to chew. What woman could be expected to put up with that?

Grapes caused Aunt Elvie concern. She had always been fond of them and had eaten them as everyone else did, swallowing the pulp without extracting the seeds and savoring the sweet cool slipperiness as it went down. Now this enjoyment was threatened by the rise of appendicitis. The earlier name for what became appendicitis was "inflammation of the bowels," words with a chilling sound. Whoever had this inflammation died in great pain, almost at once. Unexpectedly, it seemed to our community, the disease changed to appendicitis. The inflamed appendix could be cut out and the patient saved if the trouble was identified quickly enough. The hope of recovery was encouraging, but what caused the appendix to go wrong? All sorts of theories were advanced by medical men, and an equal number of guesses put forward by the public that might be standing in the need of an operation. In our town the accepted belief was that seeds of some kind got wedged in the appendix and set up the inflammation. The thing to detect was—what seeds? The Henderson sisters, both Em and Addie, fixed on tomato seeds and grape seeds. Tomatoes could still be eaten if the seeds were scooped out. Grapes were not so easy, since each grape required the active cooperation of tongue and teeth in casting forth the unwanted. Aunt Elvie did not reject tomatoes; they were strengthening and could be made safe without too much work. But grapes with the seeds out left a sour residue in the mouth, and if teeth were as poor as hers, it wasn't worth it to struggle. She never had appendicitis and neither did the Henderson sisters.

In spite of village laughter over Elvie's cup of hot water and cracker, her diet was far better than the family realized. She lived on milk, eggs, bread, cereals, fruits, and vegetables, and of these she ate so sparingly that she was rail-thin. What she omitted, after all, were the fats and sugars.

Her teeth may have been a factor in her giving up meat. They failed her quite early, and she would not go to a dentist. Submitting to pain voluntarily was beyond her power. The result distressed us, and Ethel and I tried to persuade her that the process of having her teeth out with an anesthetic would be quite simple and she would not suffer. Finally, as the teeth grew worse and worse, Ethel interviewed a dentist and explained Aunt Elvie's fears. He promised the kindest treatment and was sure she need not worry about being hurt. After much argument, Aunt Elvie consented to go to him and the date was set. We were to take her to the city and stay with her every minute, and we bolstered her courage by emphasizing all that the dentist had said. On the morning of the day, as we were getting ready, our telephone rang. Aunt Elvie was sick in bed with a violent headache and was throwing up. It was so clear a case of fright that we never attempted to get her near a dentist again. One by one her teeth fell out and gradually the gums hardened to stone. Aunt Elvie chewed vigorously with them, just as well, she said, as if she'd had false teeth like Welt and Ellen, and she didn't have the fuss of putting them in a cup of water every night either.

Underlying the tooth misadventure was the permanent dread that "something" might happen. The "something" was death. Granted that life was full of disappointments and sorrows, Aunt Elvie loved it and wanted to go on living. She never went to a funeral or looked at the dead, not even the dead she had loved dearly in life. She was upset if flowers from a funeral were brought to her. She knew the flowers were sent in kindness by someone who did not understand her feeling, and she received the gift politely—and got rid of the flowers as soon as she could.

It hurts to think of how much happiness she ought to have had and of the persistence with which her pleasures were flawed in ways unforeseen and impossible to avoid. She had always longed to go to the Woods, as we called the Adirondack Mountains, and one summer day I suggested that we go up there in my car and stay overnight. Aunt Elvie was delighted with the prospect. She wanted to see Old Forge, the most talked-of spot in the Woods among her acquaintances who traveled. The weather was sunny, the roads good, and we reached Old Forge quickly. But Aunt Elvie could not believe it really *was* Old Forge. She had pictured the place to herself set in thick forest beside a sparkling mountain lake. It was nothing of the sort. Much of the area had been lumbered over, and the ugly buildings offered little of interest and afforded her no enjoyment. Aunt Elvie was ready to cry to think that the Old Forge of her imagination was swept away by raw reality. Aunt Welt had once said to me that the Moultons were all under a curse. If it were so, the curse that fell upon Aunt Elvie displayed itself in never giving her the fullness of joy that corresponded to her hope.

There was the Easter when I took her and mother for their first visit to New York. Easter was late in April, and that should have meant sunshine, warmth, and green leaves. But with Aunt Elvie along, the weather turned windy and hesitated between snow and rain. Central Park, where they had expected to see flower beds in full bloom, was as barren and bitter cold as Grant's Tomb; the Statue of Liberty guarded arctic water; and the ferry ride they had counted on was out of the question. We stopped in a nice place to get thawed out with malted milk for Aunt Elvie and hot chocolate for mother and me. Aunt Elvie spooned her malted milk gratefully, and then all of a sudden she discovered there was blood in her mouth: she was going to have a hemorrhage! The tiny spot of blood on the napkin undoubtedly came from a tooth, but Aunt Elvie was too frightened to be reasoned with. We went straight back to the hotel. The hemorrhage did not occur and later on, after Aunt Elvie was herself again, we found a movie nearby where John Barrymore substituted dream for reality—to Aunt Elvie's comfort.

Her serious illnesses began when she was already elderly and they followed a pattern: there was a slight cold, it worsened, and pneumonia developed in its most severe form. Incredible as it was to the doctors and to us, she survived five attacks of the disease in pre-penicillin days. Each time the doctors decided there was no hope, and each time the church friends wrote in their diaries: "Elvie Moulton is not expected to live through the night." She recovered, but with the constant dread of having to go through another attack. She did not have pneumonia again, and two days before her ninety-sixth birthday she was anticipating her birthday party and the new red sweater that was to be a present from her Indiana grandnieces. She was not ill, only things did not seem to be quite as usual with her. One sign was that at supper she ate only a mouthful of her favorite johnnycake that Ethel had made for her. At bedtime she asked me to sleep in her room that night. In the early morning she called me, and as I raised her up she died in my arms. The long terror of death was over at last and the end was not fearful at all.

Sarah Marie Moulton

WHEN MOTHER was eighty-eight years old, she began to be tired of what she called a do-nothing life. She was able to read by a skillful moving of a magnifying glass along the lines, but although she read lavishly there was still too much unoccupied time left that could no longer be filled with the household tasks of sewing, knitting, or rug making.

For a day or two she enjoyed trying to see if she could write down the capital cities of all the states in the Union and their location, which she had learned eighty years before in district school. She sailed along smoothly from "Maine: Augusta on the Kennebec" through the list of the states as they had been admitted to about 1875. The memory test ended with a perfect score. What could she do next?

I suggested that she try writing some account of her childhood, a page a day, setting down the stories she had told us and anything that she remembered from her youth. Mother objected that things often were not straight in her head and what she wrote would be muddled. I assured her that it wouldn't be any more muddled than the stream-of-consciousness writing then establishing itself in current literature, and mother finally agreed to try. She could not use ink, but with a pencil and a big sheet of paper laid on a book she could sit in her armchair and write a little every day.

The plan worked better than I expected. Before she grew tired of it, she had covered many pages on both sides of the paper. But it was disappointing to find that the stories as she had written them were far less interesting than as she had told them to us. Mother was a born storyteller, delightful to listen to, when voice and gesture and the expression of her face made the story come alive for us. These things were missing in the writing, and so were the homely details that created reality. The stories lacked the special quality that had charmed us in childhood. As she had feared, the sequence in time was confused or disregarded; yet occasionally some of the things she wrote pictured clearly that vanished world of which I am speaking.

She had begun to read so young that she could not recall the process of learning, and one of her earliest problems was to find a safe place where reading would be uninterrupted. To hide in plain sight—almost but not quite—was the solution. There was a window at the foot of her bed, and by crawling under the bed close to the window she found light enough to read by and dimness enough to escape notice. Lying flat on her stomach, with the book on the floor before her and her head propped on her hands—the time-honored position of secret readers—she read in peace any book she could get hold of. She always spoke of *The Children of the Abbey* and *Thaddeus of Warsaw* with affection. Ethel and I tried them on her recommendation and thought them terrible.

At the time when my mother started to school, a parent paid a tax for each child's education. Grandfather had always paid it cheerfully. But when the law was passed making education in the common schools free to every child in New York State, grandfather was highly indignant. Why should he be taxed to provide education for his neighbor's children? He had looked after his own children's chance at school; let the neighbors do the same. As a matter of fact, the school tax levied in the district hardly justified grandfather's emotion, since the salary of teachers was meager, fuel was cheap, and teacher and pupils did the work of keeping the schoolhouse clean and the educational fires burning.

During her school years, mother had all the experiences that a snow country afforded children in the 1850's. When the snow piled high, grandfather's oxen were hitched to a long, low bobsleigh and came to the school to carry home all the children from her neighborhood. It must have been after dark when the last infant was deposited at home, for school was "kept" till four o'clock in the afternoon, and Buck and Bride set their own pace. Mother had chilblains, and on the days not bad enough for the oxen to be sent she would stop at a little wood-colored house halfway between school and home. A kind old Irish woman lived there, who always welcomed mother warmly, gave her a slice of bread and butter, and put her feet in the stove oven to get warm. Very comforting, but probably not the best treatment for chilblains.

She was very happy in school though it lacked everything now thought requisite for either health or learning. It had, however, the priceless ingredient: a remarkable teacher. Miss Harriet Loomis, who presided there for many years, was a superior woman. She was still alive, a very old lady indeed, in my early childhood. Once she described her first teaching to Ethel and me. She was fourteen years old and ruled over a log schoolhouse that stood on a road accurately called The Cowpath. She received seventy-five cents a week.

Miss Harriet stressed the achievement of excellence, particularly in reading and writing. To the end of her life, mother was disturbed because both her daughters wrote so untidily and illegibly. Her own writing was fine, clear, delicate and even as an engraving. If she had been Chinese she would have understood that the artist's signature is a true part of the drawing. This is the way Miss Harriet taught her pupils to write, as mother recalled it in her autobiography:

> In those days we were taught writing and each scholar had a writing book. It was a number of sheets of paper fastened together with a cover. At the top of each page was a written saying like "As the twig is bent the tree inclines." We were expected to copy this as well as we could on the lines below. The last line we wrote was usually much better than the first. Each day at a certain hour the writing books were passed out and at the end of the period gathered up and laid in the drawer of the teacher's desk. It seems that learning to write well is very much neglected in the present day.

I'm afraid mother had Ethel and me in mind when she wrote that last sentence.

Miss Harriet made it a point to have company every two weeks on Friday, and then each child had to speak a piece or write a composition to read to the visitors. She brought glimpses too of the outside world to the geography class, for she had read of far-off California and could tell of wonderful trees and flowers and show them murmuring shells from the ocean. None of the children had ever seen a pineapple until Miss Harriet brought one to school and shared it among them. Best of all, Miss Harriet had beautiful manners and a belief that good manners and discipline must accompany education. She was never paid very much in money, but all who went to school to her spoke always of "Miss Hattie" with a love and respect any teacher would be proud to inspire.

A new pleasure began for mother when she was about eight years old. She had gone across the road one Sunday morning to see our friend Clara Wright. She found Clara getting ready for Sunday school, with her mother buttoning her into a white dotted muslin dress. Mother wrote about the effect on her.

> I think I must have gone home and talked about it and wished that I could go to Sunday school too. Mother promised that she would try to have us go the next summer. As I remember, when the time came, I had a new dress of challis-delaine to wear. That was a name given to a soft cotton or cotton-and-wool stuff—often with a pattern of flowers woven in it. We all had shakers. I don't suppose anyone knows now what shakers were, and after eighty years I doubt if one could be found unless some museum has preserved one as a curiosity. Shakers were worn on the head instead of hats. They were shaped in a half circle made of straw and trimmed with red, blue or green chambray. Chambray was gingham with a linen finish. On top of the straw circle was a band and bow and in the back a cape about a foot long. The shakers were tied like bonnets. They sound queer as I write about them, but we thought they were very pretty and becoming to wear to Sunday school.
>
> The Sunday school was held in the Universalist Church and the Superintendent was Warren Wright, who afterward

married my sister Sophia. He had a democrat wagon and carried all the children that went from our way—a big load at times. There were seventy-five or more scholars at church each week. We had songbooks and catechisms and often had to learn verses from the Bible. Some weeks I learned as many as ten verses besides the regular lesson.

One result of this Sunday school training was that mother regularly quoted the Bible to us. Her favorite verses were those that approached poetry. She was fond of explaining a mystery of human nature by repeating: "The wind bloweth where it listeth and ye hear the sound thereof; but cannot tell whence it cometh or whither it goeth: so is he that is born of the Spirit." Another verse that she loved also dealt with the unexplainable: "Who knoweth the spirit of man that goeth upward or the spirit of the beast that goeth downward to the earth?"

There was one verse she used a bit irreverently to remind Ethel and me when we had forgotten or neglected some work we had been told to do. Mother would set about doing it, saying loud enough for us to hear, "Let him that is greatest among you be the servant of all."

In September of 1865, when mother was thirteen years old, men from Oneida County came into the neighborhood to hire all the girls that were willing to go hop picking for two weeks. Many acres of hops were raised in Oneida. Hops were used by breweries everywhere and in yeastmaking and were a profitable crop if they could be picked before the first early frosts. There was so little chance in those days for girls to earn cash money that a considerable number of them agreed to go. Aunt Sophy was relieved of cooking for the hired men at the Thomas farm so that she could be a hop-picker and she decided to take mother along with her. As a preparation they made a number of pairs of thick gloves from factory cloth, which was a heavy unbleached muslin cotton of stout wearing qualities. Such gloves would protect their hands that otherwise might blister.

The ride to the Oneida hopyard was in lumber wagons, springless and with no seats except boards laid across from side to side. The thirty-mile journey, behind farm horses walking all the way, left the girls so tired that their employer told them work would not begin till the next morning.

The hop vines grew around poles and sometimes ran from one pole to another. Boxes which held seven bushels were used to pick in, and four of these boxes were joined together. The men who pulled the poles would let a pole down over each end of a box so that two pickers could work at the same vine. Mother said that when the hops were firm and hard the boxes filled quite fast. Sometimes, however, the hops were soft or infected with lice, and then it took her all day to fill one box. In the two weeks diligent Sarah earned two dollars and fifty cents.

This hopyard was not far from the famous Oneida Community, about which highly controversial opinions were held. It was a period everywhere of experiments in communal living, and because the ways and customs and purposes of the groups differed so widely from those of ordinary folks, the countryside around such communities was likely to be critical and hostile. Apparently this particular hopyard owner did not share in the prejudice, or else he wanted to make the girls feel they had seen something of the world while away from home. Whatever his reason, when Sunday came he offered to take them all to visit the Community. Mother wrote that she was too young and strange to notice very much. She thought the buildings were nice and large and such a lot of them! The people in the Community were dressed in plain ordinary clothes and acted like other people as far as she could see. What stood out in her memory was the beautiful chapel she went into and the singing of the children.

When she was ten years older, in 1875, she went hop picking again. That year the hops were good, and mother picked the most of anyone in the yard. She earned over thirteen dollars in less than two weeks, and she loved the smell of hops all her life. But as the years passed hop picking attracted a rougher and wilder type of worker until it was no longer regarded as desirable work for a well-brought-up girl to undertake. In my own childhood hops were still grown, but the Hop Growers Picnic at the end of the season was thought of in our neighborhood as a tough, barely respectable outing from which careful citizens stayed away.

Spring of 1868 came, and mother went with her friend, Delia Talcot, to a nearby town to try the examination for teachers, and both she and Delia were given certificates by the commissioner. There were certificates to fit every need. Lowest of all was the third grade, good for six months, and in great favor with young women who wished to earn money for their wedding clothes. The second grade certificate covered a few more subjects and presumably asked harder questions and was valid for several years. The crown of educational achievement was the first grade certificate which granted the holder the right to teach in any public school in the state for life. It was about the equivalent of a high school diploma. The only teacher in a district school that I ever knew of who possessed a first grade certificate was my sister Ethel.

Lest the commissioner be left without teachers, the law kindly gave him the power to grant permits with no examination at all. These permits could be bestowed upon the daughters or nieces of those to whom the commissioner owed a political debt, or wherever he perceived future usefulness in a friendly gesture. The permits were renewable without examination. I do not know what kind of certificate mother drew, but certainly she had no intention at that time of using it. It turned out otherwise. Grandfather, as I have said, had taken pains to secure the Pine Grove School for Aunt Ann. After all his foresight, he was somewhat taken aback when Aunt Ann accepted a much better position near Syracuse. With instant recovery, Grandfather said, "Well, it doesn't matter. Sarah can take Ann's place at Pine Grove."

Sarah heard her sentence in dismay, but naturally made no protest. School was to begin the first week in May, three weeks before mother's sixteenth birthday. The trustees accepted grandfather's substitution of one daughter for another, and the family hurried to make a new calico dress for mother to appear in at school. On the first morning, grandfather took her to Pine Grove. They stopped in the village at the general store long enough for grandfather to buy her a pair of shoes. Mother said there was no fitting of shoes at the store; the only thing to be sure of was to get them big enough. So, arrayed in the new calico dress and fortified by the firm new shoes, mother began her teaching. She did not guess that she would follow the occupation through the next ten years.

What did she look like as she stood before her pupils? To

the children, she probably seemed completely grown up. She was tall and slim; her brown hair was looped in braids about her head; her decorous skirts came to her ankles. Her eyes were very dark and she was the only one of grandfather's ten children to inherit his aquiline nose. It was of slender and delicate lines and lent distinction to her features. A picture that I have of her at eighteen shows a very touching expression on her young face, at once grave and innocent.

So far as the school itself was concerned, no teaching experience for a beginner could have been more agreeable. It was the summer term, when only the little girls and boys came. They were well behaved and eager to learn, and mother loved them all. The only cloud in her sky was that, in addition to her salary of two dollars and fifty cents a week, she was expected to "board around" in different homes in the district, staying a week for each child the family had in school.

Fortunately for mother, the first place to which she went was the Skiff farm. The Skiffs had been family friends for three generations, the farm was large and prosperous, and staying there was almost like being at home. Polly Skiff, the mistress of the household, was a notable cook and a kind and motherly woman. Some of the daughters were mother's age, and two little Skiff children went to school as her pupils, so for two blessed weeks mother was happy and comfortable.

Mother's stay at the Skiff farm had not prepared her for what was to follow. In the next place, the family lived on intimate terms with the chickens. At supper on the first night, mother was horrified to have a chicken fly up on the table to share the meal. The food, oddly enough, was good, but the chicken took away her appetite.

Once when she was to change boarding places, mother had a bad sick headache. The house was three miles from the school, and there was no means of getting there except to walk. The children were her guides, and all the long way mother looked forward to a cup of hot, hot green tea to help her headache. But at the house she found that the woman was away on an afternoon visit and had left her husband to get a makeshift supper for the teacher.

The man said, "Well, Miss Moulton, she let the kitchen fire go out, and if you don't mind drinking water for supper, I guess I won't build it up again." Mother said she didn't mind.

Not all her experiences were like these two. There were pleasant interludes where she was welcomed and liked because she made her own bed and wiped the dishes for her hostess. But "Aunt Polly" Skiff had her own notion about the fitness of some of the places and presently invited mother to come back and spend the rest of the term with the Skiffs. On the last day of school there was a grand picnic under the pine trees. Everybody in the district brought food, and grandmother Moulton sent a clothes basket loaded with chicken pies, apple pies, cheese, pickles, and doughnuts.

With the first money she earned by teaching, mother bought three maple chairs for grandmother's parlor. The chair backs were carved in a rose pattern that caught mother's fancy. Chairs of this type were called side chairs because they were placed against the wall instead of standing out in the center of things like rocking chairs.

Mother's teaching suited the trustees well enough so that they offered her the school for the next year. She accepted, but instead of boarding around, she lived at home and went back and forth on the stage that ran conveniently for school hours. She never complained that boarding around had been hard. Instead she turned her experiences into funny stories that she told us. When we said how horrid it must have been, mother always said yes, it was, in a way, only at sixteen she learned a great deal about parents and children from boarding around that otherwise she might never have known. Could a meeting of minds in a PTA say as much?

After the Pine Grove sessions, mother decided that she did not know enough to go on teaching without more education. The village school in Cicero was two miles from her home and the only one mother could afford to attend. Yet mother's choice was wise. The village school of the period did not represent any special advantage over the district school, except that it had a "downstairs" for young children and an "upstairs" for older pupils. Its great merit was that a man taught the upstairs pupils and therefore offered a superior knowledge compared to what any woman teacher possessed. In the middle third of the nineteenth century, unusual teachers sometimes appeared in village schools. Such was the case in Cicero. From somewhere, nobody knew just where, a young Irishman named Francis Lantry had come to take on the principalship of the school. Professor Lantry, as he was called, captivated all hearts; and his former pupils in later years named their babies for him. Over the almost grown men and women who were his pupils, his discipline was perfect. Mother said they all stood a little in fear of him, though she did not know why, unless it was that he knew so much more in books than anyone else they had ever seen.

He spoke three languages besides English, taught Latin and philosophy or any other subject desired, and was one of the rare examples that prove the truth of the saying that all subjects are interesting with the right teacher. When Professor Lantry found that mother had already been certified as a teacher, he handed the geography class over to her to be heard in a little recitation room. Mother was certain she taught the class badly, but I feel certain the state capitals were mastered.

That year was the last of her formal education. Professor Lantry was leaving, and anyone after him would have been worthless. The rest of his story was strange, as it drifted back to the village that had admired and loved him. He went to New York City to live and there committed suicide. He took some sort of pills to cause death, and on a sheet of paper he wrote down what his pulse was after swallowing each pill. Mother said it was an extraordinary act for so intelligent a man. But no one ever knew the story that must have lain back of it all.

Meantime mother's oldest sister Jane was writing home to urge mother to come out to Indiana for a long visit. All was well with Aunt Jane. She was happy with her little boys and Uncle George was prospering; but she missed the big family she had always been surrounded by. She suggested that Sarah could get a school nearby and would be paid better than in New York State. Why couldn't Sarah come? It sounded so exciting and adventurous that mother was persuaded to go in February in time for the spring term. Before the day to start arrived, however, she was so homesick by anticipation that she almost gave up going until her brother Bill said he would go with her and deliver her safely to Jane. This was a kindness of Uncle Bill's that mother liked to remember.

The journey to Chicago meant sitting up all night in the cars (a train was referred to thus in 1870), eating two or three meals out of a lunch basket, changing trains in Chicago, and not arriving at Goodland, Indiana, till after dark the next day. Uncle George met them with a lantern fastened to the dashboard of the wagon, and the farm horses plodded two miles along the muddy road to the farm. When mother described the lamplight shining out in welcome and the hot supper waiting for them, we saw it all—Indiana hospitality that never failed. Uncle Bill stayed two weeks. He was fond of his oldest sister, and like all the family, respected and admired George Welch.

After he left, mother had to consider getting a teaching certificate since her New York license was not valid in Indiana. At five o'clock on a dark morning, Uncle George harnessed the horses and drove with mother the long miles to the place of the examination. The certificate acquired, mother secured a school within six miles of Goodland. The distance was too far for her to come back to Aunt Jane's except for the weekends. She found a boarding place with a Southern family named Russell that had moved to Indiana after the war. Mr. Russell was an old soldier, a Confederate, I suppose. Mother liked him and his wife very much. Her only trial was Mrs. Russell's cooking. The lady had not been brought up to cook, and from Monday to Friday, when she got back to Aunt Jane's, mother struggled with sour bread, heavy cake, half-baked pies, and burnt meat. There was no cellar in the house, and the hot Indiana summer reduced the butter to such a melted state that it came to the table in a saucer. Only a curious succession of jams or preserves, called by sunny names like apple butter, plum butter, cherry butter, helped mother to swallow the food. Ethel and I thought these new kinds of butter must have been wonderful. Mother shook her head and said we hadn't tasted them.

Indiana was still prairie country, and she never tired of looking at the flat landscape stretching unhindered to the sky or listening to the prairie chickens calling to one another. Most of all she enjoyed her school. The salary of seven dollars a week approached luxury, and the children, she thought, were the most intelligent and best mannered she had ever taught. Mother stayed until September; then, as Aunt Sophy was planning to be married in November, she went home. In many ways the long stay in Indiana was one of the happiest periods of her life.

Home again—and after teaching in various district schools for several years, she finally came back to her own district. I seem to see grandfather's arranging hand in that. The school had grown much larger than in mother's childhood; there were some forty scholars. To manage that number and teach classes that ranged from toddlers to big boys and girls called for physical and mental stamina. Since mother held out for three years, she must have had something of grandfather's power to quell a riot.

The end of her teaching came when she was married, on October 8, 1878, to my father, Jacob Sneller. The evening of the wedding was a beautiful fall night. Mother had not spent too much on her wedding dress; it was a soft grey wool made with the tight unornamented bodice and flowing overskirt of the 1870's. Again, as for Aunt Sophy's wedding, grandmother cooked a twenty-eight pound turkey for the feast, and there were enough relatives on both sides present to deal with the turkey. After supper the bridal pair left to take the cars at Brewerton and set out for the prescribed honeymoon at Niagara Falls.

The glory of mother's traveling attire was her wedding hat. Five garnet-colored ostrich plumes soared above the wide black velvet brim, and the hat, mother would tell us rather guiltily, had cost *seven dollars*. And this in spite of the belief of all the Moulton sisters that three dollars at the outside was a great plenty to pay for a hat for any occasion. The plumes lasted beyond the rest of the hat and were carefully kept in an upstairs bureau drawer to be used again from time to time as ostrich plumes went in or out of style. Mother was always glad of a chance to wear them, for the color was becoming to her and she felt dignified under their protection.

The trains that specialized in getting bridal couples to the Falls ran twice a day from New York City to Niagara Falls. One arrived in the morning, one in the afternoon, and each was known as the Honeymoon Express. Cabs stood about in numbers to receive the passengers, and as they came down the steps from the car, the cab drivers ran forward shouting, "Hurry! Hurry! The Falls are going to be turned off in an hour!" A timid bride, clinging to her rushing husband's arm, must have found it as much as she could do to make haste in her long full skirt in order not to miss seeing the Falls pour over themselves before turning-off time came.

No couple could have seen the wonders of Niagara more intensively than father and mother. They rode on *The Maid of the Mist,* a boat which then went much closer to the Falls than is now considered safe. Clad in rubber coats and hoods to protect the bridal raiment (how was The Hat safeguarded?), they walked back of the Falls to the Cave of the

Winds, visited the Whirlpool Rapids, and to crown all left their country by crossing the bridge into Canada. Then before they started for home they had their picture taken. The photographic print was on glass and is still very clear. Father had hired an open carriage when their feet gave out, and the carriage is an important part of the picture. It includes father and mother sitting side by side in the rear, the coachman on a high box seat, two good-looking horses with unhappy bobbed tails, and in the background, slightly obscured by mother's plumes, the Falls.

Father and Mother and the Farms

ALTHOUGH FATHER and mother had been engaged for four years, at the end of that time neither had any clear understanding of the other's nature. There had been no objections from mother's family to her marriage. If anyone was dubious about Sarah's choice, he practiced a wait-and-see policy. There was little to criticize in the beginning. Jacob Sneller was a good farmer and a hard worker, clever in school, particularly in mathematics, a thorough reader of newspapers although not of books. He had no interest in religion except for the social activities of the church; his real interest, aside from his farm, was in politics. It was evident to all that he was ambitious and determined to succeed. Who could quarrel with this equipment for life in a farming community?

But he was German. There was a considerable German population in and around Syracuse, respectable and respected, and in Cicero the Mud Mill Road had a succession of German-owned farms. Yet the Germans were not accepted as socially equal to families of English descent. The Irish, of course, were out of the running altogether. The German citizens in our town were always referred to as "Dutch." Either the neighbors knew no difference between Dutch and German, or they used the word in a derogatory sense to indicate a foreign speech or a variation from their own standard of doing things. Father spoke excellent English without the slightest accent. To his father and mother he spoke German, but never a German word to Ethel or me. His conviction that he was far more intelligent than those who called him Dutch made him resent the name. He was quick to see slights where probably no slight was intended, and he treasured up every criticism to hurl back later at his critics. In his home while growing up with his brother and sister he had been distinctly the fair-haired child. His opinions and judgment had been accepted by his family, and he was ill prepared for the contradiction or indifference of outsiders to what he advised or approved.

Does he sound objectionable? He was not. In the earlier years of marriage the temper that later became violent did not often show itself. The disasters that it brought lay far ahead. Like mother, he was unprejudiced toward any race or religion, so that Ethel and I never had to unlearn fears or hatreds based on the color of skin or differences in ritual or dogma. He was generous and hospitable, as the tramps who came to the kitchen door very well knew. He was handsome too, with black hair, piercing grey eyes, regular features, and perfect teeth. His good teeth, father explained to us, came from his childhood diet of black bread and loppered milk, a thick, sour curdle not unlike yogurt and with all the vitamins intact. It was usually called bonny-clabber, not a German word but Scotch in origin.

Nature had bestowed upon father great physical strength. When I learned about Caesar, I used to think father was built like one of Caesar's soldiers. He had the medium height and flat back that go with the power to lift and carry heavy weights. Sometimes he would put across his shoulders the wooden yoke grandfather Sneller had brought from Germany and then he became a figure in a drawing, somehow different and remote from us.

He had begun to "work out," that is, work away from home on a neighboring farm, when he was eight years old. The little "Dutch" boy had been set to hoeing corn alongside the grown-up hired men, and he took pride in telling us that he had kept up his row with the others, and at the end of each day had earned fifty cents.

But there was an element in his character which, if mother had understood, might have meant a happier relationship for them. Father loved praise. He needed it to bolster him against the feeling of inferiority that dogged him. Sadly enough, the Moultons were not given to praise. They believed firmly in the old saying,

> Praise to the face
> Is open disgrace.

Once I discussed the matter with Uncle Alfred. I tried to persuade him that a little praise sweetened hard work, and that it was a comfort to a man to know he was appreciated. Uncle Alfred said no: if a man was doing all right, there was no need to say anything; if he was doing a job badly, it was time to correct him and show him the right way.

Mother followed the Moulton technique. She was not critical, but she failed to give father the approbation that his efforts warranted and for which he longed. She often praised my uncles' achievements to him, and father resented that what he had done even better was passed over without a word. Most important of all, perhaps, father was unaccustomed to female domination such as Aunt Welt exercised over the Moulton family. He was his own man and restless under a sister-in-law's advice, however sound and well meant. But mother could not lay aside her lifelong faith in the rightness of her family's opinions.

Very early in their married life, he began to engage in politics. He enjoyed the minor intrigues and modest triumphs of village democracy and found office holding a means of advancing socially and financially. The bookish girl he had married had no social ambitions. She did not quarrel with old friends, as father did, because of political differences, and though she was pleased and gratified when father was elected to something, she stood in a curious way apart from it.

Father's mother and sister had often worked out in the fields when a crisis in planting or harvesting occurred; women had done so in Germany. Mother never did. Father would not permit anything that could be stigmatized as Dutch. It was just as well, for mother was not an outdoor woman, aside from picking berries or currants and tending two small flower beds. She did every kind of housework excellently, and she thought the well-kept fields beautiful and loved the blue of the flax crop in blossom. Hers was not the farming eye; her enthusiasm was for the loveliness of an apple orchard in May or sheaves of wheat golden in the sun; her lasting wonder was for the poetry of earth.

During their four years' engagement, father had saved

enough money to purchase his parents' farm. They had allowed him three thousand dollars on the purchase price— an unusually generous wedding gift, and his tireless energy and good crops quickly paid off the rest of the debt. Mother had saved a hundred dollars from her teacher's salary, and with that they bought a walnut bed and bureau and three parlor chairs, besides plain things for the kitchen. So equipped, they set up housekeeping.

Mother loved everything about her new home, where the first seven years of her married life were spent. It was truly a storybook place. It was on a crossroad not far from the homes of the relatives, all living within a square mile. If you turned at the corner by the schoolhouse where both father and mother had taught and followed a bending dirt road with orchards on one side and stump fences on the other, you came to a little hill. A spring that never went dry flowed at the foot of the hill and along it peppermint grew in abundance and made a green line to mark the water course. This wild mint was gathered regularly as a specific against colds and sore throat. The house at the top of the hill faced south and was painted a mellow dark red. A little brick walk bordered with sweet-scented polyanthus led from the road to the parlor door, and the lilac at the window was in its proper place. Around the house were towering maples and butternut trees, and high above the gray barn a windmill rose. In May the big orchard fluttered pink and white in the spring winds, and on a slope to the east was a vineyard where red, blue, and white grapes grew and a few tiny Delawares that Ethel and I thought were meant especially for children because they were so little. Ethel and I were born at this farm. The farm was, and still is, quietness itself. Only one other house was on the road, which turned into a grass-grown track after passing our house. Looking south across the fields, you could see woods and pastures and a pond fringed with cat-tails and beloved of the cows. A view to remember.

The new house grandfather Sneller was building was not finished in time for my grandparents to move into when father was married, so they stayed on with father and mother until the next spring. Mother was warmly attached to grand-mother Sneller and glad to have her company through the deep winter. It is a little odd that we knew from mother more about her mother-in-law than about her own mother. Perhaps grandmother Moulton was too busy to talk much of her youth, or perhaps it was so like the experience of every child at that time that it did not seem worth talking about. But grandmother Sneller had grown up in Germany, and Germany was far away and different; and mother loved to ask questions and learn how things were done there. An eager listener to grandmother's tales could not have been too frequent, and so while they cooked and washed and sewed together, grandmother talked and mother remem-bered.

In later years people spoke of grandmother Sneller as beautiful. I was nearly six years old when she died, and my memory is of her softly curling white hair and dark blue eyes. She had too what I would now call an expression of lovely serenity, though I could only feel it then. It is an ex-pression that more often characterizes European faces than American.

Grandmother's maiden name was Rosina Barbara Roller. She was the daughter of the burgomeister in her native town somewhere in Württemberg and not far from the borders of

Alsace-Lorraine. Her book education had been limited but thorough, and what she told mother of the punishments inflicted for poorly learned lessons sounded painfully cruel. The schoolmaster had a pair of scissors, and a failure in lessons meant that he would snip the end of an unlucky child's finger till the blood came. The story mother liked best was of grandmother's journey as a young girl, along with other pilgrims, to see the great cathedral at Strasbourg. To save their shoes, the pilgrims walked barefoot the entire distance, a matter of several days, all carrying their shoes and necessary food and extra clothing. Grandmother described the whole story of the Crucifixion as it was told on the marvelous cathedral clock—the betrayal of Judas, the crowing of the cock and the denials of Peter, Christ and His disciples and the Roman soldiers moving in and out to the notes of the bell— glorious to see. Mother saw it through grandmother's eyes.

Grandmother's three brothers were already in America when she decided to come. She had had an unhappy love affair of which she never spoke beyond saying that it was the reason for her leaving home. Ethel and I somehow had the impression that a nobleman had fallen in love with the beautiful Rosina, but could not marry her because she was not of his social class, and therefore grandmother resolved to leave Germany forever.

Her father provided three oak chests to hold her possessions for the long journey of ten weeks on a sailing vessel. On the front of each chest her name was painted in black Gothic lettering, followed by *nach Bremen,* the port from which she sailed. Into the chests went clothing and blankets and quilts and linen, brass kettles and iron pots, and bags of coffee beans and a coffee grinder. Grandmother was not sure

133

whether coffee was easily obtainable in America and did not propose to be without it. As long as she lived, she roasted coffee beans on a little shovel glowing red hot from the wood fire. It was exciting to stand by while the hot beans were put into the grinder on the kitchen wall and to sniff the delicious smell of the coffee. But I cannot remember that we children were ever given coffee to drink.

Grandmother had been very lonely at first. Everything was strange and since she could not speak English, the process of becoming familiar with her new life was slow. Her brother Martin had been in America long enough to own a farm on the Mud Mill Road and it was through him that grandmother met grandfather Sneller. His name was then spelled Schnierle, but like many foreign-born citizens he had chosen to change it for a simpler spelling. Just as the Scheldts became Shields, so grandfather Schnierle became grandfather Sneller, easier to say if little more musical.

Grandfather was greatly his wife's inferior in mind and character, though shrewd, sober, and industrious. In Germany he had been a shepherd and had come to America to escape military service. Grandmother's loneliness and dependence led her to accept his offer of marriage and she bore his infirmities of temper and his unkindness unflinchingly all their life together.

But she found happiness and sorrow too in her children. She named her oldest son Martin for her brother, and the family always said that he was the dearest to his mother of all the children. His death in the Civil War was an unhealed grief. Her other children, Uncle John, father, and Aunt Kate, loved and revered their mother as their ideal of kindness and goodness.

Grandmother had been brought up in the strict Lutheran communion, and when she could she went to a Lutheran church in Syracuse where the service was familiar and the preaching in German. But twelve miles was a long way to drive a farm horse on Sundays, and she gradually ceased to go. She missed Watch Night particularly, she told mother, when the New Year was brought in at midnight with prayers and hymns of praise. After a time she turned to the Methodist Church and there is a memorial window to her in the village church.

Every day in the year except one grandmother knitted. On Good Friday she sat with folded hands and her German Bible open before her. At first the Sunday knitting seemed irreverent to mother. The Moultons did not knit on Sunday. But mother accepted it: that was the way they did in Germany.

The six months that grandmother and mother were together were very valuable to mother. Grandmother taught her much about cooking, especially German dishes such as homemade noodles on chicken, potato soup with dumplings, and Dutch cheese, which is now universally known as cottage cheese, but was then specifically Dutch. Sometimes balls of this cheese were put out on a board to dry in the sun until they turned a golden brown. They were then taken to market to sell among the Germans in Syracuse.

When grandmother moved to her new house, she left as a present for mother the largest of the three chests she had brought from Germany. Up in our garret the old chest stands safe and sound and still stores blankets and woolens and keeps them free from moths.

After the grandparents left in the spring, the pace of life

at the farm quickened. Outside there was the heavy spring work of preparing the soil and getting the crops in; the spring flush of milk and the new calves meant early rising and early going to bed, since all farmers regarded chores as something to be added to the regular day's routine in the fields. Father always had two or three hired men, usually the same ones from year to year, and they lived with the family and mother cooked and washed and ironed for them. She found it pleasant to keep the house clean and in order, but one thing did not suit her. On the plaster of the west wall of the parlor a spreading green willow tree had been painted. It covered the whole wall, and the two windows did not interfere with the artist's design. This sort of wall painting was common in such old houses. The other walls of the room and the ceiling were whitewashed. The parlor by today's standards would have been artistically correct. But mother thought painted walls were old-fashioned, and she sighed for Victorian gilt paper. After a year or two, father was con- verted to the idea, and the parlor was made elegant with paper. In time, layer after layer of paper was added, each on top of the last, and it was not until after father's death in 1923 that the paper was torn off down to the original plaster. There were still traces of the tree left, enough to make us wish that mother had let it alone, but not enough to make re-creating it possible.

In June of 1880, Ethel was born. Only rarely does a child inherit so wisely a mixture of looks from both parents. Her beauty held something of each. She had mother's silken hair, but instead of being straight as mother's hair was, Ethel's curls were golden in babyhood and later brown touched with sunlight. Her grey eyes and perfect nose repeated father's, and along with the unblemished Moulton skin went the delicate bone structure that was to remain the basis of her beauty till death. Her hands were so shaped that no matter what rough work they did—and she never spared them—it was a delight to watch them, for to their beauty was joined the strength of *doing* hands. Yet Ethel was utterly without vanity. She was gay and fearless and high-spirited, and as quick in mind as in her motions. Small wonder that from the day she was born she was everybody's darling, especially father's and Aunt Welt's. Grandmother Sneller, who could not easily manage the English *th,* called her *Ed*el with a long *e,* and all the other relatives pronounced her name *E*-thel, with the same long *e*. It is a good Saxon name and Ethel always liked it, and when she learned that it meant noble, she liked it even better. Grandmother had told her that children who ate the crusts of their bread would have curly hair. Though Ethel's hair curled already, she ate her crusts conscientiously and so did I—with no effect on my hair.

Ethel was three years old when I was born in July of 1883. The circumstances of my birth were more dramatic than hers. Doctor Blynn, who attended mother, was both a general practitioner and a surgeon who had made a fine record in the Civil War. He had used chloroform when he could get it in performing the countless amputations on wounded soldiers, and he regarded it as suitable and desirable for lessening pain. He suggested to mother that she permit him to try chloroform if things got bad. The proposal was startling. No such thing as a woman's escaping the pangs of childbirth had ever been heard of in the village. Chloroform was dangerous. Who knew what it might do? But mother was no fonder of pain than most women and she was, besides, courageous and open to new ideas. She agreed at once, and I suppose father must have agreed too. The objections came from Aunt Sophy. She was to stay with mother, and the thought that her dear sister might be lost under the influence of a medicine no doctor had ever prescribed before for such a purpose frightened her into protests and prophecies.

"Sarah," she wept, "if you let the doctor do this you will die, or if you don't die, the baby will be an idiot!"

In spite of Aunt Sophy's implorings, mother decided to take the risk. Dr. Blynn's method was simple. He called for a clean white cloth, which Aunt Sophy tearfully produced. By mother's account, he sprinkled chloroform on the cloth and laid it over her face, and the idiot baby was on its way. The only thing that turned out wrong was that father had set his heart on having a boy.

All went well with father's farming. He paid his hired help rather better than most farmers and put in as hard a day as they did. Mother had a hired girl most of the time. A hired girl at two dollars a week was not a luxury but a necessity when there were always two or three men to be cooked for, two small children to tend, and all the sewing to be done for the family.

My father was a proud and happy man when at the end of seven years he was able to buy a farm on the main road—twenty acres for three thousand dollars. He had to go in debt for it, but he believed always that one of the few cases where debt was justified was in the purchase of a home. He implanted in Ethel and me a horror of debt that never left us. A grocery bill that ran for months unpaid was, father said, like paying for a dead horse. Another sentence that he often repeated expressed the philosophy of country folks: "If you have a dollar and spend ninety-nine cents, you are a capitalist; if you spend a dollar and one cent, you are a damned fool and will be in debt all your life."

In retrospect, my memories of the farm where I was born seem very clear though I was not three years old when we left it. But after we moved to the new home, father worked both farms, and for many years we children went back and forth with him so that there is no definite line between the first impressions I actually had and those that came afterward.

For a long time father's chief hired man had been Adney Eggleston, blue-eyed, blond, kindly, and faithful. Adney was a cherished part of life for Ethel and me. Mother said she always felt safe about us when Adney took charge of our riding on the high loads of hay or watching the farm operations. He was unmarried and father installed him with his parents in the old farm house. A hired man's wages in such cases included the house rent free, garden ground, a place to raise a pig if he wanted one, a plot for a potato patch, a quart of milk a day, and all the apples and fruit he could use. The actual cash payments ranged anywhere from fifteen dollars a month in winter when farm work subsided to chores, to twenty or twenty-five dollars a month from April to December. The heavy fringe benefits were as good as money. The hired man's wife or mother usually looked after the hens, and the eggs were divided equally between owner and worker. Since practically all the food for the hens grew on the farm, it was a fair arrangement.

Adney's father and mother were rather queer old people,

and I was a little afraid of them for no reason at all. Everyone called them by their first names, Zeb and Roxy, reduced from Zebulon and Roxana, but Ethel and I of course said Mr. and Mrs. Eggleston. Old Mr. Eggleston—he *was* very old, with sparse hair, a grizzled beard and bloodshot eyes—was clever with his hands and tools and won my timid affection by mending my broken doll carriage when I had accidentally sat down on it. While he worked, he said things that I thought were wonderful and used to repeat at home. One was a wish he often made: "I wish I had a meeting house full of needles and every needle worn up to the eye making sacks and every sack was full of gold." The splendor of it took away my breath. A meeting house full of needles that must have been gold-eyed! When Mr. Eggleston was out of sorts, he would declare that he was going to leave the United States before long and go to Californy. I think that meant infinite distance to him.

Father often laughed over the way Zeb divided the eggs. He had a method of his own in counting. It went like this: "Egg for Zeb; egg for Jake. Egg for Zeb; egg for Jake. Egg over. Egg for Zeb. Too bad there ain't another egg for Jake." But father never said anything to the old man about it. Eggs were worth only around ten cents a dozen, so it did not matter.

Poor Mr. Eggleston died of cancer. When mother took me in to see him in his last illness, he insisted on showing me how the bone of his leg below the knee had been eaten away. It was a sickening sore and caused him horrible pain, yet he had a kind of mournful pride in displaying it, so that I would know what tortures he was enduring. The sight was unforgettable.

Mrs. Eggleston had a protruding lower lip that gave her face a cross expression she did not deserve. She had lost a little girl many years before and liked to show us the child's picture in a frame set with tiny shells. We thought the ringleted little face very pretty and the shell frame a marvel of beauty. In the spring when the lilac tree blossomed, we used to walk down to the farm after school and ask Mrs. Eggleston for a lilac, since there was no lilac tree by our new home. It never occurred to us that father owned the lilacs and we could take them without her permission They were as much Mrs. Eggleston's lilacs as the geraniums she raised. She was always kind about parting with the lilacs.

There were various reasons that had led father to buy another farm. He wanted more land for raising tobacco and grain; the apple orchard on the new farm promised a good cash crop; and the farm was located on a hard gravel road that made going to market much easier than the mud of the sideroad in spring and fall. Underlying all these sound reasons was his undeclared wish to improve his social position. The main road separated him more definitely from all that was Dutch on the Mud Mill Road.

The white house on the new farm stood in a thick grove of gigantic maples; seven huge elms rose like a row of green fountains along the roadside, and there was a tall orchard beyond the elms. Scattered everywhere were butternut trees and hickories, Flemish Beauty pear trees (sweetest of all varieties!), and many basswoods. Basswood is not so pretty a word as linden, its European name, but by any name a great basswood covered with white blossoms in spring scents the air with fragrance and calls the bees to gather the best honey that can be made. A white picket fence ran in front of the house; it had two gates, a wide one where a wagon could drive through and a smaller one just the right size for a child to swing on. From the little gate a board walk went to the front porch. A white railing enclosed the porch and an indomitable woodbine, which still thrives, grew at its south end. There was no lawn——Mr. Loomis had the only lawn in town—but the large dooryard was grassy and father mowed it with a scythe often enough so that it kept pleasantly green and attractive.

The barnyard was grassy too and shady and had a never-drying spring from which water was pumped for the cows. The watering trough charmed Ethel and me. It was a log from a forest tree hollowed out by hand, to judge by its irregular sides and bottom. At one end a hole had been cut and a plug made to fit it. Moss grew constantly on the trough, inside and out, and it was a favorite job of ours to clean it off. Father would pull the plug to let the water out; then, armed with blunt knives we attacked the moss and scraped it off as well as we could. Naturally we left the moss on the outside alone. But the inside had to be rinsed clear of dirt and the pieces of moss, and that was a nice ending. At night the cows would have clear water to drink.

Bright as the farm looked, we thought Mr. Raleigh, from whom father bought it, must have been a peculiar man. There had been a grove of chestnuts west of the orchard. Since the boys of the neighborhood regularly invaded it every October, one of Mr. Raleigh's achievements was to have the trees cut down so that the boys could not annoy him by stealing some of *his* chestnuts. A perfect example of a nose operation to spite the face. Only one chestnut tree escaped, and that because it stood near the house. Its fertilizing comrades gone, this tree never bore well afterwards. Some years there would be a few dozen nuts for us to pick up and eat on the big rock under the tree, but no abundance to excite us. We spoke ill of Mr. Raleigh as we munched.

The Raleighs had only one child, the Gertie Raleigh whose immaculate care of her aprons had made her name familiar and odious to us though she belonged to an earlier generation and we never saw her. She was still quite small when her mother died. In the time between the death of Gertie's mother and his second marriage, Mr. Raleigh had engaged my aunt Jane to keep house for him and look after the little girl. Aunt Jane was then waiting for Uncle George to return from the Civil War, and was glad to earn the money. It must have been a very small sum, for Mr. Raleigh had a tight-fitting hand over money and even the food was scantier than Aunt Jane was used to. Curiously enough, he made no objection to Aunt Jane's having mother come frequently to stay overnight and keep her company.

Mother remembered very well how the Raleigh house had looked when she first knew it. The blinds were always closely drawn lest the sun fade the carpets, and parlor and sitting room were painted a green so deadly dark that the effect upon entering was like arriving in the middle of the night. It was all a part of the economy the Raleighs lived by. It could never have crossed mother's mind that some day she would be mistress of the white house. But there she was and welcomed the nearness of neighbors after living seven years on a lonely road. She could walk north, south, or east and be quickly among relatives, and on a nearby farm lived Frances Loomis, who became a dear friend and companion.

Before the moving, father had enlarged and extended the

downstairs bedroom, and later on, as he had money to spare, he bought new furniture that he thought would improve the house. Mother was not consulted in the choice; father produced the purchases as a surprise. She liked the walnut parlor table and the marble-topped commode and the hanging lamp very much, and the elephant armchair not at all. About the oak secretary, a combined desk and bookcase, she was noncommittal. But everyone in town was getting a secretary.

Father had also a passion for machinery. As fast as a new farm machine was put on the market he was eager to try it and see if it made life easier. All kinds of farm tools and machinery were undergoing rapid changes in the eighties and nineties; each change meant that more work could be done better and faster. This was especially true of plows, mowers, and reapers. Father's first reaper was a triumph and the sound of it music to his ears. He bought a tobacco setter before most farmers had heard there was such a thing.

Tobacco was the big money crop that paid off the mortgage. It was a precarious crop, for a sudden hailstorm in August could cut it to pieces or an untimely frost destroy it without remedy. Crop insurance was unknown. Raising tobacco, father said, took more out of the land and more out of the men than any other crop. Tobacco required an early start in spring. Because the seeds are so tiny they were mixed with cornmeal or something similar so that they would show up when scattered broadcast on the beds. The beds themselves had been prepared with extra good dirt and banked at the sides with boards. Cheesecloth was stretched over them to protect the seeds, and if everything in earth and air combined favorably, they sprouted rapidly. Weeding came soon. A flat stone was placed on each side of the bed and a board laid from one stone to the other. Along the board the weed puller could crouch to work until every weed within arm's reach had been dealt with, and stones and board could be moved on to the next station.

Before the setter came to help, the seedlings had to be planted by hand in the field. This was one of the very few kinds of outdoor work that Ethel and I ever took part in, and we were proud to be thought equal to it. We each carried a pan of plants, which had been pulled with great care to prevent injury to the roots. The plants were dropped about eighteen inches apart in rows, and the hired men followed us with trowels or hoes to set them in. The men dug a small hole for each plant, sprinkled it, and pressed the dirt around it. Hoeing began not quite the next morning, but as the plants grew, the hoes were steadily needed to keep down the weeds. When the plants were about three feet high, they were topped. The six to eight inches broken off at the top left the plant strength to broaden the leaves instead of wasting it on nicotine blossoms. But nature does not accept defeat easily. The plants, deprived of their tops, sent out shoots at the base of the leaves. These shoots were called suckers, and suckering a field of tobacco required going up and down the rows and disposing of the shoots. Worming was waiting —the most disagreeable business of all. Big tobacco worms in their handsome pale green coats are repulsive to touch and crush. Last of all came the cutting. The plants fell under the big tobacco shears and lay in straight lines throughout the field until they had wilted enough to be put in small piles. Wilting was necessary to avoid breaking the brittle leaves.

As soon as they could be safely handled, the plants were strung on laths. A lath was stuck firmly in a jack and a very sharp, pointed steel needle slid over one end. It took stout steel to pierce the thick tobacco stalk. The knife-like needle and lath together did the work of needle and thread. Occasionally under threat of storm Ethel and I helped for a little while handing the stalks to the men. Since the stalks were almost as heavy as we were, it was harder than dropping plants, and our work hours were accordingly brief. Not more than four or five plants could be strung on a lath, and the weight of the load was about twelve pounds. When all the tobacco was at length hung on poles in the shed, the men had to make sure that the plants hung separately and did not touch one another. Otherwise they would poleburn to the ruin of color and texture. Every tobacco shed had ventilators to let in air and cure the leaves slowly and evenly to a color ranging from golden to dark brown. But curing was not the end. It was the halfway mark when the farmer could say, "So far, so good."

If it survived the curing, on a damp, foggy day in late fall chosen for the moisture it would give the leaves, the tobacco was taken down from the shed, the stalks stripped, and the harvest of leaves carried to a room in barn or shop for the long process of sorting. A little stove kept the place warm for the men to work and held pans of steaming water for the benefit of the tobacco, which must not dry out. The leaves were sorted and graded into wrappers, binders, fillers, and lugs. Wrappers were the finest in size, color, and quality, and were used for the outside of a cigar. Binders became the cigar's inner wrapping and held together the fillers that took up the center. The fillers might be used too for pipe tobacco. Lugs were the poor relations destined for scrap or chewing. It was often difficult to decide whether a leaf was a wrapper or a binder, but you could always tell it from a lug. A number of leaves of the same kind made a "hand" and were fastened together by winding a long leaf securely around the top and threading it back into the hand.

When enough hands accumulated, they became a bundle and were covered with heavy glazed paper ready to be cased. It was like the multiplication table, I thought:

> Leaves made a hand
> Hands made a bundle
> Bundles made a case
> Cases were shipped away.

The final packing was done in strong wooden boxes about four feet square. When they were nailed down and labeled, the last step had been taken: the tobacco work was over. All these things Ethel and I learned without knowing we learned them. Thinking it over now, I wonder how the days were ever long enough for all that had to be done to and for tobacco.

Selling his crop did not depend entirely upon the farmer. In early winter the tobacco buyers would arrive from New York or elsewhere and begin inspecting the tobacco while it was still spread out in the shop. They were shrewd, dark men whose sharp eyes missed no defect. They would engage a local man to drive them about from farm to farm, and it was sometimes suspected that the driver gave them information about the farmers' financial condition which enabled them to drive a hard bargain. Whether this was true or not, ill feeling often arose when one man's crop sold for much more than another's. Sometimes in a bad year the price would not rise above ten cents a pound, and that did not pay the farmer for his time and labor. Ordinarily tobacco was shipped in

March and the farmer did not receive his check until that time—almost a year after the starting of the crop. One never-to-be-forgotten year father's tobacco check was twenty-two hundred dollars. Mother and Ethel and I pressed close to him to look at the check in his hand. His face was shining and he said triumphantly, "This will cover the last payment on the mortgage. The place is ours."

Tobacco is no longer grown in our part of the country. Farmers turned from it to cabbage raising, and a tobacco setter was easily transformed into a cabbage setter. Cabbage requires less work and care than tobacco and much less risk. Both cabbage and tobacco crops in their prime are beautiful. The blue-green spreading leaves of cabbage suggest enormous roses, and the stately stalks of brilliant green tobacco changed our cool northern landscape into tropical fields.

Woman's Work

A CHILD once upon a time saw her elders at work in field and house and knew very well how food grown outdoors by the men was transformed indoors by the women and brought to the table. The relationship between a crop of ripe buckwheat in early fall and pancakes in winter was clear to her.

When she was a child there was nothing mother had liked better than to watch her mother or the older sisters at work on homely tasks that required skill. The processes of cooking she had found fascinating. The smells, the colors, the mixings, the promise of something good to eat at the end had held her close in watchful waiting at the scene of operations.

So she spoke lovingly to Ethel and me of grandmother's making cider applesauce. It was before the era of canning in glass jars. First a good fire was built out in the yard, and over it on poles a great brass kettle was hung. Into the kettle went the sweet cider to boil down until it was thick. Constant care was necessary to keep the cider skimmed and to add fresh cider if it started to boil over. A child's quick eye may have

149

been **helpful** in detecting the crucial moment. When the
cider was thick enough, very sweet apples were dropped into
it and the sauce would keep all winter long. Each year grandmother made a barrel of this sauce to last through the pan-

cake season. Altogether the sauce-making sounds gypsyish and like a pleasant October job.

Another of her memories was candle making. Grandmother made all the tallow candles that the family used. Each candle required hand servicing. The wicks were dipped and redipped in the hot tallow, each dipping making the candle larger until the proper size was attained. It was backbreaking work. When candle molds were put on the market the work was cut in half, for the wick was fastened in the center of each mold and the liquid tallow poured around the wick. Then the candles were let stand until they were cold and firm.

When grandfather brought home the first kerosene lamp, the family felt that illumination could go no further. Still they all rather expected that the lamp would explode at any minute. As lamps finally replaced all candles, the womenfolks learned to their surprise that filling, washing, and trimming lamps every day and polishing the lamp chimneys took more time than lighting a candle and blowing it out—or even cleaning the dripped tallow off the candlesticks. But lamps had come to stay.

Women were not called upon to pick up stones, but stones weighed little more than cheese and Aunt Welt made cheese. Even for a man that is not easy work, and it demanded all her skill and strength and the special techniques that must be followed with the greatest care and accuracy. The milk was carried in big pails from the stable to the cheesehouse. Mother was the carrier. Aunt Welt had to lift the heavy pails to the vat and manage the long process of dealing with curds and whey, getting the cheese into the presses and out, turning them on the shelf, greasing them and paying them all the attention that was needed to insure perfect flavor and texture. She made two cheese a day. People drove miles to get a piece of one, and there was always a cheese to be cut. But the greater number of them were taken to the city of Syracuse, where they sold rapidly at a high price.

Every large family then needed a steady seamstress. Among Aunt Jane's duties as a girl was the making of white shirts for grandfather. His sons, like their neighbors, wore colored shirts for everyday; white ones were reserved for Sunday and special occasions. Since colored shirts could not be boiled without danger to their brightness, a white shirt was called a boiled shirt. Grandfather, for reasons best known to himself, would never wear anything but a boiled shirt. Aunt Jane was an exquisite seamstress, and every stitch of every shirt was the work of her hands. The high point in shirt making was the "bosom," a sort of ellipse in shape, sewed on the front of the shirt with infinitesimal stitches. It was sometimes tucked, sometimes plain, but its real purpose was to be the starched, glistening expanse that showed when waistcoat and coat were buttoned.

Some time after the war, when Aunt Jane was married and gone, a "sewing machine" was brought into the house. They all stood around and looked at it in happy excitement. Never again would sewing be tedious or hard, they thought; here was a machine to put an end to drudgery forever. Aunt Welt had taken over as the maker of all things for the family, and the machine was logically regarded as her special property. While, as hoped, it did do away with the toil of invisible stitches on shirt bosoms and dress hems, it also increased the number of things to be sewed!

One story often told to us concerned the knitting contest

held by Aunt Jane and Aunt Sophy in their girlhood. They were both rapid and expert knitters. Which was to be regarded as the champion? The girls agreed to see which one could knit a sock in a day. That did not mean that they could sit down after breakfast and knit steadily till night. They must carry on their regular household tasks and knit only as usual in whatever spare time was left. The result of the race was that by sundown each girl had her sock completely finished without a flaw. Since the whole family wore knitted stockings, a pair a day could be readily used.

Tatting was a popular kind of work to do in the afternoon on a visit when knitting might seem too cumbersome or engrossing. It was a particular specialty of Aunt Ann's. Tatting was done with a shuttle—Aunt Ann's was ivory—and she was skillful at the delicate work. Among the possessions that were treasured after her death was a pair of pillowcases of fine cotton now grown soft with their century of age. Above the hem are set perfect little wheels of tatting so exquisitely made that at first glance they look like lace, and every stitch holds fast in its place. They were always thought "too good to use."

But most of all and worst of all for women were the washings and ironings. These I remember well. The process of washing began with putting the badly soiled colored clothes—the men's work clothes—to soak on Sunday night. All water had to be pumped from cistern or well and heated on the kitchen stove. On Monday morning the tubs were emptied, hot water brought from the big copper boiler that had been filled and was waiting on the stove, and in this the white clothes were thoroughly rubbed on the ridged zinc washboards. Meantime the boiler had been filled again and shaved soap added—all ready to receive the white clothes, which remained in the boiling soapy water until they were spotless. Mother kept a special smooth stick known as the clothes stick for poking and turning the clothes so that each piece had its fair share of exposure. While the white clothes boiled, the colored clothes had their chance at the washboard. Colors often faded badly despite care, for no color was guaranteed. As a preventive against fading, mother sometimes soaked yards of pink or blue or red calico or gingham in salt water before the material was made up.

Next came the sudsing to remove the soap. The sudsing done, the rinsing followed. It had to be thorough, and often two rinsings were necessary for special things. Rinsing included bluing from a small cloth bag that held cubes of real indigo.

The final step was starching. The starch had to be cooked carefully so that it was clear and free from lumps or scum that would otherwise cling to one's best white apron and stick to the flatiron. Starch was much beloved by all the Moultons, and everything that could take it was duly dipped in it: the calico dresses, the gingham aprons and sunbonnets, the rustling petticoats and long tucked drawers. Old tablecloths were strengthened and their youth renewed by being starched, and not a curtain, not even the lace ones, escaped, but stood out away from the windows in pride of their starchiness. My Aunt Sophy's aprons were remarkable for the amount of starch she was able to get on them and were often referred to as "Sophy's glass aprons." Of all my aunts, Aunt Alice was the only one who actively disliked starch. Her muslin curtains hung so much more gracefully than ours or the curtains at grandfather's that I once asked her the reason for it. She confided to me that it was because she never starched them. But then, she was an aunt only by marriage.

In all, the clothes on washday were subjected to five complete baths and then carried out to the lines to be pegged firmly against the wind. Altogether Monday was a day of carrying, bending, and lifting. It was good to get it over with after a day of rest. But the smell of clean clothes dried in the sun and wind is one of the most refreshing in the world.

Soap for washing was sometimes homemade, sometimes Mr. Babbit's product. Mother made both soft soap and hard soap. Soft soap was slippery, semi-liquid brown stuff used on the dirtiest garments, and as distasteful to look at as it was to feel on the hands. I disliked it so much that I have always thought a certain type of conversation known as "soft soaping" was accurately described by the term. The quality of hard soap depended on the skill of the maker. Aunt Welt's hard soap was pure white and fine grained as toilet soap; in fact it was used as a toilet soap by the whole family. She always scented it with something nice to smell of—usually sassafras oil if she could get it.

Ironing followed washing as the night the day, and Tuesday was dedicated to it. The heavy flatirons were heated over a very hot fire, and the combined temperatures of fire and irons on a July day called for grim endurance. When I learned that flatirons were once called sadirons, I assumed that the name reflected the ironer's state of mind. Everything had to be ironed. There was no putting by any nylons or drip-drys and going on one's carefree way. No housewife ever wondered what she would do on Tuesday: she knew. The finished ironing hanging on the clothes bars or about the kitchen was satisfying to eyes and pride. Mother taught Ethel and me to iron while we were still quite young, and of all household tasks I liked it best. After the skills were learned, the mind could be permitted to roam where it pleased.

Unceasingly busy as women were, they liked to know about the proper behavior for all occasions whether such occasions would ever arise in their lives or not. It was therefore natural and suitable that the prize Aunt Ann was once given at Sunday school should be a book entitled *True Politeness or Etiquette for Ladies.* It is a very tiny book, three and a half by four and a half inches. The print is small, but clear and distinct and easily read. The date is 1847, and it is a complete guide as to what was expected of women in the middle nineteenth century. Not working women. These are rules for a formal social life of dinners, balls, elaborate costumes and servants. Much of the advice, as is true of all good etiquette books, is as sound today as in 1847; it is only surface fashions and styles that sound funny nowadays when the whole background of accepted customs and manners has changed. These are samples:

Bow with slow and measured dignity; never hastily.

Be not ostentatious in the display of jewelry—let your ornaments be more remarkable for the taste with which they are chosen and worn than for their profusion.

Conversation is a difficult art, but do not despair of acquiring it. It is better to say too little than too much: let your conversation be consistent with your sex and age.

As a hostess, avoid all appearance of anxiety, yet let nothing escape your attention.

Your handkerchief should be as fine as a snowy cobweb. Your gloves for the ballroom of white kid, your shoes small and fitting with the nicest exactness.

Let your movements in the dance be characterized by elegance and gracefulness rather than by activity and complexity of steps.

Do not make a public room the arena for torturing a simple swain who may perchance admire you more than you deserve. Recollect that while you are wounding another's heart, you may be trifling with your own peace.

If you are engaged to a gentleman, do not let your attention be paid exclusively to him. The object of your love should alone perceive it.

Ladies do not wear gloves during dinner.

Never give away a present which you have received from another; or at least so arrange it that it will never be known.

Excellent advice indeed. Yet, considering how much was required of women in sheer hard physical work, did Aunt Ann and her sisters ever find time to read *True Politeness or Etiquette for Ladies?*

Strange Images of Death

WHAT DID THE FOLKS find to talk about after farm work and household matters and neighborhood gossip had been disposed of? Wasn't it very dull? The world, as Robert Louis Stevenson observed, is dull only to dull people. The talk on farms was not bounded by stump fences or overflowing creeks. Besides the subjects that plain people have always occupied themselves with, there happened over and again, close at hand, events so unusual and disturbing that they offered unmeasured material for a lifetime of talk and reflection, the mind returning to them as experience brought a new point of view or age suggested a new interpretation.

Modern novelists have made it very clear that the lovelier the country landscape, the more peaceful and kindly the outward aspect of village and farm, the more certain it is that underneath all this smiling beauty lie secrets which the memory shudders away from, unable to reconcile them to conscience or humanity. In the neighborhood of grandfather's farm perhaps such events did not seem so terrible when each was a separate story and in the course of years was crowded out of the thoughts as a new tragedy occurred. Set down together, as if one had followed another closely, they chill the mind.

In what order these old unhappy things took place there is now no means of knowing. They were recalled and told to us many times, unimplemented by explanation or suggestion when something said or done brought them back out of the past.

First of all there was the case of the baby in the woods. My Great-uncle Emery's farm was near my grandfather's and in some places bordered it. It was heavy with woods, much of it virgin timber. Every year in the spring, woodcutters went there to cut down trees enough to supply the family with fuel for a year. The men carried big dinner pails and always built a thatched, open-faced hut in front of which they could have a fire and enjoy their dinner in comfort. There seemed to be no likelihood that on a special March morning there would be anything in the woods either surprising or different from usual.

The snow was gone except in the hollows, and the men walked easily some distance into the woods. They were looking about, trying to decide which tree to attack first, when something at the foot of a tree caught their attention and they went toward it.

There on the leaves fallen the autumn before lay a baby, a beautiful little creature, without wrapping of any sort. If this story were a classic myth, the baby in the forest would have been found alive, rescued by the kindly woodcutters and taken to the palace to be reared as the king's son. But the baby was dead and there was no doubt in any woodcutter's mind that it had been put out to perish in the March cold. But whose baby? They were men of the neighborhood and knew of no baby expected or suspected. The womenfolk would have told them or at least hinted such a possibility. But not a word had been said.

One of the men picked up the baby and wrapped it in his coat—so much of the decencies at least must be preserved. Then the whole group went back to Uncle Emery's house with their story.

If any work was done the rest of the day it must have been only the brewing of one big pot of coffee after another, so that everybody could sit around the kitchen table and discuss the question of the baby's identity and how it had come to be put in the woods and what should be done.

Nothing was done. There was no investigation except to have the story of finding it told over and over by the woodcutters with whatever detail of the discovery each man could remember or suggest. Somehow the part of the story that made the strongest impression was that the baby was not wrapped up. No protection from the bitter cold night! There was, the women thought, an extra cruelty in that.

Nobody referred to the child's death as murder; that was too harsh a word for so pitiful a crime. A burial in Uncle Emery's garden bound the baby to the community and the mystery remained a mystery. Speculation took the place of solution.

When I was old enough to read *Adam Bede,* I came to the chapter where Hetty Sorrel carried her newborn child to a wood and there buried it in a shallow grave. Later she returned because she thought she heard the baby crying, and she stayed by the grave until she was arrested. I thought of the baby in Uncle Emery's woods and wondered if it was the mother who had laid it under the tree to die—and if the baby had cried.

Among the men who worked for grandfather was a Scotchman named Lovell. He was an excellent worker who had been installed with his wife and two boys on one of grandfather's farms several miles from the main house. Mrs. Lovell was Scotch too and given to occasional drinking when chance offered. Sometimes she would take the morning stage into Syracuse where her sister lived and enjoy the rare opportunity of having a glass of whiskey.

She was not altogether to be blamed. Work was hard, wages were low, and comforts were few. The infrequent solace of whiskey helped her to escape for a while into an easier world. So it happened that on a stormy day in deep winter, my aunts saw Mrs. Lovell coming along the lane and passing through the gate and the yard out to the road. She was waiting, they knew, for the stage. They shook their heads and sighed a little for the boys and their father. She would be sure to come home unfit to do anything except sleep.

As the day wore on, it grew bitter cold, and the snow was so blinding that the track through the yard was completely covered. By the time the afternoon stage halted to let Mrs. Lovell off, the storm had risen to a frenzy of wind and snow.

Grandfather and the uncles hailed Mrs. Lovell when they caught sight of her and urged her to come into the house and stay all night. They pointed out how dangerous the storm had become and how soon it would be dark. She shook her head and plodded on.

Apparently no one at grandfather's worried about her particularly. They had the comfortable belief that the whiskey she had drunk would protect her from the cold, and bad as the storm was, she would get through it all right. The storm lasted well into the next morning, and it was afternoon before Mr. Lovell came to find out if grandfather would let him take the oxen to break a road around his house. They were snowed in over there, he said.

Grandfather agreed and asked casually, "I suppose your wife got home all right last night?"

Mr. Lovell shook his head. "She didn't come. I guess she must have thought the storm was too bad to try it and stayed with her sister."

Grandfather and the family looked at him with shocked faces.

"But she did come," grandfather said. "She got off the stage and we tried to get her to come in here and stay, but she wouldn't. We'd better go and look for her."

The oxen were got out, the men armed themselves with shovels, and they started down the lane. They ran alongside the ox sled looking right and left and stopping to examine any large heap of snow. They found nothing and came at last to the Thomas house where the little boys had scraped frost from the window pane and were watching for them.

In front of the house was a picket fence with a small gate —hardly visible in the drifts. But as they opened the gate, one of the men gave a shout and rushed along the fence for a little distance. The others followed. They had found the poor woman. Blinded by snow and dulled by drink, she had not been able to see the gate and had felt her way along the fence looking for it until the cold and storm overcame her and she had sunk down in the snow at last and frozen to death.

A sad tale's best for winter.

The Acts of God created awe and wonder among the neighbors and perhaps—as is still true—a secret thankfulness that God had not included them in the Act. There was none of the hushed horror that they felt over the fearful acts of men. Still, a death in the field under a spring sky startled everyone into thinking of the uncertainties life held even in places as remote and seemingly secure as grandfather's farm.

It was sad, we thought, that by the time we heard the story of the hired man his name had been forgotten. The event was remembered, but the man to whom it happened had ceased to be a personality.

Grandfather had sent one of the men into the field to plow. With him went George Welch—not yet my uncle—to harrow a strip already plowed in the same field. It was late spring, a day with a high hot wind, far too early for a thunderstorm, grandfather said. But the afternoon grew hotter, the wind blew dust into the men's eyes and made plowing and dragging a smarting hardship. The hired man evidently thought that Uncle George had the easier job. When the two teams were near each other he suggested that they change work. Uncle George agreed and took over the other team. The strength of the wind and the darkening sky did not suggest to them that they had better stop work and go back to the barn.

It was only a little while before a tumult of thunder and plunging lightning filled the sky and then came sheets of rain. The hired man's new work as he drove around the field had brought him near a fence corner where a great oak tree stood. He threw the reins of the team on the ground and made a dash for the shelter of the oak. Just as he reached it there was a crash of thunder and at the same second a blinding flash of lightning. The tree was split in half and the hired man died with the tree.

Except for the change of work Uncle George might have been in the same spot. Grandaunt Jane Wright, who knew the Bible as minutely as if she were an embodied Concordance, said it made her think of the two women grinding at the mill—the one should be taken and the other left. And Aunt Jane Moulton, because of her secret attachment to George, was fervently thankful that he was not the one taken.

Through all the violence of the storm the horses stood quietly where the hired man had left them and were uninjured. Everyone said how providential it was for Mr. Moulton that in such an awful accident the team was not hurt.

I have spoken, in connection with the Civil War, of Charles Wright, the Copperhead neighbor across the road who was such a thorn in grandfather's side during the four years of conflict. But the war had ended and with it Mr. Wright's animosity toward grandfather and his malicious enjoyment of grandfather's anxieties. So far as anyone knew, his life was moving along prosperously and as happily as most lives.

The Wright home was a big old-fashioned white house and his beautiful daughter Clara, my Aunt Ann's dearest friend, was his special treasure. Her death at twenty-one from consumption was a sorrow to the whole neighborhood, and to her father a grief beyond explanation or endurance.

It may have seemed to him, although no one could know what went on in his mind, that with Clara gone there was nothing left worth living for. The death of the young, the beautiful, and the good was too overwhelming for his philosophy to accept, although he had been completely philosophical over the death of the young on battlefields.

But he could not, the neighbors heard him say over and over, regard Clara's death otherwise than as a cruel stroke of heaven directed sharply against him. They found him in the barn hanging from a rafter—death in the ugliest manner possible.

It was easy to suggest a reason for his act, but not altogether easy to believe the reason when suggested. Other men too experienced human sorrow as deep as his and went on with their duties and responsibilities. Why seemed it so particular with him? Was there, the neighbors wondered, something in his life far back in the past, something terrible enough to make him believe that Clara's death was the long overdue punishment that had been silently coming toward him down the years?

The Moultons were too honest to profess more regret for him than they felt. They were not indifferent to his wife's sorrow, and they had mourned the lovely Clara like one of their own. Nor could they cease talking over the death and repeating the unanswered question: Why should he have hanged himself? It was not so much that they missed him. Still and all, he had lived near them a long time and except during the war, wasn't a bad neighbor. And what a dreadful thing to happen right in the neighborhood.

The Carmichaels lived a little way down the road from grandfather's. Their farm was one of the best in the town. The white house was very large and lay low along the ground shaded by elms and chestnuts and locust trees. There was a beautiful old doorway belonging to a happier period of architecture, and in the parlor was a fireplace that matched the doorway. The land was rolling and of unmatched fertility, and the Carmichael woods in their height and girth might have been those that greeted the Pilgrim Fathers. I was ten years old when those woods were sold and cut down, and mother and I cried together over their slaughter.

Mrs. Carmichael was the mother of several daughters who continued to be called, in the kindly American fashion that makes the best of age and spinsterhood, "the Carmichael girls" as long as they lived. The family had more money than most of their neighbors and the girls were sent away to school. They were envied a little, but also liked and admired.

Still, it had to be admitted that there was a queer spot in the family. Not in the girls nor in their efficient mother, though she tended to grow silent in her husband's presence.

Mr. Carmichael himself was a subject of discussion behind the hand covering the mouth. The talk did not concern itself with exact physical or medical terms, but the rumor persisted through the years that he had "a bad disease," and

bad in this case meant moral as well as physical. How anyone could have known this or whether it was a fact was
never clear, but it was taken to be the truth and believed.
Whatever the tales and surmises, Mr. Carmichael was held
to be an agreeable man enough, better educated than most
of his neighbors, but always friendly and ready to help if
help was needed. Not a man to be distrusted in the ordinary
affairs of life.

Imagine then—and it is almost impossible to imagine—
how great the shock and horror when, late on a summer
afternoon, word was spread up and down the road that Mrs.
Carmichael had drowned herself in the well. It was not, as
it proved, a sudden mad impulse that overpowered sense
and reason: the more that was heard of the details, the more
dreadful it seemed. For this was only too plainly an act long
planned with everything carefully worked out.

There was a well in the front yard close to the road and
of no use to a woman who wished to make away with herself.
This well was in active service in my childhood when, three
minutes after leaving home for school, we were seized with
the consuming thirst of children. But back of the house was
another well not too far from the kitchen door. It had no
pump and the well curb was covered with boards that could
be pushed aside when water was wanted. Then a pail fastened to a rope was let down and hauled up full. Certainly
not an easy method of getting water, but not much harder
than the old oaken bucket. The water used by the Carmichael
family was mostly taken from this well, which was always
deep and cold.

Mrs. Carmichael had to wait for her departure from the
world until a day when every member of the family and all

the hired men were safely out of the way. On the chosen afternoon the girls had gone berrying in the woods and along the fences, and the men were getting in oats in the lot at the end of the farm—far enough away to guarantee no interruption. She had arranged it all in her mind. The well cover was shoved back and the rope tied tightly to the knob of the kitchen door. Then, taking the rope in both hands, she walked to the well and lowered herself into it, till the water was over her head.

Later in the day the men drove up to the barn with a load of oats. One of them volunteered to get a pail of water so that they could have a drink. Mrs. Carmichael had been dead for some time.

What followed removed any doubts that she was entirely sane. All the clothes for her burial had been laid out; even her stockings were neatly turned down so that they would slip easily over her feet. There was a long letter of instructions and advice for her daughters, bidding the oldest take the best and tenderest care of the others. But all this was insignificant compared to the astonishing last command. Her funeral text, she wrote, was to be a verse from II Kings, the fourth chapter and the twenty-sixth verse. This is the account of Elisha's healing the Shunammite's son. She had written down the part of the verse that she wished used: "Is it well with thee? . . . Is it well with the child? And she answered, It is well."

A psychiatrist might have explained her choice of a text by the recurrence of the word "well." The neighbor women who made Mrs. Carmichael ready for the grave explained it another way. They said nothing to the family, for the girls were too stricken to bear anything more, but later on they told what they felt to be the true cause of Mrs. Carmichael's death. They were experienced matrons, and in caring for the body they believed they had found sure indications that she was well advanced in pregnancy. There had been a considerable lapse of years since her last child, and her experience of childbearing was little compared to Mrs. Jackson's fifteen or Mrs. Wilson's seventeen or even Grandmother Moulton's ten. But something, some secret despair, had led Mrs. Carmichael to determine never to bring another child into the world. Was she afraid this child might inherit some taint from the father? She would make certain that all should be well for the child and, in doing so, she could believe that all would be well for her.

There was nothing to do but to burn the rope and fill up the well.

The last remaining log cabin of the countryside was still standing in my childhood. It was exactly like the pictures in our history book. It faced due south, and the logs used in its construction were cut from primeval forest and chinked with mud. When I knew the cabin the logs were moss-covered with age, but they were sound and the cabin still snug against all weathers. It had belonged earlier to Mr. A. J. Loomis, who was a large landowner and employed what the neighbors called a raft of hired help. Men liked to work for him. He was easygoing and kindly, never exerted pressure, but somehow work got done and the men had one another's company to lighten it.

The log cabin was used to house one of the hired men and his family. There were also frame houses for the help, small and ugly but painted white and with garden space—decent in all respects. The hired man who got a frame house to live in instead of the cabin felt he had gone up in the world.

One spring a young Irishman applied to Mr. Loomis for work and was hired. It happened that the frame houses were already occupied and so John Kaliker and his family moved into the log cabin. They were not too long away from Ireland and famine and bitter poverty, not long enough for their tongues to have forgotten the Irish lilt and rhythm or to have been touched by the farm speech of the countryside.

To the eyes of the Kaliker family the cabin looked pleasant enough for a new home. It was set in the shade of tall trees with a row of pines to shield it from the west wind, and ribbon grass grew in clumps by the doorstone. The sun shining squarely in at the south door told them when it was noon, and if there was no turf to burn, there was wood for the taking.

The summer went happily. The other men liked John, though they teased him for his clumsiness in handling tools whose like he had never seen before. But in their own rough way they were good to him and showed him the right and easy method of doing things.

The dairy on the farm was important. The eighty cows had plenty of pasture and ponds to drink from and were contented without any inquiry as to the world beyond fences. But Mr. Loomis kept a bull. Not all farmers kept bulls, partly because they could not provide separate pasture and stabling for them, and partly because of the very real terror that bulls inspired. They were regarded by most farmers as savage beasts and treated accordingly. It is not pleasant to remember how bulls were treated, both the intended cruelty and the unconscious cruelty that roused in the animals a ferocity so dangerous that it seemed to justify the farmers' fears.

It was customary to thrust a copper ring through the bull's nose. To this ring a chain could be attached and the bull fastened in his pen in the barn or on occasion staked outdoors with a heavy chain made tight to the stake. With even a slight movement on the bull's part, the nerves that centered in the nostrils were set quivering and kept him in a state of bellowing and pawing. Because of the fear felt of him, he was not allowed the freedom that might have made him, if not gentle, at least less likely to turn vicious. In the summer when he was staked out it seldom occurred to the owner that without water or shade the scorching heat of the sun could raise the bull's temper to madness. The men who took the bull out to pasture or brought him back to the barn always carried pitchforks for their own protection.

The bull on Mr. Loomis's farm was treated neither better nor worse than most bulls. He was a huge red beast, but as he was regarded as reasonably safe he was sometimes turned loose in the narrow field at the back of the barn where the fences were stout. This field reached past John Kaliker's cabin. Four o'clock in the afternoon was the time set to get the bull in and penned up for the night so that the men could start milking at five o'clock.

Now it happened one very hot afternoon that, of the two men who regularly went for the bull, one had stayed in the back field to help finish the last load of hay, and the other back in the barn had wrenched his arm and shoulder in lifting. John Kaliker had been getting things ready for milking and he saw the man's face twisted with pain. He offered to go after the bull.

"Think you could get along with him alone?" the hired man inquired. His arm was hurting badly.

"Sure I can," said confident John.

"Well, I'll let you then. I guess the old fellow's feeling good. Take your pitchfork and be sure you get behind him and don't hurry him."

John took his pitchfork and started. After a few minutes the hired man's mind began to trouble him almost into forgetting his arm. The bull hadn't acted up for weeks, but you never could tell about a bull. Mebbe he shouldn't have let the greenhorn go alone. Mebbe he should have waited and got one of the other men to go with him.

He went out the barn door and up the little knoll that overlooked the field. One half of his mind noticed that John Kaliker's wife was standing opposite by the fence on the far side watching her husband.

John had obeyed orders. He had gone along quietly till he was about even with the bull. Then he saw his wife waving her hand to him and in return he lifted the pitchfork high and waved back to her.

But the hired man realized in panic that there was something strange about the bull. He had been standing statue-still, eyeing John. The sudden movement of the pitchfork fixed his attention for a second, then with a mighty roar he charged upon the enemy. It was so swift and frightful that the man and woman who witnessed it could not move or speak while the bull trampled John's body, tossed it in the air, ripped and tore and gored it with his great horns.

When help came it was too late to be of any service. John Kaliker was dead and beyond all recognition. The story always ended with the same words: "There wasn't nothing of his clothes left on him except the wristband of one shirtsleeve."

The rest of the story was sad too. The poor wife died only a month later. The old grandmother went to live in a little wood-colored house near grandfather's, earning what she could by helping the women of the neighborhood. The young daughter was placed in a church orphanage for a time and later came back to live with the Loomises. But the log cabin remained untenanted.

The Talcot house was once white, but with age it had put on grey, trimmed in springtime by lilacs blossoming at the parlor window. It was surrounded by currant bushes and grapevines and stood in the midst of forty fertile acres, separated only by a row of rhubarb from grandfather's garden. If a curse was going to settle on this sunny house, no one but my grandmother would have believed it.

The land was rather better than grandfather's holdings and his wishes may occasionally have followed his eyes when he looked across his neighbor's flourishing fields. But it is unlikely that he ever expected the house and land would some day be his, bid in at the final auction, together with a cherry nightstand.

Earlier, the farm had changed hands more than once, though not at times when grandfather was sufficiently in funds to purchase it. The Talcots had been living there long enough for the place to be called by their name. They had come from down-east a way, folks said. There were three pretty daughters: Delia, about sixteen, Catherine, a year or two younger, and Charlotte, only a little girl.

Delia wished to be a teacher and had passed the examination at the same time as my mother. But Delia Talcot's certificate to teach was never put to use. Mrs. Talcot had always been an ailing, sickly woman, and she died suddenly the week after the examination. As the oldest, Delia must stay at home and look after her father and sisters.

Mrs. Talcot had never taken any part in neighborhood affairs, and Talcot himself made no attempt to be friendly with anyone and was thought sour and sullen. It was the girls that people knew and liked and felt sorry for. But after their mother's death, the girls, except little Charlotte, seemed gradually to draw away from the life around them. They went nowhere and invited no one in to see them. Those who came felt unwelcome, so that by-and-by visits of sympathy and interest ceased altogether. This did not happen at once. The change could be seen only by looking back and comparing the new manner with the old.

By the end of two years Delia and Catherine were almost recluses. Little Charlotte still came down sometimes to grandfather's and was petted and fed large sugar cookies. When the family inquired about Delia and Catherine, Charlotte explained that pa didn't want them to go away from the house, he always kept them busy and besides, they both had bad coughs and Delia had spit up a lot of blood.

Someone else had had a glimpse of the two girls and reported that they didn't look like themselves, they were so thin and pale. He guessed they wouldn't live too long. His report and Charlotte's account worried the neighborhood women. It wasn't natural that two young girls should shut themselves away from their friends when they were sick and motherless too. Some of the older women ought to go and see if they didn't need help.

Mrs. Jackson and Mrs. Wilson considered the matter and decided to go. One morning when they had seen Talcot drive away with Charlotte on the seat beside him, they put on their sunbonnets and walked up the road and along the path to the front door. Neighbors were in the habit of going to the back door and entering without knocking. That morning the visitors thought best to choose the front door and knock. After some waiting the door opened and Catherine let them into the sitting room. Delia sat there in a rocking chair, huddled under a quilt and holding a bloodstained cloth in her hand. Catherine pointed to chairs for the women, but began coughing so violently that speech was impossible.

The women said afterward that they knew in a minute what the symptoms meant: the wasted figures, the bright spot of color on their cheeks, the cough, the blood—all that was the sure sign of galloping consumption, which killed the young with a swiftness that could not be overtaken. In concern and distress they looked from Delia to Catherine and said what they had to say, however useless.

"Have you had the doctor?" The girls shook their heads. Mrs. Wilson said, "The doctor could mebbe give you something to stop your cough."

Before the sympathy and affection they saw in the friendly faces, some barrier in the girls' minds yielded to their terrible need to talk to someone older, to find relief in telling what had happened to them.

Delia spoke between gasps. "A doctor—wouldn't do us

any good. We know we've got consumption—like Ann and Clara. We're going to die—just as they did—and—we want to."

"But why? Why?" the women said in amazement. "You are too young to feel that way. You have everything to live for."

Catherine answered between sobs, "No—no! We haven't—it's—pa." She stopped and covered her face with her hands.

"Your father would be willing you should have a doctor," Mrs. Wilson protested.

Delia struggled to get the words out. "You don't understand. It's—what pa has done to us. It's too awful to tell you—but—since ma died—he's made us take her place—in his room—at night."

Her hearers could not at first absorb the meaning her words contained.

"But—but," they stammered, "he couldn't—you didn't—oh, you poor things—why didn't you tell us! Why didn't you tell us?"

"Pa said—he'd kill us if we told—anybody. We wanted—to run away, but we didn't have any money—and we couldn't leave Charlotte."

"Haven't you anybody to turn to? Didn't I hear that your mother had a sister back East where you came from?" Mrs. Jackson asked in an effort to say something.

Catherine said, "Yes, but we—couldn't bear to tell her. We hoped she would—take Charlotte—after . . ."

"I'll write to her," Mrs. Jackson promised, "and we'll see that you girls are looked after. You needn't be afraid any more."

She and Mrs. Wilson waited with the girls, trying to

comfort where no comfort was possible, until Talcot drove into the yard. Charlotte climbed down from the wagon and came running to the house. The women went out where Talcot was unharnessing the horse. Mrs. Jackson was the speaker and she wasted no words.

"There isn't anything I could call you bad enough to fit you. But you'll be tarred and feathered, if you aren't hung, if you ever dare . . ." She did not finish, but she had said enough.

That there were laws for such cases everybody knew, but Delia and Catherine were too ill to endure the shame of telling their story in court for all to hear. One of the neighbors took the two girls into her home and cared for them tenderly. As far as the neighbors could, they soothed the suffering and they tried in every way to distract the girls' minds from the hideous thing that had been done to them. Charlotte stayed contentedly at grandfather's.

A fury of anger and revulsion swept the community when the truth was known. The word "incest" was in the vocabulary of some, but was not a word to be taken on the tongue. Instead, when the matter was talked of, men and women alike fell back on the words that had been substituted for generations: their own father had used the girls!

Delia and Catherine were dead before any plans could be made for them. Mrs. Jackson wrote the full story to their aunt and she came at once and took Charlotte home with her. Talcot shut himself up at the farm and never spoke to anyone if he could help it.

His end was in keeping with the Old Testament and a God of vengeance. He was hoeing in the field one day when a dog came running out of the woods. Talcot was not directly in the dog's path, but near enough so that he picked up a stone and threw it at the animal and brandished his hoe. The dog turned, rushed at him and bit him savagely again and again. In a day or two it was reported that a mad dog coming from Cicero way had been shot by a farmer at Pine Grove. Talcot may have hoped to escape his fate. It caught up with him. So far as was known, he was the first and only victim of hydrophobia ever in the town.

Because he was human, the neighbors volunteered to tend him. Uncle Charles and Uncle Tim tried once to describe the man's death to me. Five or six men were needed to hold him while he struggled, raved, and cursed. Even in recollection years later, the uncles found the scene too awful to say much about. When he died, the grim-faced men wiped the sweat from their faces, and one of them voiced the feeling in the minds of all: "Sometimes a man gets what he deserves."

Of course the full story of the Talcot girls was not told to us as children. We knew the house by their name and that Delia had driven the old white horse when she and mother went to try the teachers' examination. We knew too that Delia and her sister Catherine had both died of consumption like our Aunt Ann and her friend Clara Wright. The dark background was never spoken of until we were grown up.

Charlotte's story had a happy ending. She was carefully brought up by her aunt and married well. As long as she lived she wrote now and then to Aunt Elvie, who had especially loved her. There is no reason to think that she ever knew the tragedy of her sisters.

The house where the Talcots lived has been torn down;

the wild rose bushes that made the June air sweet about it disappeared with the widening of the road. Only the night-stand is left to prove that the Talcots once lived hereabouts. It had stood in their bedroom, and after grandfather bought it, it was stationed by his bed and held the candle or the little brass lamp that lighted him up the stairs each night.

Now the nightstand has become an antique in my sitting room and is covered with books and flowers. I can reach out my hand to touch it as I write. It is well that tables cannot speak.

All these stories seemed to us as children so long ago and so far away from our own lives that there was no need to feel fear—only the brief sadness that any tale of sorrow sheds for a minute on the hearts of happy children.

But the last scene of all that ends the strange eventful histories affected my imagination so deeply that I carried it in my mind for years, and whenever I think of it the old shiver of horror returns.

This story, unlike the others, did not happen in the immediate neighborhood so that we could look at the field or house or barn and think what had gone on there. Yet the place was not distant either, perhaps some five miles east of the village.

Gathered there at this time was a sect that called them-selves Free or Shouting Methodists, not, so far as I know, a part of the organized Methodist Church nor subject to its discipline. The followers in this sect were characterized almost equally by poverty, ignorance, and intense fanaticism. They held camp meetings in woods or open fields where they shouted and prayed and danced before the Lord with the uninhibited abandonment of uninhabited minds.

Chief among them were a preacher and his wife, whose fervency in supplications to the Almighty was marked even in a group whose gift of tongues filled the air. This couple had a little boy about three or four years old. The children of the Free Methodists were expected, almost from their first word, to call upon the Lord and make public protestations of their love for Him and confess their unworthiness as sinners to be saved from a burning hell.

With such parents the little boy may have been incapable of making a prayer of any sort, or the fear of hell may have paralyzed any mental energy he had. Whatever the reason, his efforts failed to satisfy the father and mother and presumably their God. He must be made to pray. They resolved to give him a taste of what hell would be like and then he would understand what he must do.

It is difficult to judge the ferocity that can seize men and women in the name of religion. If it hurt these two to do what they did, they may have taken that as a sign that they were to be punished for the child's sins. Or it may be that the cruelty of the God they believed in was a part of their own nature.

They had a kitchen stove in which wood was burned and they started the fire until the top of the stove was red hot. Over it the two of them held the boy's feet and watched them burn until the flesh was seared and until the agony of the child frightened them from their purpose.

The burns were so deep that the child died almost at once, the only merciful part of the story. When this became known, something was done. The preacher and his wife were arrested and finally adjudged insane and sent to a mental hospital. Perhaps all cruelty *is* insanity, or to say it more simply, a turning to the devil.

Now this thing happened not very long before I was born so that it took on flesh and blood in my mind. We had a tall coal stove in the sitting room, and in the evening the red coals shone out clearly through the isinglass that sur- rounded them and were beautiful to look at. At that time I had not been promoted to nightgowns like Ethel, but was still wearing a humiliating little buttoned garment that ended in legs. My feet were always cold, and often at bedtime father or mother would rub them and hold them close to the stove to warm them. The fire looked *very* close to the feet, and I was terrified lest the same thing that happened to the little boy should by mistake happen to me.

I knew mother never made any fuss about our saying our prayers, and sometimes if we were tired she would tell us to go to sleep and she would say the prayers for us. But in a world that I had already learned held unexpected and fearful things, they might make a mistake and let my feet burn. I am sure I never said so or they would have talked away my fears. As it was, the fate of the little boy threatened me as long as I was small enough to have my feet held to the fire.

Growing Up

"Aunt anne," said my young grandniece with pity in her eyes and voice, "you and grandmother had a very stern, rigid childhood, didn't you?"

How can I make her understand that her grandmother's childhood and mine was neither stern nor rigid; that a disciplined childhood, such as ours was, could be both free and happy? For the word "disciplined" suggests to her severity and punishment. Ethel and I grew up without either. We were expected to obey, and since we knew the rules and they were few and reasonable, it did not occur to us that we were mistreated in having to keep them. They were largely concerned with behavior and property. Father forbade us ever to throw stones at people or windows. It was no hardship to refrain. I doubt if we would have done it anyway. If we found a gate open in our rambles, it was to be left open; if it was closed and we opened it to pass through, then it must be closed after us. If possible, we should climb over it instead of running the risk of not being able to shut it again. Misbehavior and punishment at school, we were told, meant that a second punishment would await us at home. The teacher was always right and we were sent to school to study and to behave ourselves. As all the children in the neighborhood grew up by this same rule, reasonable peace prevailed at school and the second punishment never took place. We were allowed to spend long afternoons in the woods and fields, and if we got home by suppertime all was well. In fact we were so surrounded by aunts, uncles, and cousins that it would have been difficult to get ourselves lost, strayed, or stolen if we had tried.

In the woods I was never afraid, but I did fear that the gypsies might take a fancy to me and spirit me away. They came by in springtime in long wagons covered with black canvas, a threatening color in itself. The gypsy women would come to the kitchen door to beg food or offer to tell fortunes. From a safe position protected by mother's skirts I loved to look at them. They wore bright kerchiefs on their heads and hoops of gold in their ears and had many chains and bangles and short, looped-up skirts. Seventy years later their costume would have been completely fashionable, but at that time they were wholly unlike the sunbonnet-and-ging-ham-apron world I knew. They never showed any desire to annex me. Still there was the frightening tale of Charley Ross, the child stolen, it was believed, by the gypsies and never seen again. There was a woeful ballad about him which the sight of the black wagons always brought to my mind.

Like the tramps who stopped, the gypsies were always given food at our house. Most people thought they helped themselves to milk from the pails left cooling in the watering troughs at night, or eggs if they were convenient to get at.

Beyond such petty thievery no graver charge was ever laid against them. People were inclined to like their coming, for they brought with them a suggestion of a free and mysterious kind of life remote from farms.

School began for Ethel at the age of four. She walked up the safe road from the old farm and was delighted with school and all its ways. The schoolhouse stood on the same spot where father and mother had taught, but a new building had replaced the old one in 1881. It was painted white; never again would the children in the district have the historic privilege of going to the Little Red Schoolhouse. Except for being white, however, the new building was similar to the old one. On one side of the entrance was a space for coal and wood to be stored. The square hole through which coal was shoveled and wood thrown was just large enough for a small child to crawl through and unlock the door for other pupils. In winter we all felt it was too cold to wait outside for the teacher to come. Because of my size I was often selected to climb up and squeeze through the hole and open the door. A heap of coal made a slippery landing place.

Another door, not locked, let us into the schoolroom. There were two windows to the north and to the west and the south. A potbellied stove stood near the door and from it a stovepipe ran the full length of the room to a chimney in the west end. There were no lights except the sun, no clock except the sun. If a storm came up and it was too dark to study, we closed our books and the teacher led us in singing. Blackboards on three walls provided for arithmetic examples and spelling lists. Teacher's desk was a flat table flanked by recitation benches. The three rows of desks started with very small ones that the four-year-olds fitted into, and grew larger toward the back of the room. Only the teacher could see out of the windows in all directions; the pupils faced nothing that could be supposed to distract from the purpose of their being there. But a seat near a side window commanded a view of the spring sky and the fall of the first snowflakes.

The school year was then about thirty-six weeks. In February, the worst of the winter months, the roads were so drifted that no attempt was made to keep the school open. The summer vacation lasted from mid-June to early September. A scant nine months of education was entirely satisfactory to parents and children.

Teachers received their pay—four to six dollars a week was average—in the most inconvenient way possible. All public money intended for education was sent to the supervisor of the township, who in turn checked it out to the teachers once a month. Sometimes the money was late in arriving, or the supervisor might be away from home when the teachers of the fourteen districts in our township came for their checks. Then they had to make a second trip. In a world without telephones or rural free delivery of mail this was often a hardship and always an annoyance. During father's four years as supervisor, the visits of a string of teachers each month were highly interesting to Ethel and me. We could compare the others with Our Teacher and debate whether an exchange might be desirable. As each district was usually paying its teacher at a slightly different rate, the supervisor was required to do considerable figuring. Father also offered financial advice to some of the young women. One girl from the district next to ours was using her meager wages to help her father hang on to a worthless farm at the edge of the swamp. Father urged her to sell the farm for whatever it would bring and to stop pounding sand in a rathole.

Textbooks were not furnished to us. Some of the pupils whose fathers were hired men and moved often never had a complete set. Ethel and I took it for granted that we would have new books whenever it was necessary. To keep the books from getting soiled, mother covered them with pieces of pretty calico or gingham. It took a big piece of leftover cloth to go around the geography, but all the books looked attractive when mother had finished with them. The covering of schoolbooks was general in the neighborhood. Some mothers, however, used pieces of ugly bedticking because it was thick and stout.

Every child had a slate, large or small. All of them had inch-wide wood frames that made a loud noise when they were slammed down on top of one another in the rush of an arithmetic match. When the wood frames began to be bound with strips of red wool they looked less drab and made less noise. But slates had to be companioned by slate pencils, and of all the sounds to rasp a teacher's nerves, a squeaking slate pencil was the most trying. Any slate pencil could be made to squeak if you held it just right and it was one of your bad days. The law requiring a flag flying over every school building did not exist in our earlier schooldays. The nearest thing to it was the paper picture of the Stars and Stripes pasted around the top of our slate pencils.

A pencil was not enough for a slate. It demanded the constant use of a slate rag. On almost every child's desk stood an old bottle filled with water and with a folded paper wedged in its neck in place of a cork. Water could be poured on the slate rag and all the mistakes and sorrows of misspelled words and wrong answers to arithmetic examples could be wiped out. Slate rags were repulsive to sight, smell, and touch. The alternative—only employed by a child who had not been taught better—was to spit plentifully on the slate and rub it off on a sleeve already dirty. Pencil and paper were thought too expensive except for some special purpose. A penny would buy a pencil that had a tiny rubber eraser in the end, and five cents bought a tablet of ruled white paper. To make the tablet last longer, we used any scraps of wrapping paper we could find at home. But the slate remained the backbone of our school equipment. On it we worked our arithmetic examples, drew our maps for the geography class, and constructed diagrams for sentences in the grammar lesson. Some of the pleasures of the slate were not for the teacher's inspection. Such were the houses that covered both sides with an upstairs and a down or a floor plan for playing tic-tac-toe should the opportunity arise. Our slates were our all-in-all.

By the time I was four and ready to be educated we were living on the main road and school gradually assumed its daily routine. In the beginning of my school life I loved to hear the older children recite. My little front seat was a listening post. I could not bear to have the physiology lesson come to an end just as it was in the middle of talking about the hammer, anvil, and stirrup inside our ears—of all places! —and the twenty-four vertebrae and thirty-two teeth. The numbers sounded like arithmetic, but the class didn't have to work them out.

Everything in school was wonderful except arithmetic

and that was too wonderful for me. In later years trials-by-arithmetic darkened my life. If our teacher was new and teaching on a six-months' license or a permit, she started us in the fractions which she had learned to manage. If she was experienced and had weathered a crisis in numbers before, we might find ourselves facing square root or cube root or compound interest and partial payments. I dreaded most the review problems where two trains running in opposite directions at different speeds and starting at different hours were expected to meet somewhere along the way. Where was the trysting-place for the trains? Instead of trains it might be pipes filling a huge cistern, each pouring in a different quantity of water. The big pipe worked in gallons and the smaller pipe in quarts. If there was yet a third pipe it mustered only pints. How soon could they reconcile their differences and get the cistern filled?

And then A, B, and C took over. All three had toiled happily by themselves and had got the job done in five, seven, or ten days. The arithmetic wanted them to unite, and how many days did A, B, and C working together need to finish the whole business and in what proportion would they be paid? Arithmetic was the blot on my happiness at school, for how could a child be at ease in her mind when she knew that trains, cisterns, and A, B, and C were waiting for her?

We carried our dinner to school though the distance was short enough so that we might have gone home to eat. All the children preferred eating at school and having the rest of the hour-long nooning for playing. In warm and pleasant weather we ate in squat old apple trees, climbable and comfortable, along the side road. Hard-boiled eggs nested in everybody's dinner pail. Burke Hamilton had a knowledgeable trick of cracking his egg in one blow against his forehead, a skill we strove to imitate but could not. It hurt. The dinner pail held varieties. Sandwiches were infrequent except bread and jelly. Our bread and butter was cut into quarters and could be eaten with the slices of cold ham or cold sausage or dried beef tied up separately. The Egg was certain to be there and a piece of cheese, an apple, a pear, or a bunch of grapes. We got through this part of the dinner in a hurry and went on to the cookies, ginger or raisin-decked sugar; a piece of cake and a saucer pie, a whole pie baked in a saucer that had lost its cup-mate. Last of all we ate the best of all: the cinnamon rolls that were mother's specialty. They were made of piecrust and inside them was a thick sugar syrup flavored with cinnamon. The piecrust was folded into neat oblongs to cover the syrup completely and then baked to a pale golden brown. The double jelly tarts we did not like so well; they were pretty but messy. It is clear that our lunches ran heavily to sweets. No child ever carried milk. The water pail took care of washing the final crumbs down our throats.

The water pail stood on the shelf beside our dinner pails in the tiny closet where we hung our wraps. Next to the joy of going after a pail of water was the importance of passing it. In the interests of democracy the carriers who fetched the water did not pass it. The pail was set on an empty desk in the schoolroom and a child appointed to distribute it. He filled the dipper and the smallest slobbering front-seater had the first drink. Though there was supposed to be only enough water in the dipper to satisfy one child's thirst, it never worked out right. A child wanted less or he wanted more, and if any water was left in the dipper it went back into the pail. The longer it took to go around with the water, the shorter the time for me to hear the physiology class follow the circulation of the blood from the right auricle to the right ventricle or thereabouts! I fussed over drinking from the common dipper and hit upon using my dinner pail cover instead. This private elegance did not save me from the common cold or any of the other common ailments that went up and down the aisle with the dipper.

In winter when the stove was red-hot we improved on our cold lunches. At recess time the ashes in the pan were glowing, and in them we buried the big potatoes we had brought from home. By noon the potatoes were done, light and mealy and needing only to have the ashes wiped off. We scraped butter from our bread over them and ate them skins and all. In addition to roasting potatoes, we sometimes opened the stove door, thrust a stick through a quarter section of our bread and butter, and toasted it to a crisp. The butter sizzled and sometimes the bread slipped off the stick and fell into the fire beyond rescue, but usually we had nice hot toast. Toast was a treat. It had no place on the average farm table; toasters, even tin ones, were rare and many women held that toast was indigestible. The only time we had toast at home was when we came back from school with a sick headache and a violently upset stomach. Mother would put us to bed on the sitting room sofa and lay a cloth moistened in camphor on our foreheads. Camphor was such a sure cure for headache that she could safely leave us to sleep away our misery. It was dark when we woke up and time for mother to bring our headache supper—a baked potato softened with cream and butter, a cup of pale hot cambric tea (a combination of a little green tea and warm milk), and a slice of perfect toast made by holding the bread on a kitchen fork over the wood fire. Ethel had more headaches than I, for her eyes were bad and there was no school doctor to examine them. Her eyes ached at home as well as in school; but they looked so clear and bright that mother was inclined to be doubtful about their aching. Ethel was sixteen years old before mother and father realized how seriously her eyes handicapped her.

Subtract from the nooning hour twenty minutes or less —time enough for any child to eat dinner in fair weather— and there remained forty minutes to do as we pleased, provided we did not go beyond the sound of the bell that would call us back to an afternoon of geography and spelling. The schoolyard, where we might decide to play, was open on all sides but for a board fence separating school property on the south from the neighboring farm. The yard was a good-sized oblong, partly grassy, and in games that required taking sides the schoolhouse supplied one side and the fence directly opposite served as the other.

The games we played must have come down through many generations of children, and in the course of time had arrived at wide variations from the starting point. There was motion of one kind or another in all of them; it might be running or forming a circle and going round and round singing as we went. Running was restful for legs that had been stationary all the morning, and singing in the circle games rescued our voices from the forenoon silence. We sang now high, now low, together and apart, but always stopping promptly when the circle came to a halt. A modern playground director would say the best feature of the games was that everybody could join in—unless one child had a mad on some other child. Five-year-olds could run when ten-year-olds ran, trying hard to keep up, and five-year-olds could make a joyful noise alongside their elders.

One of our favorite games was "King William Was." That sounds as if the name had been cut in two, but it identified the game. We formed a circle, a boy stood in the center, and we began to sing:

> King William was King George's son,
> Of all the royal race he run—
> He wore a star upon his breast,
> In gold and silver he was dressed.

We had no idea whether King William was the son of George III who had mistreated us so badly in the history book or who he was. He just *was*. It didn't matter, for to wear a star and have gold and silver clothes made King William a splendid person to sing about. At the end of the four lines, however, he dropped out of the game and became a bystander while we went on without him to sing the rest of the song.

> Go choose to the east, go choose to the west,
> Choose the one that you love best.
> If she's not here to take your part,
> Choose another with all your heart.
> Down on this carpet you must kneel,
> Sure's the grass grows in the field.
> Salute your bride and kiss her sweet,
> And now you may rise upon your feet.

The choosing of the bride and kneeling on the grass were carried out; the salutation was always a bow, and the kiss was omitted altogether.

The rhymes in our singing games were often faulty—not much more than a doubtful likeness in sound—and the words frequently made no sense. But rhymes and words were easy to say and we were not critical. It was easier to say "Buckety, Buckety, Water" than to go to the trouble of prolonging it to

> Bucket of, Bucket of Water

and in a short nooning too!

"Buckety Water" was a two-children game. It took up so little room that several pairs of children could be playing it at the same time. In each pair the children stood face to face and clasped hands, right to right and left to left. Then they swung their arms back and forth, cradle rocking fashion, while they sang:

> Buckety, Buckety Water,
> Buckety, Buckety Water,
> My father's a king, my mother's a queen,
> I have a little sister all dressed in green.
> One berry bush,
> Two berry bush,
> Please step under the rosy bush.

The "rosy bush" meant that the arms were brought over the head and a second later the children stood back to back, hands still clasped, inside the rosy bush.

A king or a queen was present in many songs. The words rhymed well and the world had been familiar with kings and queens a long time. Besides, what child could have sung something that rhymed with "president"?

"Old Witch" was not sung. We chose the Witch, or a girl selected herself by saying, "I'll be the Witch"; next we chose the mother, and the rest of us were the children lined up beside the mother on the schoolhouse side. The Witch lived opposite by the board fence. She came across to our house and knocked with her stick and demanded a piece of pie. While the mother went to get it, the Witch grabbed a child and ran off with him to her home. If the mother could catch the child before the Witch reached home, she could take him back, but if the Witch got him to the fence he had to stay with her and help her catch the other children.

This continued until all the children had been stolen and were in the Witch's house. Then the situation was reversed. The mother knocked at the Witch's door and asked for a piece of pie.

"What kind?" snarled the Witch.

"Oh, apple pie," said the mother.

The Witch brought out a child and the mother biting the air cried, "This tastes like my girl Sally. Run home!" and away they ran.

We repeated this over and over till all the kinds of pie we knew about were eaten and all the children saved. It was a very long game full of shouting and dodging and clutching and laughing.

As I think of it now, this game reflected that dark backward of time when the ancient terror of witches was everywhere. A child disappeared and the mother knew that a witch had stolen it, and in despair the mother left home to search for it—and all in vain. The story was transformed before it came to us and our game ended happily. Today the true and fearful stories of our own century are made into plays for the theater, but the things that have happened are not yet far enough away from us to warrant a happy ending.

Odd as it may seem, we enjoyed playing games that dealt with sickness, death, and funerals. The details as we understood them were interesting rather than frightening and did not disturb us by any sense of sadness.

"Miss 'Ginia Jones" was a very agreeable game. It had a good deal of motion and singsonging and much talking back and forth. Whoever was to be Miss 'Ginia Jones lay down on the grass and a nurse sat beside her. The rest of us, friends of the invalid, took hold of hands and came forward singing,

> We've come to see Miss 'Ginia Jones,
> 'Ginia Jones, 'Ginia Jones,
> We've come to see Miss 'Ginia Jones,
> And how is she today?

The nurse answered, "She's very sick." We took up the strain:

> We're very sorry to hear of that,
> Hear of that, hear of that,
> We're very sorry to hear of that,
> We'll come some other day.

We moved back a little and returned for further inquiries. The tune almost sang itself and each verse had the same repetitions.

> We've come to see Miss 'Ginia Jones,
> . . . We hope she's well today.

The nurse broke the news to us that Miss 'Ginia Jones was dead. We made a circle around Miss 'Ginia and began to arrange for the funeral.

> What shall we bury her in?
> . . . For it must be today.

The exciting part was choosing the right color for burial. If the nurse suggested pink, we shook our heads in rebuke.

> Pink is for babies, babies, babies,
> . . . And that will never do.

The other colors brought more headshakings and objections. Blue was for sailors; red for firemen; green for Irishmen;

yellow for Chinamen; grey for old folks; black for mourners
—and none of them would do. Finally, at the end of the
rainbow, the nurse had nothing to propose but white. We
agreed at once.

> White is for dead people,
>   Dead people, dead people,
> White is for dead people,
>   And that will always do.

We helped Miss 'Ginia Jones up and started over again.
Although she was the central figure in one sense, no one
ever particularly wanted to be Miss 'Ginia, for she did nothing more dramatic than to lie still and watch us.

It is clear that repetition of motions and words was
highly important in learning a game. The tunes had to be
easy, half-talking, half-singing, and the rhymes, real or
synthetic, helped us to remember. The lasting gift of our
games was to our imagination. We became brothers and
sisters of kings and queens, witches, and friends of the sick,
and stepped at will inside a rosy bush. The bell always rang
too soon.

Our play was not confined to the schoolyard. Woods
were near and orchards were handy. Directly across the
road from the school was a tumbledown house that had
reached the state just right for children to play in—windows
gone, broken stairs leading to a floorless second story, queer
paper—queer to us—clinging to the parlor wall, and outside,
flower beds full of blossoms from spring till school closed
in June. Some woman once upon a time must have chosen
lovingly the sweet of the year to look at, for daffodils and
hyacinths and white stars-of-Bethlehem, sweet williams,
and double buttercups had survived climate and time and

neglect. A great bush of June roses offered material for wreaths to decorate our hats. Our school hats had only a dark ribbon band for trimming and a wide brim to shield our complexions. The June roses beautified them.

Study hours were subject to interruptions. Once a year a man with a dancing bear would stop at the school. Then the teacher would declare an extra recess and we would rush out to see the bear. From what I know now of the cruelty that accompanied bear training, I do not see how we could have enjoyed his dancing. But we had met bears only in fairy tales where they had a habit of turning into princes after the wicked witch's spell was broken. It never crossed our minds that the bear was not as pleased to be dancing for us as we were to witness it. The bear man always looked foreign and always carried a sort of club which we thought served to guide the bear like an orchestra conductor's wand. We were still happier when the hand-organ man and the monkey came. First the man would set up a pole to which the monkey was fastened by a long chain. Next he let down the organ from his shoulders until it rested on a peg that was attached to it like a wooden leg. Not until then did he begin grinding out a tune, while we watched the sad-eyed little monkey run up and down the pole and do tricks. Since none of us ever brought money to school, it could not have been very profitable for the bear leader or the organ man to perform for us. Perhaps they got satisfaction from the delight of an uncritical audience, and we did have remnants in our dinner pails to feed the monkey and the bear or their owners. The seldomness of things, the almost-neverness of seeing before us what we had read of, made bear and monkey and organ man a greater source of excitement than if we had been accustomed to hand-organs and animals. How lamentable it was, we felt, if some child born to ill luck was at home with whooping cough when the schoolyard became a stage upon which strange creatures took their parts before our enchanted eyes.

The last day of school was never sad. No one was moving away, and ahead of us the summer vacation stretched endlessly into time. Perhaps the teacher would give us presents. The presents seldom failed. At four my present was a china doll in a white satin dress; at seven it was a copy of *Oliver Twist,* and at the same time Ethel was given *Jane Eyre.* Do they sound too old for our years? I admit that the descriptions were slighted and some episodes and conversations were not clear to us. But the story was there to read. Both books begin with the childhood of hero and heroine and that made it easier for us to be interested in them. We never outgrew our devotion to Oliver and Jane. As children we laughed over Dickens' characters and scenes, but when we grew older the terror and cruelty of Oliver's London left no room for laughter. *Jane Eyre* was not then a subject for smiles, and yet the other day I picked up the book and read again Jane's closing comment on Adele: "A sound English education corrected in large measure her French defects." England under Victoria was in that sentence.

Our teachers must have loved their pupils. Some of them were young enough to make friends of us, and they would invite us in pairs to stay at their homes for a weekend. Under their direction we wove garlands of oak leaves to decorate the schoolroom for the Last Day. The stem of each leaf was broken off and used as a pin to fasten it to the next leaf. True garlands to hang in shining loops upon the walls and transform the room. Our mothers came on the Last Day and admired our work. They praised the pieces we spoke and the songs we sang without any accompaniment, and they said no accompaniment was needed because our voices were clear and sweet! A good Last Day.

In the record book of the district, beginning in 1867, Grandfather Moulton's name appears over and over again as trustee or clerk of the school meeting. Later by many pages comes my father's name in the same offices, and the names of uncles and cousins and neighbors, all doing their duty by the school. Reading through the book gives a picture of the changes in the neighborhood. The familiar names of relatives and friends give way to another generation and yet another until the little school is at the end of its history. The closing entry in the book is in Ethel's handwriting. As clerk, she recorded the names of those present, the motion, and the vote taken upon it: the school is to be shut and the district joined with other districts in a central school. Buses are to carry the children away from the world that was—that world of woods and meadows and undirected play—to the world in which these children must grow up.

Pleasures and Palaces

INDIANS HAD NOT been a danger in our part of the world for well over a hundred years. We were concerned with them one summer largely because we liked to handle a bow and arrow. When, very rarely, news came of a flare-up of Indian trouble in the West, our spines crinkled with fear and hope that the Indians were on the warpath again. If they were, they never stayed there, and we did not really believe they were coming our way. But a semi-belief was a help at the "Let's Pretend" age.

We had shortened the name of our weapon by reversing it, and "arr'an'bow" had the sound of a flying arrow. Father had provided us with superior arms. From a battered old umbrella he took two ribs for the bows; the ends of each rib were fastened together by a stout cord, and it bent at once into a perfect curve. The arrows came next. Father notched and pointed maple sprouts and fitted them to the bows, and we were ready for the attack.

The best position to take up—just in case—was the roof

of the corncrib, which stood close to the board fence at one side of the barnyard. To climb from the fence to the corn-crib was easy, for the roof slanted so low that landing on it and getting to the top offered no risk except that it was exposed on all sides to the enemy. We drew our bows and aimed our arrows at the first brave who showed his feathered head around the corner of the barn. "There! There he is!" we cried to each other. "Shoot! Shoot!"

But an arrow shot from the bowstring must be retrieved and that meant climbing down from the outlook post and hunting in the grass while the Indians crept nearer. We took turns in gathering the arrows: one of us at least must escape scalping. Another way to escape was open if we were hard pressed. The tall corn in the field nearby would hide us securely. No Indian, no matter how keen his eye or how swift his moccasined foot, could track us to the middle of the big cornfield. But the little bird that tells secrets—a crow straight from the cornfield in this case—informed us that our greatest peril was what father would say if we dashed through the corn and broke the stalks down. Instead, in the last desperate moment when the worst had happened, we blew our whistles to alarm the other settlers.

Like our bows, our whistles had been constructed before our eyes. Father's sharp jackknife had cut limber basswood growths, whose pith slipped easily, and he had whittled and trimmed until there was a whistle for each of us. A faint breath into the whistle made a noise like an onrushing train—a cry for help that would rouse the United States cavalry at the fort ten miles away.

We were a little vain at being the only children in the neighborhood that had arr'an'bows made from umbrella ribs and maple sprouts. That was probably why we outwitted the Indians and survived the summer.

Time ever flowing had not yet left behind the Age of the Organ. There was an organ in most homes that had musical inclinations or the wish to keep abreast of what the family owed itself. Our cousin Grace had an organ and was able to play the hymns in Sunday school; our cousin Ray had an organ and could accompany himself when he sang at church socials. I did not like the architecture of organs very well, but I lingered over the stops, whose names were all melodious madrigals. Ethel, like father, loved music and she yearned for a piano. Her hopes soared above an organ because she associated a piano with gayer and more dancing strains than a staid organ consecrated to Sundays and funerals. Father drove a bargain with her. He said, "I'll get you a piano as soon as you learn to make good bread." No challenge was ever presented to Ethel that she did not instantly resolve to meet. Mother had not been consulted about the possible purchase of a piano, but she enlisted all her powers to turn Ethel into an accomplished bread maker. Ethel had a cooking sense and a skillful hand, and by the time she was twelve years old she could set on the table before father a golden-brown, fine-textured loaf of bread all of her own making. She had won her piano. Father went to the city by himself to select it, and if mother felt hurt at being ignored she did not show it. The music of poetry and of old ballads and singing of almost any kind deeply appealed to her, but for music divorced from words and voices she cared little.

The piano arrived. It was the upright type, a little lumbering and taking up too much space—a great reckoning in a small room. The case was near-mahogany and had scrolls on the front, combining musical notes, horns, and flowers. We thought it a very handsome addition to the parlor. I never expected to play on it, for father said that at nine I was too young to have lessons and I did not want them. To run my fingers up and down the piano keys was enough. Ethel was many heavens beyond the seventh in her delight over the new piano, and lessons began at once for her. There was an excellent teacher in the village, a graduate of a music college, and under her instruction Ethel practiced steadily and learned quickly. In what seemed a very short time she was reading notes almost as easily as she read print. That was her greatest musical talent. Her touch was not rippling and springlike, such as our cousins possessed; instead it was firm and sure. I, being mother's child in music, was happy to lean over her shoulder and sing the songs she played— "Clementine," "Sweet and Low," "Juanita."

Father belonged to the village band. The band was a democratic organization made up of those who could play fairly well, those who could play a little, and those who were tone deaf but hopeful of improvement. They met for practice each Thursday night and tooted and drummed till eleven o'clock and they were ready to make music on all occasions in the village. Father had chosen the cornet as his instrument of performance—more complicated than a trumpet, only somehow not so stirring. About the time of the piano advent he decided that he wanted a better horn than the brass one he had learned on, and accordingly, after more inquiry than he had made about the piano, he discovered a cornet that looked like silver and had the name of some master maker or owner engraved on it. Whether it was as valuable as father believed, I do not know, but as soon as Ethel could play well enough to follow the cornet or the cornet follow the piano, he found great satisfaction in conducting a concert in the parlor, to which mother and I listened full of admiration for what they could do.

In many ways father's band was one of the unspoiled pleasures of his life, for he liked the bandmaster and his companion players and was not troubled by the jealousy or suspicion of slights that too often attacked him. He felt that his silver cornet was the best instrument in the band, and he was proud to show it off when called upon either at home or in public. He would sometimes sit on the front steps after supper and send the notes of his cornet, softened by being out of doors, across the fields and into the glimmering sky.

The place for any band to perform is in the open air, and it was at picnics and celebrations and in parades that our bandsmen were regularly heard. The G.A.R. yearly clambake gave them their finest hour. The picnic was held on Frenchman's Island in Oneida Lake and everyone went, for besides the band there was the boatride to the island, and there were clams.

Clams were cheap, though not commonly bought for private parties but kept for picnic crowds where the men vied with one another to see how many clams each one could eat without quite passing the margin of explosion. Actually the clams were steamed rather than baked, and it required considerable work to get enough ready for the hungry processions. A good-sized but shallow pit was dug and stones put in the bottom. On these a fire was built and by the time it had died down and the ashes had been raked off, the stones were red hot. Clams by the bushel were spread over them and covered with wet lake grass and left to cook. The steam forced open the shells and the clams were then ready to be swallowed. In the process of their being lifted out, much of the juice was lost, but butter from the waiting picnic baskets took its place. A prize was given for the man who downed the most clams. Four dozen was about the limit. After the clam consumption, the members of the band had to find breath to play the required pieces; the horn blowers in particular must have wished they had eaten one less clam. The afternoon ended with a stirring rendition of "Should Auld Acquaintance Be Forgot." The clambake was always a glorious day.

Education was not taken so seriously that any parent raised objections to our being excused from school to see the afternoon parade of *Uncle Tom's Cabin* in the village. The play was to be given in the evening in a tent set up on a patch of grass beyond the creek. Everyone expected or hoped to see the show (all entertainments acted out were "shows") but the parade was free. We crowded up on the steps of stores or houses, out of breath from running to get there on time. First came a wagonload of black men, perhaps Negroes, perhaps not, singing and playing banjos. Then came the mammies, their heads tied up in red bandannas, and after them Eliza, holding her child on high and desperately crossing invisible ice. Miss Ophelia clung tightly to her bandbox and beside her Topsy sifted flour over her very black face to turn it white. Uncle Tom was in chains and Legree flourished a bullwhip over him. Last of all, riding a white pony, was Little Eva. She had golden hair and wore a light blue dress. I could not begin to describe how beautiful she was. Every little girl who saw her wished more than anything else in the world that she were Little Eva and the white pony hers.

Father took us to the play that night and we shed tears over Uncle Tom's sufferings. At the very last we saw Little Eva in heaven; she had long white wings folded about her,

her hands were laid upon her heart, and her gaze turned upward. For the minute or two that the scene lasted a rosy light shone around her, which father said was stage fire. Whether it was that or a gleam straight from above did not matter to us. We knew that Little Eva was safe among the angels.

One reason why Ethel and I were so well prepared to enjoy the play was that mother had been reading the book aloud to us every evening. We were thrilled and horrified by it. We got from it an impression of slavery that never left us, nor was it, as is sometimes argued, an unjust picture. If two of Uncle Tom's three masters were good and kind men, that was better luck for the slave than was likely to happen in most cases. The book took such hold of us that we could not bear to have mother stop reading and say it was our bedtime. One night we pleaded so hard to hear more that mother said she would sit on the stairs outside our bedroom door and read for a little while. The next night she had to read the same chapter over again. We had gone to sleep and missed it.

Today it is fashionable to turn a superior eye on *Uncle Tom's Cabin* and refer to it as melodramatic or exaggerated and really nothing but folklore. Let those who have never given a thought to what slavery meant, or felt in imagination the enormity of its evils, speak lightly of a book that fell upon the heart and conscience of America and changed an abstract question into a living reality. Well, if Mrs. Stowe had not written the book, Little Eva would never have come a-riding down the village street and her bright image would not have been fixed forever in our minds.

Not equal to *Uncle Tom's Cabin* but still worth seeing

was the medicine show of the Kickapoo Indians. It was held in the ballroom of the Parker House and went on all day long. Father took Ethel and me to the show on Saturday morning as the least crowded time. For some reason mother did not care to go. She said she had not the right kind of mind to accept a medicine of such far-reaching powers. Usually the Indians came in the winter and were dressed in full costume of feathered headdress, leather jacket, fringed trousers and moccasins, and overhung with beads. I did not know then that the Kickapoos were a branch of the fierce Sioux. We all thought it was a made-up name. They were stalwart men, striding swiftly through the audience and proffering bottles of Kickapoo Indian "sagwah." This was their miracle medicine that cured whatever evil had seized you. Buying in faith or in kindness, the onlookers treated the medicine respectfully and were inclined to think that since Indians knew so much about herbs and things it would probably do them good. Undoubtedly it was no harder to believe in the efficacy of sagwah than in the drugs advertised now on television. The Kickapoos were orderly and well behaved, but they played their drums like the redskins falling upon the settlers. We were glad that father bought a bottle of sagwah even if he did call it a cure-all when he handed it over to mother.

Once a new kind of entertainment was announced, to be held at school in the evening. News of it had spread from other school districts, and it was reported that the tickets were to cost five cents for children and ten cents for grown-ups—and each family was asked to bring a lighted lantern. The schoolhouse was crowded when we got there, after gathering a procession of neighbors, children, and lanterns as we went along. A white sheet had been stretched across the front blackboard, and in front of that was a queer-looking brass tube affair. The man in charge told us that he was about to give a magic lantern show, the only one that royalty had delighted to honor. None of us had ever heard of a magic lantern. Lanterns belonged to barns, or they lighted paths at night; or, fastened to the dashboard of a carriage, they showed where the road was. The word "magic" changed all that.

The man must have thrown many pictures on the screen with appropriate comments on the enthusiasm kings and queens had expressed for them, but I have no memory of them until he said, "Now we will go around the world." Then there appeared what looked at first like a map of the hemisphere. Meridian lines in red and black were marked off on it; part of North and South America could be seen and bits of Europe at the edges. While we stared at it, a little ship came into sight at the North Pole and began sailing clockwise around the outside of the circumference. It was at the South Pole and back at the North Pole before we could take in what was happening. The ship was sailing around the world! "Do it again," we begged. "Make the ship go around the world again!" The man laughed and sent the ship around two or three times. The capsule in orbit could not have been more bewildering or astonishing to us than the white-sailed ship of our World Cruise.

No one has ever discovered how children out of their own heads invent names for places, sometimes fitting exactly and sometimes not fitting at all until through time and use the name seems entirely suitable.

The King's Palace may have been pure inspiration or it may have been a memory of the king's house protected by thorny hedges in a fairy tale. Whatever the reason, the King's Palace it was and we loved the name. We went to the woods in spring for flowers and in the fall for nuts, but in the heart of summer we went to the King's Palace for nothing except the joy of going. When one of us said, "Let's make an Expedition," we all understood that the Expedition was an afternoon at the Palace. None of our other explorations was called by such a high-sounding title.

The Palace was a perfect circle of hemlock trees standing on a knoll and overlooking the rest of the scattered woods of pine and hemlock. The ground sloped slowly to a swampy stretch of alders and maples which we had to cross to reach the Palace. If there was water in the swamp, we jumped from hummock to hummock, but it was usually dry and covered by great sheets of moss which we tore up and piled for houses—ignorant children that we were—never dreaming of the years it would take before moss grew there again.

Our preparation for the Expedition emphasized food. We needed a pail of water for cooking and for washing our hands—the boys who carried the pail thought handwashing wasteful—and every one of us was certain to be thirsty. Then we needed matches to start our fire and newspapers to roll tightly and put under the dry wood that had to be picked up when we got there. Sometimes mother let us have a little bottle of kerosene oil to hurry the fire along. It was a settled habit that we should always take the same things for supper. Each of us brought eggs and potatoes and sweet corn in season to be cooked. Besides those substantials, Aunt Kate made German potato salad for Blaine's contribution; Aunt Mary sent caraway cookies by Emery; Mrs. Millen put bread and cold meat and a can of cold coffee in the basket

Helen and Georgia and Mildred carried; and mother baked red raspberry shortcake in quantity for my share. The biscuits came hot from the oven and were split and buttered and wrapped in a towel to stay warm. I gave one hand to them and the other to a quart of rich canned raspberries. The load would have been heavy for anything but a picnic. The short-cake was put together at suppertime, and suppertime arrived early.

Till that happy hour we climbed our trees. Each of us laid claim to a special tree in the Palace circle. The hemlocks were still young enough to be reached easily from the ground and tall and strong enough to bear our weight and let us swing back and forth high in air as far as we could go without breaking the treetops. They never broke and we never fell out of them—and the rhythm of a swaying treetop is music and dancing and poetry and all the arts. Tree-climbing lasted till wood-gathering time. Twigs and brush and pine cones lay all about and we scattered to collect them. The wood fire urged on by matches, oil, and paper burned successfully and all we had to do was to watch it and see that it did not spread.

We had heard that the gypsies, who knew much more about outdoor cooking than other people, had a particular way of cooking eggs. They wrapped them in layers of wet paper and when the fire had died down, they tucked the eggs carefully into the hot ashes to steam. We followed the gypsy method—how pleasant to be a gypsy even briefly—and the corn too was roasted in its own husks and the potatoes in their jackets. The only drawback was the waiting for everything to get done. We ate in sequence: the eggs were ready first, then the corn, and finally the potatoes. None of

213

them were overdone, but accompanied by whatever needed no cooking, they tasted delicious. The shortcake crowned all.

What a terrible risk we ran, you might say, of setting ourselves on fire and burning the woods up. Not at all. I might not advise it today—other times, other dangers—but we had grown up with wood fires and had all been taught about them. We knew that we must never reach over or bend across a fire; never put little stones around or under it lest they heat and burst in our faces; and we must never, never leave a fire till the last spark had died out and the ashes had been doused with water. We never had a burn or an accident, and the woods were none the worse for our coming.

The King's Palace is gone. Many years later when a new highway was put through, moving and destroying the known world, the walls of the Palace crumbled. After the road was opened, I saw Georgia at church and she said to me, "We drove along the new road yesterday. I looked to see if the King's Palace was there—the road runs so near—but I couldn't find it. They must have cut it down."

Nor could any of us ever find it again.

Not all our tree-climbing was done in the King's Palace. There were trees to climb at home so that our skill was not confined to hemlocks. Apple trees were safe and maples even in old age. Hickory was extra strong but often too high for us, and cherry, pear, and plum trees were not to be trusted.

Safety for the climber lay in his keeping his foot close to the trunk of the tree as he went from bough to bough on his way up. If he planned to drop from the tree, he must be wary of getting so far out on the limb that it would break in bending. There was one exact spot to choose—not too near, not too far—and country children learned it by experiment and experience.

I know now that we lived in a world of extraordinary beauty and what we heard and saw as the year went by remained deep in heart and mind. The farm tools and machines had a music of their own: the click of hoes in springtime; the swish of a scythe in the deep grass of the fence corners; the sound of a mower traveling across a meadow, and most beautiful of all, the melody of the reaper at work on the harvest. Mother used to call me to listen to it. The four rakes of the reaper turned like a wheel, now high, now low, and after the reaper had passed, the grain lay prostrate in the shorn field.

In June when the dew fell, the haycocks smelled of roses. In the late August afternoon the sheaves of wheat were golden enough for the courtyards of heaven. By October the shocks of corn surrounded by pumpkins rose into an Indian wigwam village. Everything was something else and yet itself. But for the men who worked on the land, summer was hard. To pitch great forkfuls of hay up to the loaded wagon and then to mow it away in the barn; to bind and set up sheaves all the long day—these were tests of a man's strength.

Today people riding by in cars stop to watch hay pressed and baled in one operation in the field and piled up ready for the barn or for shipping. They stare at the wheat, cut, threshed, and sacked and taken away only a few steps short of being bread; and the lookers-on exclaim, "How interesting! How wonderfully efficient!" But no one says any longer, "How beautiful it is!"

The Ways of Churches

DURING HER SEVEN YEARS at the old farm, mother was not often able to go to church, and Ethel and I were too young to benefit by Sunday school. Now in the new home on the main road, mother began churchgoing at once, and we were henceforth a part of the Universalist Sunday school and eventually members of the church.

On a Sunday morning the bells of the three churches in the village called to all to come to meeting, for the church was still spoken of as the meetinghouse. The bells did not interfere with one another; whichever bell started ringing first would pause after two or three minutes and let the others take up the summons. All three bells had individual tones easily identified. The loungers on the hotel steps, who never went to church, not only recognized the notes of each, but were able to interpret what they said. According to their insight, the Methodist bell shouted "Repent! Repent!" The Presbyterian bell urged "Church time! Church time!" Only the Universalist bell held out a cheerful promise. "No hell! No hell!" it said. The loungers felt safe in staying where they were.

The church bells sounding across the countryside set Sunday apart from other days. The faithful did not stand still with folded hands to pray, but they were reminded that they belonged to more worlds than one and it was time to consider that other world. The bells no longer ring. Like the vanished sleighbells, we hear them only in memory.

Father went to church irregularly when there was a minister he liked to hear. Most of our ministers were callow young students coming down from the St. Lawrence Theological School a hundred miles away. Very little in the way of education was then required for entrance to the seminary, and young men went there straight from farm or village and were shortly preaching the gospel. Some of them became surprisingly successful in their profession, but a considerable number of them gave up after a few years and turned to other occupations. Whenever the news came of their change of heart, father was accustomed to remark that they had reached the bottom of their sermon barrel. Over and over again, however, students who had practiced upon a patient congregation would ask permission to be ordained in our church. If the student was well liked, everybody was willing to help start him off properly in his ministry and consent was readily given. Ordinations occurred almost every year.

Insofar as there was any hierarchy in the Universalist Church, the highest ranking dignitaries came from the Theological School together with any nearby General Superintendent or Universalist minister who was well known. Besides these, the pastors of the other village churches were invited to be present and countenance the event, and all our own church members were there in force to watch a pale-faced young man solemnly set apart for Christian work. The ordination service required a good deal of extra work from the women. To them fell the cleaning of the church—washing the windows, brushing the pew cushions, sweeping the carpets, and preparing the ordination dinner that rounded out the day. They arranged the appropriate white roses on the altar and saw to it that the candidate's father and mother were welcomed and comfortably seated where they had a good view of their son. But women were not expected to have a share in the religious rites of the occasion.

All Sunday school classes were held in the body of the church, the only place there was for them, and large enough so that the sounds from one class did not disturb another. The Infant Class gathered on the front seat, where their legs dangled in space unless they sat on them. At six, Ethel was eligible as an Infant, and I was added to the class in due time. Ethel used to declare that she never was promoted, but remained in the same class during the whole of her Sunday school life. I doubt that. I think she enjoyed the early experience more than anything that came later and chose not to put any other class in competition with it. Our teacher was a sweet old lady with the lovely name of Mercy Hawn. She wore her iron-grey hair strained tidily back under a little round black hat indifferent to the change of seasons, and she had a paisley shawl fastened with a jet brooch.

Every Sunday we were given a bright-colored card showing a scene from the lesson. Below it was the text for us to learn, and on the back of the card a brief account of what the Bible said about the picture. A few simple questions and answers followed. We looked at the picture, listened while Mrs. Hawn read what was printed, and repeated the text after her. Then she asked the questions and we read the answers if we could read.

I do not remember Ethel's difficulties with Nebuchadnezzar, but she told the story so many times after she was grown up that I feel I must have been there when it happened. The picture card that Sunday showed Nebuchadnezzar in the glory of robe, crown, and scepter, and Mrs. Hawn read what was said about him, which included a brief mention of the Hanging Gardens of Babylon. Question-and-answer period went forward smoothly until Ethel's turn came. Instead of answering "But the king did evil in the sight of the Lord," as the card ordered, Ethel said, "Mrs. Hawn, how did the king make the gardens hang? What were they fastened to?"

Mrs. Hawn must have been startled. Never before had any Infant in her charge displayed the slightest interest in how Nebuchadnezzar's gardens operated. She was too honest to pretend she knew, and she said, "Ethel, I don't think I know. I never thought about it before." Unlike a modern teacher, she did not say, "We will look it up and see." She would have had no idea where to look.

Ethel retired mentally from questions-and-answers, but just as the lesson was about to end, she said, "Oh, Mrs. Hawn, do you suppose the angels let down ropes from heaven with baskets of flowers fastened to them—and they could have hung?"

Mrs. Hawn was relieved. "I think prob'ly that's just the way it was," she said.

She loved Ethel, and basket gardens hanging from heaven presented less difficulty to her faith than Nebuchadnezzar's being turned out to eat grass. She had always found trouble with that.

The village churches differed as much in appearance as in belief. The Methodists and Universalists worshipped in old-fashioned white buildings of wood. The Methodist Church was square and somewhat squat; the Universalist Church was high-roofed and had a soaring tiered steeple that could be seen for miles in all directions. The Presbyterian Church was also of wood but of jigsaw and gingerbread architecture and painted a kind of greyish-buff, set off by red around doors and windows. But inside, the Presbyterian Church was, by comparison with its rivals, the handsomest church in town. In the first place, it had colored glass windows—we called them stained glass—and when the sun shone in, it cast warm bright rays of light through them that fell on the wide oak pews and red carpet. And of all miracles, the Presbyterian Church had a pipe organ —gilded pipes that accounted for its deep tones. On Sundays a young boy stood in the corner by the organ and worked the handle of the bellows to fill the pipes with air and produce the wonderful sound. Any boy could pump the bellows as easily as he could pump water for the cows at home, and boys, Presbyterian and otherwise, clamored for a chance at the organ, and later in life claimed that they belonged to the Organ Pumpers Guild.

Aunt Alice was a devout Presbyterian and had the Young Ladies Class. Occasionally she took me to church with her, and when I sat beside her and looked up at the peaked roof and at the windows and listened to the organ, I thought Aunt Alice's church was so much nicer than ours that I wished we were Presbyterians instead of Universalists.

Presbyterian families were as a whole well-to-do, well dressed, and well mannered. If there was one thing they prided themselves on, it was their gentility. They measured the propriety of an action or an event by whether or not it could be termed genteel and anxiously questioned speech and manners to be sure they conformed to this idea. Aunt Alice told me that once when she was cutting cake at a church tea, one of the ladies approached her and said, "Mrs. Sneller, do you think that way of cutting cake is genteel?" Aunt Alice had been dividing the layer cake into generous triangles. It would have been more genteel, the questioner thought, to have cut the slices at right angles to each other— as if it had been marked off for a game! Since it was too late for Aunt Alice to change her method of cutting, the cake was set aside for the last table when the waiters ate. They would be too tired to notice the lack of gentility.

At the height of their pursuit of The Genteel Life, the Presbyterian ladies entered on a campaign to have their husbands and other women's husbands address their wives at home or abroad as Mrs. Smith, Mrs. Brown, or Mrs. Whatever. Even in the presence of close relatives and old friends the formal title was to be used. Uncle John was coerced into accepting this stylish idea and many other husbands underwent treatment and were cured of saying Jennie or Nellie or Bessie. Only, when Uncle John called Aunt Alice "Mrs. Sneller" before us it sounded cross. Mother thought it was a rather nice form of speech and would have been pleased to have had father adopt it. Father said it was silly and declined to cooperate. He was not fond of the Presbyterian ladies. I think their gentility increased the resentful feeling of inferiority that he was always plagued by.

The Presbyterians were markedly more dignified in their social relations than the Universalists. Could it have been because they never danced? I loved to see them walking in stateliness to their pews. The Widow Driesbeck was my special admiration. There were other widows in town, but when people said "The Widow" they meant her.

The Widow's Sunday dress was a striped green silk that rustled softly as she moved down the aisle—perhaps a trifle late, but that gave everyone a chance to see the latest fashion. Over her shoulders was a black lace shawl that did not hide the dress, and on her handsome head was a gay bonnet. She carried a fan, not a plain palm leaf, but a decorative creation which wafted her gently along till she sank back in her pew. The Widow lived in a large white house set among many trees on a wide lawn, and she had various suitors. One of them was a neighbor of ours who was always dressed up and could not have been just a dirt farmer. He was a handsome man, a lover of fast horses, and often enough on the road to give us children an occasional ride. The village thought that The Widow favored him, but said she could not accept him because her husband had made a mean will. By our standards the husband had been wealthy, and he had left all his property to his wife with the provision that if she remarried everything was to be taken from her and distributed among their children. Since the husband owned all the property and a wife at that time could hold nothing, it was natural that Mrs. Driesbeck was reluctant to leave her spacious house and its good furnishings, her horse and phaeton and carriage barn, and start life again with fewer comforts and less freedom than she had as a widow. Although the village regarded the will as unjust—"trying to hang on after he was dead," they said— they spoke of The Widow's romance, foundering on legal rocks, as rather funny. Still, they sympathized with her in her hard choice between sentiment and security. She never married again and neither did her suitor.

The Methodists were rich in doctrine, but much poorer in a worldly sense than the other churches. They were largely farmers and, with the exception of Uncle Jim, poor farmers. The women, again with the exception of Aunt Kate, were extremely poor cooks. The Presbyterians were excellent cooks and the Universalists were superb cooks. As Aunt Kate was a Methodist, Aunt Alice a Presbyterian, and we were Universalists, each family went to the church teas and socials at a relative's home and had an opportunity to sample the offerings. The judgment on them never varied.

I understand now why Methodist cooking was so plain and tasteless. The materials that make food good—eggs, cream, sugar, butter, the free hand that uses them unsparingly —all these the Methodist women did not have or could not afford. Even the butter contrived to be astonishingly bad.

The whirligig of time has revenged the Methodists. The Presbyterian Church has descended into a slovenly Grange Hall; the Universalist Church has been bulldozed out of existence to make room for a new post office. Only the Methodist Church remains and flourishes, enlarged and improved beyond recognition. Its modern kitchen and dining room have equipment worthy of a fine hotel, and the church suppers and dinners draw crowds from a long distance. But this lay far in the future.

Methodist ministers, like other country ministers, were paid—very slowly—some four hundred dollars a year and had a gaunt old parsonage to live in. Many a bitter winter day Uncle Jim went with a bobsleigh to move the minister and his family from the death-dealing cold of the parsonage to his own warm farmhouse, where Aunt Kate fed and cared for them till the cold snap had passed and they could be safely taken home, supplied with apples and potatoes and a pan of sausage.

Our church had no evangelists and therefore no revivals. The Presbyterians at wide intervals had a series of sermons designed to strengthen their faith or sometimes joined with the Methodists in financing an exhorter. To the Methodists, revivals were the lifeblood of the church. The meetings were always crowded. Some came in the fervent hope that sinners would be transformed into saints, and some came out of curiosity to see whatever might happen during the evening. Ethel and I were not often allowed to attend. Father and mother disapproved of the excitement and emotion revivals produced. But from time to time they yielded to our pleadings and the aunts and uncles took us along with them.

There was always a sermon on the awful penalty of unbelief and then from all parts of the church familiar figures went forward to the mourners' bench amid entreaties of "Save 'em, Lord!" from the sobbing congregation.

The choir sighed:

> Almost persuaded now to believe—
> Almost persuaded—

and lamented that those who delayed might be rejected.

Late, late, so late! And dark the night and chill!
Late, late, so late! But we can enter still!
Too late! Too late! Ye cannot enter now!

Bony old men with streaming white beards and wild eyes would burst into long prayers and gradually become possessed of what the village called "the Powers." Women too were subject to the Powers, a shriller and more fearful kind, that in the dim light of the smoking oil lamps made the church seem a battleground where angels and devils fought for their souls.

One old man never failed to burst into the most frightening hymn of all—

> There is a fountain filled with blood
> Drawn from Immanuel's veins;
> And sinners plunged beneath that flood
>   Lose all their guilty stains.

Once when Ethel went with Uncle Jim and Aunt Kate, she came home much disturbed. "I think it was mean of Mr. Dermott," she said, "to keep praying and praying for his second wife when Mrs. Dermott was sitting right there next to him."

Father began to laugh. "He wasn't praying about a wife. He was praying for his second *life*—his future in heaven— making sure of it. He's got reason to be anxious. And you needn't worry over Mrs. Dermott. She can take care of a second wife, if it's necessary, or even a third one." Ethel felt easier.

A revival was never connected in my mind with anything I had been told about religion. Yet I shivered over the strange singing, the evangelist's voice, now high, now low, and the cries of joy when someone was converted and saved.

After the evangelist had left town and the excitement had died down, a fair number of the converts returned to their old ways—"backslid" was the technical term. But even a brief experience of a deep emotion may have been good for them. It is hard to judge.

It may be thought that in our church we sometimes spoke lightly of what other churches held dear. We were not irreverent in our hearts, and we never meant to sin against the Holy Spirit. The mission of the Universalist Church was to free the minds of men from the cruel prisons of dread and fear and to help them to understand that God is kinder than they had supposed. To the degree that the mission was accomplished the church was justified.

Christmas

CHRISTMAS was a joyful time. It started early in September when the butternuts began falling, for the butternuts furnished most of the money to buy our Christmas presents. For some reason, the butternuts were our special property, perhaps because children could pick them up more easily than grownups could or would. Butternuts are large and a pleasant shape for the hand to grasp, and they filled bushel crates quickly. At the time of falling they are a soft green color that turns black as the nuts dry. The only drawback to the butternut harvesting was that they were very sticky— a kind of glue-like stickiness that attached itself at once to the gathering fingers. At the end of a session with them, we had to go to the house for kerosene oil and wash our hands liberally in it. The kerosene was almost as disagreeable as the stickiness, but only kerosene could combat that successfully, and then soap and hot water had to wash off the kerosene. On a fall morning or after school when the wind had blown down the nuts and the yellow fan-like leaves, it was highly agreeable to omit dishes and dusting and go out to the butternut trees to work. Father furnished the crates and sold the nuts for us on the city market at twenty-five cents a bushel. Usually the proceeds were two or even three dollars, and each Christmas present had the same value as a bushel of butternuts.

After the butternuts were picked up, it was time to begin on the cider apples to add to the Christmas fund. The orchard trees were grafted on wild fruit and the apples were almost entirely free from blight or insect. The trees were so tall that long ladders had to be used and the apples were brought down carefully to be packed in barrels on the barn floor. Those that fell off through wind or overripeness were used for cider and taken to Mr. Loomis's cider mill a short distance away. Father had two big barrels of cider made every year and stored in the cellar. He paid Ethel and me five cents a bushel for picking up the fallen apples. No care was taken to throw out any apple unless it was far gone in decay or extra dirty or had been nibbled by the cows. Although cider apple work paid us less than butternuts, it was easier, and sometimes Adney or Archie would help us a little when they came down from the ladders.

It might be thought that the cider made from these apples would have had an unpleasant taste, but it never did. My dearest playmate's father ran the cider mill for Mr. Loomis, and we would go up there after school and drink all the sweet cider we could hold. Then we would climb into the apple bins and hunt for a perfect apple that had somehow escaped the pickers and joined the cider group. Once found, we bit into it as if it were the first apple we had ever tasted. The mixed colors in the bins were a blended picture—English Streaks and red Spitzenbergs and Rhode Island Greenings,

Roxbury Russets (not much juice in them!) and dark Baldwins and yellow Bellflowers and a rare Northern Spy, much too good to be wasted on cider. The cider was drunk by father, the hired men, the neighbors, and visitors. By late winter it had turned hard and sharp like a primitive champagne, and Ethel and I did not enjoy it. But we would bring up two glassfuls from the cellar and put a teaspoonful of baking soda in each glass. Instantly the cider turned a dark brown and was once again sweet to the taste. Soda was held to be good for gas and indigestion, and mother let us drink our preventive in peace.

The butternut money and the cider money together were enough to buy presents for mother and father and the aunts and cousins and for each other. The next step in the Christmas progress was to go to the village and pick out the presents at Mr. Coville's store. Mrs. Coville always helped us make the right decision and was enthusiastic over the cup and saucer, the little bottle of cologne, or the vase we fixed on. When our choice was made, she would hold it up for our admiration and her own, and say, "Isn't it bootiful!" Mrs. Coville wished to speak genteelly and the sound of bootiful gratified her ears. She was the kindest of women and always had time to make our shopping a part of the delight of Christmas. Today there are more things to choose from in the dime store, but no Mrs. Coville to guide and help a child and approve his selection.

Sometimes we bought a deck of cards in a fancy case for father or a big red handkerchief for him to wear in threshing time; a pipe for grandfather or a pincushion for the aunts; and once two clothbound, well-printed copies of *Tom Sawyer* for the cousins—incredible at twenty-five cents!

I remember only one disappointment. Ethel found it hard to keep a secret, and she confided to me that her present for me was made of silk and was lilac-colored. I felt sure it must be a lilac-colored silk dress, though I didn't see how she could have bought one for twenty-five cents. Still, hope was stronger than economics, and I waited in suspense for Christmas to arrive and the lilac silk dress to be given to me. The dress turned out to be a square lilac silk necker-chief to be worn under my winter coat to church. And Ethel had recklessly paid *fifty cents* for it.

Early in December preparations began for Christmas at the church. There was always a Christmas concert at which all the Sunday school children performed, singing together, singing separately, and speaking pieces about Christmas, sometimes religious, but more often concerned with Santa Claus, hanging up stockings, and Christmas dinners. The girls' recitations were always longer than the boys' efforts, and each number was delivered with the speaker's glow of anticipation. Two tall Christmas trees were brought into the church and placed beside the altar. Candles were not used on them because the fear of fire in the old wood build-ing was strong and also because candles to our unlighted thought belonged in Catholic churches; nor was there elec-tricity to take the place of candles. Strings of popcorn and tinsel and Great Expectations made the trees bright to our eyes.

Early in December, too, a Committee on Presents for the Sunday School Scholars was appointed, usually Franc Loomis and mother, since Mrs. Poole and Mrs. Klosheim took charge of the concert. The committee spent a day in the city buying presents. They seldom had as much as ten cents to spend for each child, more likely five cents, and they bought according to classes, hoping that children of the same age and tastes had landed in the same group. It was surprising what interesting and attractive articles five cents could buy, and they were never moral presents like thimbles and holders. But however desirable they were, Ethel and I often took home nothing from the Sunday school Christmas tree. The reason was this. The committee shopped early while things had not yet been picked over, and they bought prudently one present for each child enrolled as a Sunday school pupil and provided no extras.

Now it happened—probably in all three churches—that a Sunday or two before Christmas, children would appear who had never been there before, but expressed their intention of being faithful comers thereafter. Somehow the committee always failed to reckon with this influx although it was a fairly certain part of the Christmas season. There stood the Christmas trees. Here were the children—and no presents for them. The same thing was done every year so that no time was lost in discussion. Franc would speak to one or two of the regular pupils, and mother would come to Ethel and me and whisper, "Little Gracie Drear and her little sister are here and there aren't any presents for them. We shall have to give your presents to them. You will have presents at home." And into the outstretched hands of Gracie Drear, that well-named child, and Little Sister went our presents. I cannot recall that we ever made a fuss about Gracie's invasion of our rights. We were comforted by knowing that no outsiders could possibly empty our stockings on Christmas morning.

Many of the church members brought their family

presents to put on the trees, and that lent both sparkle and excitement. Often the presents were more valuable than most of the church received. One year a pair of diamond earrings was given to the wife of a prosperous farmer and held up for all to see; once the tree bore a sealskin coat for Mr. Loomis's daughter. Mother did not wholly approve of having such expensive presents given at church. She thought home was the place for private gifts where the contrasts would not be so sharp and where it wouldn't look as if the display were intended to show off. She did not realize that not everyone had a Christmas tree at home, and that the whole congregation was interested to have real diamond earrings or a real sealskin coat to admire, even if it wasn't their good luck to get it. There was popcorn for everybody and we didn't have to resign our share to any latecomer.

We went home to hang up our stockings behind the sitting room coal fire. Because our stockings were small, we feared it might prevent our getting good-sized presents so we placed a shiny big milk pan directly under each stocking. Santa himself might have rested comfortably in either pan without crowding the gifts. Our home presents came in the stockings and pan; those from the relatives awaited us on the Christmas tree at the home of whichever aunt was having the Christmas dinner. What kind of presents? A red sled for Ethel or a pair of skates that would extend Christmas till spring; a red cart and new dolls for me, or the old ones in new dresses. Ethel's presents were three years older than mine; her doll's tea set was a size larger, and by the time I was finding letter blocks in my pan she was taking out a set of dominoes. The differences grew less as soon as I could read. The game of Authors appeared in a neat box and from it we learned the chief writers from Irving to Bryant and Cooper and the New England list, Hawthorne, Longfellow, and Whittier, along with Dickens, Thackeray, and Tennyson. On the card with the author's full name were the titles of his four most important works, and we learned forever what they were and found the information handy later on.

Books were standard presents for us always. Mother loved to read too well herself not to want us to grow up with the happiness reading brings. Sometimes the books were collections of stories that had passed under the purifying eye of Mrs. Alden, in the "Pansy" series, or that of Mrs. A. D. Whitney; sometimes Miss Alcott had the pans to herself, but the year that stands out above all others brought us *Andersen's Fairy Tales* and *Ellen Terry's Lady Reciter.* *Ellen Terry's Lady Reciter!* I wonder if Ellen Terry ever saw the book that bore her name. A picture of her beautiful face was in the front of the book, and we supposed, as mother did, that Miss Terry had personally chosen every poem or prose selection. Much of the poetry dealt with American heroes of war from Nathan Hale to Phil Kearney at Seven Pines. There were a few classics like "I Am Dying, Egypt, Dying" and a little patriotic prose. One of the strangest poems, strange because it did not rhyme though it was printed like poetry, was about a letter brought to a father and mother telling them of the death of their son in battle. Strange as it was, the beginning was haunting.

> Come up from the fields, father, here's a letter from our Pete,
> And come to the front door, mother, here's
> A letter from thy dear son.
> Lo—'tis autumn—

The fall of the words, the fall of the young soldier, and the falling of the leaves wove a harmony unfamiliar to us, and the poet's name, Walt Whitman, we had not heard before. Ethel and I learned piece after piece from the *Reciter*. We knew Miss Terry was an actress and the wish to follow in her footsteps stayed with us for many years. When I was sixteen and in high school, I saw my first Shakespearean play. It was *The Merchant of Venice* and Ellen Terry was Portia, a radiant figure in the scarlet robes of the law court. Watching her and listening to the magic voice, I thought how wonderful it would be to hear her recite something from her namesake book.

Christmas morning at home ended with father's taking down the brown box that for a week or two had been on the top pantry shelf. A similar one stood there every Christmas in plain sight, but we were warned not to climb up and open it. We knew it was the Candy Box and inside it were fifty sticks of candy—all kinds and flavors: white vanilla cream and black paregoric, yellow molasses, brown horehound and transparent lemon, alongside pink-and-white striped peppermint and birch and sassafras like little barber's poles in red and green and black. We knew each flavor, and the luxury of having fifty sticks at the same time was Christmas in excelsis.

Christmas Day dinners seldom differed, but there was the thrilling occasion when my cousin told us Aunt Alice was going to have *duck* for the Christmas dinner. Turkey was unknown in our community. No farmer raised turkeys and no one thought of buying them. The turkey that grandmother Moulton cooked for mother's and father's wedding supper in 1878 must have been about the last ceremonial appearance of the bird. Duck was equally unknown in our family, and the idea of eating it at dinner time made a breakfast of pancakes and sausage insignificant. When we arrived at Aunt Alice's, we found the house smelling of roasting duck, the table set in the dining room, and the relatives and neighbors already in the parlor. There were so many children that the best that could be done was to arrange a table for us in the kitchen. Aunt Alice had had no previous experience with duck and was quite innocent of calculating how many people with Christmas appetites one duck would feed. She put two ducks in the oven and waited the result in confidence. Her heart must have sunk when the ducks were ready. Each grown-up at the big table had a sliver, but by the time the platter reached the kitchen, the duck had become a family fable and poor Aunt Alice brought out some cold pot roast for us to feast on. We retired to the parlor and the Christmas tree, knowing that nothing could make up for our disappointment as long as we lived. The first present taken off the tree was for me from Aunt Alice. It was a large and brightly colored book of fairy tales, the best I ever owned. The rest of Christmas Day I sat on the floor in a corner reading my fairy book. Duck and I were no longer in the same world.

Christmas at Aunt Kate's had a special quality. For one thing her long, low sitting room ended in a large bay window which made a perfect background for the green tree and we saw it against the snow outside. Once the Christmas tree in the bay window held four dolls for me. High on the top was a golden-haired beauty for which Aunt Kate had made a white dress trimmed with butterfly pink bows along the hem and a smart little black velvet jacket. I named her

Flossy on the spot. She deserved something better, but Flossy was then my favorite name. Besides the tree and dinner, there was always the singing time at Aunt Kate's. An old-fashioned square piano stood in the sitting room, and after the dinner, the tree, and the presents, all the children gathered around it, and Aunt Kate played while we sang Christmas hymns—not the old carols, for they were no part of our tradition, but hymns we had sung in church. Last of all, Aunt Kate played "The Mistletoe Bough" and we sang over and over, "O the Mistletoe Bough! O the Mistletoe Bough!" That song, so joyous in its picture of the holly-decked castle, so sad in the fate of the bride, closed the Christmas Day.

One of my dearest memories is of the Christmas when I was in bed with the measles and unable to go to the family dinner. Mother decided that father and Ethel should go as usual, and she would stay with me. On Christmas Eve, since I could not even hang up my stocking, I snuggled down in bed to enjoy tears of sorrow and went straight to sleep. The sun was shining through frosted windows when I woke up. Mother and Ethel stood near the bed, and on a chair beside it was a little green Christmas tree with the smell of the winter woods still on it. How did it get there? Whose was it?

"It's all for you," Ethel explained. "Stuart and I went to the woods for it yesterday and everything on it is for you."

Mother took the presents off the tree, one at a time, and laid them on the bed so that I could touch them. Aunt Alice's mother had knitted a pair of white wool mittens for me; Aunt Kate had sent a little silk handkerchief with forget-

me-nots embroidered in the corners. Ethel bounced the soft red rubber ball she had bought for me. It had stripes of blue and yellow criss-crossing it like lines of latitude and longitude. It was hard to decide which of all the nice things I liked best until mother laid the last one on the pillow—a blue and gold copy of Sir Walter Scott's poems. A long extract from *The Lady of the Lake* was in our Fifth Reader and I had wanted very much to read the whole poem. Mother had remembered and the book was mine. After a chicken broth and raspberry jelly dinner, I begged mother to start reading the poem to me, but the tree, the presents, the dinner, and possibly the measles were too much, and I fell asleep to the rhythm of "Harp of the North." I like to think of Ethel planning the surprise for me and wading through the snow with Stuart to get the tree. He cut it and carried it, but it was Ethel who directed the enterprise. When the time comes that Christmas can no longer be merry, it is sweet to remember the Christmas days that were.

Festivals and Picnics

AT OUR CHURCH, printed in large black letters on a white scroll and hanging on the wall near the pulpit for all to read, was the Universalist Declaration of Faith. It proclaimed the Fatherhood of God, the brotherhood of man, and the final salvation of all from sin. That was a comfortable outcome to look forward to. It freed the church members from struggling to redeem the millions on India's coral strand; it did not demand Salvation in Our Time; and by-and-by all would be well with everybody. Our social undertakings therefore did not benefit missionaries, but were geared to raising money for the minister's salary ("The laborer is worthy of his hire," Uncle Tim quoted when he went around with the subscription paper), or for new hymn books, or for the faint, far-off possibility of some day having a new organ.

There was much for children to enjoy. Besides the festivities at Christmas, there were concerts in which we took part at Easter, on Children's Day, and at the harvest festival. At each one the children sang and spoke pieces, or if a child was too scared or too dull to speak alone he was stood in line with others in a dialogue where only a short verse was required of him and he was protected from the audience.

Easter was a more solemn occasion than Christmas. Usually in our late springs the snow still lay upon the ground and only Mrs. Loomis's primroses blossomed on the altar. Lilies belonged to summer gardens. With the buttercups and daisies and early roses of June, Children's Day in some ways was the prettiest day of the year at the church. Little girls in spotless white dresses, little boys polished to a shine, and the garlands of flowers they had gathered lent an air of innocence and sweetness no other day provided. The last concert was in October, a harvest celebration when cornstalks, pumpkins, sheaves of grain, and baskets of bright vegetables were placed about the altar. Just as primitive peoples had recognized the changing of the seasons by having their youths and maidens bring offerings to the gods, so our church in Christian fashion paid honor through the children to the endless turning of the earth.

The summit of the summer was reached toward the last of June with the strawberry festival. Wild strawberries were plentiful, but not many people had a strawberry bed in their garden. Strawberries for the festival had to be bought Over North, where soil and temperature suited their growth. In earlier days strawberries and cake alone were a treat, but as ice houses increased and ice was obtainable, ice cream was added. The custard, as it was called, was made by the women on farms, while the village ladies supplied the cakes, an easier and cheaper contribution, especially if someone brought what was known as "hired man's cake," a one-egg, butterless product that needed to be swallowed with a large spoonful of strawberries. The custard-makers used a dozen or two eggs, sugar in quantity, and as much milk and cream as they could scrimmage from more or less reluctant husbands—everything that was needed for "a good rich custard."

Each woman cooked her custard at home in the afternoon and took it the night before the festival to the Loomis house to be frozen, since Mr. Loomis always gave them a generous supply of ice and lent a hired man to chop it, pack the freezers, and turn the crank. All the custards were mixed together and poured into the two big freezers.

The flavoring of the custard was a matter requiring thought. Only vanilla and lemon ice cream were known in our town, and more vanilla than lemon was likely to be called for—so there was the problem of having the right amount of each to come out even. One year Franc Loomis suggested that they mix equal parts of vanilla and lemon flavoring and put it in all the custard. Then whichever flavor was asked for could be taken out of the same freezer. The idea worked splendidly. They called it Universalist flavoring and evidently it tasted like vanilla to those who wanted vanilla and like lemon to the lemon-lovers, and combined perfectly with the strawberries.

After most of the group had gone home those who remained, including mother and Aunt Elvie, felt that their own heaped-up, pressed-down, and overflowing custards entitled them to talk it over. Some of the custards, they said, were very much richer than others—you could tell by the color when they were poured into the freezer—and some were skimpy compared to what everybody was supposed to bring. They hoped there would be ice cream enough to hold out.

The nicest part of the festival, aside from feasting on strawberries and ice cream, was the work assigned to the girls of the Sunday school. On the afternoon of the festival evening we met to make the buttonhole bouquets. They were a regular part of the occasion and sold for five cents apiece. Each little nosegay had a background of rose geranium or lemon verbena and against that a knot of pansies, sweet peas, or mignonette—whatever flowers we had. We wound our boutonnieres tightly with thread to the right size for the buttonhole of a man's coat and provided a pin for each buyer.

The men who came to the festival were good-natured and not unwilling to have their best coats decorated. I could always depend on the uncles and our hired men to buy a posy from me. Some of the older girls who dared approach the young men made quite a sum of money. But it was happiness enough to carry around a little basket full of sweet-smelling flowers and look up with entreaty at the tall men who could afford a five-cent luxury.

Summer moved noiselessly into picnic weather. There was every kind of picnic to choose from; the Grange, the G.A.R., the Farmers', the Band Clambake; but the one that counted with us was the united Sunday school picnic. The churches had happily agreed that the children would have a better time if they were all together, and each church in turn could select the place. In the minds of the children in our church there was no doubt as to the best, the only, place for a picnic, and it was not too hard to persuade the committee to settle upon our choice.

Some fifteen miles away on Onondaga Lake was a pleasant spot called Long Branch. It was shaded by tall trees and looked out over the water and had comfortable seats and many tables. But trees, view, and tables were only the beginning of its attractions. Rows of chair swings were scattered about; there was a ball field and many stands where popcorn, peanuts, lemonade, and ice cream could be bought in quantities financially manageable. And most of all and the center of all, there was the most magnificent merry-go-round any child had ever seen.

A day at the Sunday school picnic at Long Branch went like this. In the morning father gave Ethel and me each twenty-five cents to spend exactly as we pleased. He did not often go to the picnic—it was likely to come in oat harvest time—but by ten o'clock mother had us packed in the democrat wagon along with the picnic basket and whatever other children she had volunteered to take charge of.

From year to year we had always forgotten the landmarks. As the roads grew less familiar, the happy sense of adventure increased, and when we arrived about noon at Long Branch, it looked even nicer than we had remembered. Dinner was the first thing to be thought of. Out of its towel wrappings Aunt Elvie took a huge chicken pie baked in a milkpan; mother had made fresh apple pies and beefsteak cake that morning; bowls of corn cut off the cob and cooked in cream, and bowls of ripe blackberries had traveled in safety; and there were innumerable things to be eaten out of hand, picnic fashion. Each family brought a glass can of coffee with the cream and sugar stirred in. The greenish color of the glass gave the coffee a seasick tinge before it was poured, but it came out still hot, for the newspapers rolled around the can had served as a sort of thermos. Relatives and neighbors usually ate together, and dishes were passed up and down so that sometimes there was not too much left for the family that had brought a special treat like Aunt Elvie's chicken pie. We were hungry from the long ride and we stuffed down everything as fast as we could; it was a pity to waste precious time eating slowly. With the last bite still being chewed, the boys dashed off to the ball ground, the girls started for the swings, and I ran to the merry-go-round.

There it stood—as if all the animals in Noah's Ark had decided to come together again. The music began slowly each time and quickened as the circle turned. At first the animals seemed to be putting down their feet softly, and then as they caught the spirit of the race, going faster and faster. I watched them go by—a lion and an elephant, a zebra and a deer, an ostrich and a donkey, a sea serpent and a camel—I lost count and could think only that with my twenty-five cents I could have five rides on any creature I chose, and by waiting between rides I could stay the whole afternoon at the merry-go-round. A crowd of children always surrounded it, looking and longing, but no promptings of generosity urged me to invite some other little girl who probably didn't have five cents to share my unfolding joy.

For the first ride I climbed on the camel. He was an ugly beast, I thought, but ever since I had known that the Wise Men came on camels to Bethlehem, it had seemed desirable to find out how it felt to be mounted on one. After all, people did ride on camels and they didn't really ride on

lions, handsome though they were. Yet the lion tempted me, and for my second ride he proved an accommodating steed. Three rides left—only three! I resolved to wait and think a long time before I made the great decision about them.

There was a bench close by, near enough for me to sit down and ponder and study the whole fairy group as they whirled past. Then with the suddenness of first love I saw the perfect one. Why hadn't I noticed him before? A pure white horse equipped with flowing mane and waving tail and looking ready to ride off into the air among all the winds of heaven. For my three last rides I would own the white horse. I waited until there was no other claimant to get on him, and each time the music grew more beautiful and the white horse moved farther out of the visible world. At four o'clock mother came to look for me. The afternoon had melted away; we must start for home. The strains of the carousel followed us faintly as we walked toward the wagon. Who can hold sunlight in his hand?

If, then, Long Branch offered all that heart could wish for a picnic day, why did the Methodists and Presbyterians turn their faces from it when it was their year to choose? What was the flaw? The flaw was an Open Bar Openly Arrived At. Against its back wall stood rows of bottles, and on a long wooden slab in front were many glasses and below the slab a rail on which the consumer could rest his foot. All in plain sight on three sides. Mr. John Hyatt, a Presbyterian pillar, protested that to take children to a place where liquor was sold like that was a direct defiance of "Lead us not into temptation." If questioned as to whether he had ever seen a church member dragged to the bar against his will and forced to swallow a deep glass of Rhenish wine, Mr. Hyatt, as an honest man, would have answered no. *But the possibility was there.* Mr. Hyatt's point of view was only a little more vehement than that of many of his fellow church members, who were committed to total and complete abstention from alcohol in any form. To be sure, Mr. Hyatt had advanced nearer the goal than most, for he would not permit vinegar to be brought into his house since vinegar was the result of alcoholic fermentation. His hired man reported that instead of eating sugar and vinegar on his lettuce like other folks, Mr. Hyatt poured on cream! What Mr. Hyatt did not understand was that to the children the bar was not there at all, and even if we had seen it as we rushed past it to the real enjoyments of the day, we had an absolute resistance to the thought of whiskey-drinking, a resistance received and strengthened at home, church, and school. We all knew that the man who sold liquor was as guilty as the man who drank it. The song we had learned at school proved that:

> Those who sell for the sake of gain
> Rum, gin and brandy and sweet champagne,
> Are worse than the drunkard, yes, by far,
> Who daily is seen at the oaken bar.

It would have reassured Mr. Hyatt if he could have foreseen how thoroughly temperate we would all grow up.

We did not need to inquire where the picnic would be held when the year of Long Branch was past and the Presbyterians and the Methodists had the choice. The place would be Norcross Point and there was no help for it. Norcross Point was a few miles away and jutted out rather high above Oneida Lake. It was about as it had been left on the

First Day except that at some time too many maple saplings had been planted there, and because they had been crowded so thickly together they grew spindling and scraggy and offered neither shade nor beauty. It would be difficult to think of anything about Norcross Point that could have suggested a picnic: no tables, no seats of any kind, not a solitary swing, and grass too deep to sit on. To count on having a pleasant picnic there was like being told to have a good time in a vacuum. The great merit of Norcross Point, however, was that strong drink did not rage any nearer to it than four or five miles.

The day before the picnic, the men (Methodist and Presbyterian men) had to get some makeshift tables ready and what seats they could accomplish by putting boards across sawed-off barrels. No one hurried to get to the picnic early; the day would be long enough. Mrs. Lower, one of our members, was overheard to say to Mrs. Loomis that Norcross Point had always been her idea of what the Bible meant when it spoke of the abomination of desolation. All the children stood around, unable to think of any nice game to play, as the grown-ups advised, and unwilling to go exploring as they suggested because there was nothing to explore: everything was right there before our eyes. It got to be dinner time finally, and things looked a little more hopeful.

Now a few days before the picnic Aunt Elvie had been making cucumber pickles, and as often happened in Aunt Elvie's cooking, there was a large surplus left after the family needs were taken care of. The pickles were a delectable crisp bright green and they would enliven any dull meal that had too much salt and too little relish. According

248

to the law of her nature, Aunt Elvie decided to take the big dish of extra pickles to the picnic. They would help out.

Dinner began. That at least was not a disappointment, and nobody frowned if we took a too-liberal helping. Mr. Hyatt was at the end of the table, not only engaged in eating whatever came along, but busy in pointing out to all who would listen the moral superiority of the unspoiled natural beauty of Norcross Point over the dangers of Long Branch and its like. At that very moment Mr. Hyatt was in moral danger and quite unconscious of it. Aunt Elvie's dish of gleaming cucumbers arrived at his place and he absent-mindedly speared one. Nobody warned him and the dish passed on. When Mr. Hyatt had finished his comparisons, he took a large firm bite out of his pickle. It was instantly revealed to him that *those cucumbers had been pickled in vinegar.* He choked a little, got up hurriedly and rushed off, pickle in hand, among the trees. His face was calm when he came back, but the pickle, of course, had disappeared. Not a word was said, just as if it were customary for a man to take a good pickle and then act as if it were poison. Afterwards Aunt Elvie said she didn't think much of such behavior, but Uncle Alfred said he guessed Mr. Hyatt had a right to save himself from filling a drunkard's grave if he could.

Easter and Mortality

HENS MUST OFTEN THINK regretfully of what a good life their grandmothers led. Today's hen does not set her foot upon the ground nor sit in comfort on a nest while her owner-slave brings her food and water. At the end of the rest period she does not cluck-cluck a brood of downy yellow chicks into the spring sunshine and display her offspring to her clucking neighbors. Nowadays one incubator chick is just like another, and no maternal instinct fastens a hen's glass eye on a white egg or a brown one. Mass production has replaced individual workmanship on eggs and chickens.

The little triangular coop where a mother hen lived with her family like the Old Woman in the Shoe has been succeeded by dormitories that house hundreds of hens, and there when the days grow short, electricity serves as the sun and prevents any pause in the egg business. What an automaton is the modern hen! It is true that eggs are fresher and better flavored than when grandma was at liberty to scratch happily on the manure heap, but life is less interesting for the creative artist.

A long time ago—from the original taming of the hen to the day the first patent on an incubator was granted—a hen in summer was a free creature. Eggs were gathered once a day, and a hen could amuse herself by swallowing a worm or taking a dust bath in the flower bed. Her time was her own. But when late fall came, the hen said goodbye to all that and went into retreat. No more egg-laying till spring. Straw kept the dark henhouse warm, grain was a nice diet change, and on the whole the hen was fully as comfortable as the cow or the horse.

Provident housewives like mother and the aunts began "putting down" eggs while the supply of early fall was plentiful. The eggs were wiped clean of any speck and then were sunk deep in big jars of oats or salt. This shut them away from the air and in theory kept them fresh for months. As long as the hens were laying even a few eggs, the ones put down were not touched, but in the dead of winter women were glad to reach into the oats or salt and take out something that looked like an egg.

Ethel was very fond of feeding the hens, gathering the eggs, and fussing with the little chickens; and she always waited impatiently for the spring laying to begin. We would talk hopefully of how soon the first egg could be expected and try to guess the date. When eggs were on the table, however, Ethel ate only the yolk of her egg and gave the white to me. In return I gave her my yolk and ate the two whites. We each disliked the part we gave away. We sat side by side so that the exchange was easy. Mother must have thought that children would outgrow their food tastes along with other annoying habits, for she never made much attempt to stop our trading beyond saying occasionally how nourishing the yolk was and what values the white contained.

The hens were faithful to the Easter season and started work again as the March days lengthened. The number of hens was not counted and sometimes a hen would steal her nest, lay her eggs in it, and never be missed. Presently she would come into sight followed by a dozen healthy chicks—like an errant daughter returning to the old farm with her child in her arms. There were enough eggs without hers—eggs for everything: eggs for custard pie, eggs to fry for the ham platter, and eggs for us to color to our heart's content. Some farmers kept only one strain of hens, but father's were a mixture, White Leghorns, Rhode Island Reds, and barred Plymouth Rocks—white, red, and grey as to feathers. The Leghorns laid very white eggs; the Reds and the Rocks laid brown ones.

Mother turned the kitchen over to us for the coloring hours. It was not a limited pleasure. Cousins and neighborhood children would appear and a do-it-yourself afternoon began. I am glad that commercial dyes did not rob us of getting color from whatever was on hand. Eggs boiled in water heavy with indigo became a beautiful warm blue; onion skins produced a golden brown. Sometimes mother gave us small pieces of figured calico to fasten tightly about the eggs. Cotton dyes then were not boil-fast and when the calico-clad egg was done, the pattern of the material was stamped upon it. We drew Chinese faces on the brown eggs —slanting eyes and a very red mouth with teeth and a fringe of black hair on the forehead. Very lifelike, considering that none of us had ever seen a Chinese. Most precious of all were the painted eggs, which had to be got ready a week or two before Easter. We chose the whitest eggs and with a darning needle made a tiny hole in each end of the egg. Then, taking infinite time and pains, we blew out the contents and had the fragile shell ready for our Cousin Anna to paint. Anna painted whatever flower we wanted, daisies, buttercups, pansies, or honeysuckle, and sometimes a butterfly for added naturalness.

These painted eggs Ethel and I kept to surprise each other on Easter morning. We hid them outdoors and after breakfast we knocked underneath the table and repeated the incantation: "The rabbit is knocking; he's brought an egg for you." Then we rushed out, one to search, the other to watch till the egg was discovered.

One year Mrs. Millen gave me a duck egg larger and whiter than a hen's egg could be. I took the treasure secretly to Anna and she painted on it a bunch of blue violets tied with a pink ribbon that unwound like a scroll around the egg. It was quite the most beautiful egg Anna had ever done. I could hardly wait to give it to Ethel, and I decided to have the rabbit come at supper time on Easter eve. The rabbit knocked and Ethel ran out and I followed. Tragedy met our eyes. Of all the places that I might have put the egg, I had picked one where no hen would have trusted her egg a minute. There was a stepladder leaning against the house, and to make sure that Ethel saw the painted beauty the first thing, I had laid it on one of the narrow steps of the ladder. While we were eating, a north wind had sprung up and blown it off. It lay on the ground broken to pieces. I burst into tears, and Ethel said mournfully that it must have been a perfectly beautiful egg before it was smashed. When we told Anna about it, she offered to paint another for me, but I didn't have another duck egg.

There was one thing about Easter that puzzled us for years. All the Moultons spoke of it as "Pauss." They said people always ate eggs on Pauss. Mother told us over and over what her brothers did as a Pauss surprise when she was a little girl. She thought they did it every year, though it seems as if the surprise would have worn a little thin by its annual reappearance. For two or three weeks beforehand, the boys told grandmother that the hens hadn't got to laying much yet, and there were only a few eggs for her to use for cooking. Then on the morning of Pauss they brought into the kitchen a big basket heaped with eggs that they had kept hidden in the hay mow. Mother believed there was at least a half bushel of them, but she was young and matched the size of the basket to her astonishment.

Why did the Moultons say Pauss instead of Easter? They pronounced it as I have spelled it and none of them could give any explanation of it. Easter was Pauss. As we grew older, we heard it less and less until finally "Pauss" became "Easter" to us and we almost forgot the word.

But dictionaries stand guard against forgetfulness. Years later I discovered that the word was really "Pasch," the name of the Jewish Passover, which also comes in the spring.

Ethel and I knew little of death as an interruption of life, and Grandmother Sneller had been ill so long that we did not feel her death sharply, much as we had loved her.

What I remember instead is the Easter before she died when I was not quite six years old.

Father had bought a new two-seated democrat wagon of which he was, with every reason, very proud. It was a Moyer wagon and that was equivalent to saying it was the best to be had. The seats were covered with pearl grey corduroy—just like velvet we thought—and the box and frame were a shining black. We did not believe there was a finer wagon anywhere. Father wanted to show it at once to grandmother. He coveted her praise always for everything he did and probably loved her better than he loved anyone else in the world unless it was Ethel.

So on Easter morning father and Ethel on the front seat and mother and I on the back seat started for grandmother's. That was the way families were arranged in riding then, not the father and mother in front and the children in the rear. Grandmother had been in bed for months dying with cancer. Besides the display of the new democrat, father had a present for her. One of the few things that grandmother could eat was clam broth, and father had gone to the city the day before to get clams for Aunt Kate to fix for her.

When we reached the house, father drove close to the long sitting room windows. One of them was filled with calla lilies, for Grandmother specially loved these lilies and always had them in her south window. Ethel held the reins competently while father went inside. He lifted grandmother from her bed and carried her to the window where she could see the wagon plainly and we could see her smile of pleasure and approval.

She died in June and father drove the democrat wagon

to her funeral. I hope it was a little comfort to him that grandmother had seen and liked the democrat and was glad that he had been able to buy it.

It was two or three years later that death took on reality for me. I have never understood what brought the terror of it to me without warning, for nothing had happened, no one had died, all was peaceful. I was outdoors on a summer morning, thinking, I remember, how clear the air was and how beautiful everything looked in the sunshine and how the grass waved as if the wind were patting it.

And then suddenly, never to be forgotten, the fear of death seized me violently as a physical sensation: *Everybody must die*. No one could escape. It happened to you and you had to go through it all by yourself—no one could take your place. Death was a lonely thing. Those who loved you could not help you, and they would go away and leave you under the ground—I shuddered at the thought. And if they died first, you would be all alone and how could you bear that? What a blessing it would be if you could die in a shipwreck with others near to share the dying with you, but even in a shipwreck you had to accept it: sooner or later you would die. That said itself over and over in my mind. I ran down the lane through the orchard to get away from the certainty that pursued me: Everybody must die.

The weeks that followed were miserable. I did not tell anyone what was frightening me and the cold dread in my heart did not lighten. I read the Bible constantly because the Bible told about going to heaven when you died. I tried hard to find comfort in it, but it was not my world that the Bible was promising and I had no wish to live forever in a jeweled city. In church the minister often said that death was nothing, nothing at all—you went on to a better world and a nobler life. Did he believe it? I could not.

The fall was sadder than the summer. At night the thin cry of the crickets came up to my window. It sounded lost and afraid and pitiful in the dark. The crickets would die when winter came. It was not true what people said—that everything came back to life again in the spring. The dead flower did not return, I knew, nor the dead tree.

How long this torment lasted I have no idea. It seems to me that it went on for years, but that could not have been. Time brought distractions and age has brought philosophy about leaving this pleasant earth. I often wonder how many children have suffered as I did from such fear of death.

From Summer Calico to Red Flannel

FASHIONS DID NOT CHANGE quickly in our part of the world. Hemlines were stable and colors varied little from black, brown, and grey if you were grown up, with purple added if you were old or had a purple personality. Summer calicos and ginghams were light colored, but women did not wear white dresses, and hats were almost a hundred per cent black.

Hats were important, especially at Easter—much more important than they are now and more talked about. New ones were not frequent, but a leghorn hat that had worn a wreath of forget-me-nots the year before might be brightened by changing to cherries or clover, and at Easter time the baize veils that had shrouded women's and children's heads through the winter were cast aside as a salute to spring. Baize veils were of semitransparent wool bought by the yard in all the mournful colors. About two yards of material before hemming made a veil long enough to be wrapped tightly over and around head, neck, and shoulders and would keep the wearer from getting catarrh, the winter affliction of our climate. Catarrh as a name seems to have disappeared with baize veils, or perhaps its woes have been subdivided and rechristened. It was safest to wear the veil over the face, and a woman driving her own horse and cutter could see the road plainly through the thin stuff. The only woman who risked her ears in the open from December to April was Franc Loomis, but she had a sealskin coat and could turn up the collar. It was also rumored, though not altogether believed, that she took a *cold sponge bath* every morning to ward off catarrh.

At Easter time, too, winter cloaks were likely to be shed. Many of the better-to-do women had plush cloaks, not very warm even with quilted linings, but thought much dressier than the heavy black woolen ones. Both plush and woolen cloaks in winter weather needed a blanket shawl pinned over them for extra protection. It was an agreeable part of spring to be able to get rid of the encumbrances.

Women wore black gloves to church in winter, but in summer these were exchanged for black silk mitts. Mitts were like gloves that had had their tops cut off so that there were no fingers and only part of the thumb. They went straight across the palm and almost up to the lowest joint of the fingers. The hand was much freer and cooler in mitts than in gloves, yet mitts preserved the propriety of not going out barehanded. At that time the desire to be covered was equal to the desire to be uncovered today. Children too had mitts, of blue, pink, or red silk, and we wore them in a blaze of pride and glory. In Sunday school when our hands got hot, the mitts were peeled off and put in a convenient pocket. For old or young, every dress had a convenient pocket.

The town was delightedly shocked when a woman in our church wore a bright red hat at her husband's funeral. She explained afterward that he was the kind of husband for whom a red hat was appropriate, and that she wore it as a sort of celebration because for the first time in years she knew where he was. In spite of the excitement created by the red hat *at a funeral,* the wearing of traditional mourning by women was not customary here, and black armbands for men were unheard-of. People in cities and in certain churches mourned in that fashion; our community did not. One reason was the cost. Most women could not afford to put aside the dresses and cloaks and hats they already had and buy a new wardrobe for the mourning period of a year or two. They possessed good black silk dresses, lined with fine cambric to keep them nice, and these served to express their feelings at a funeral. Black silk was standard and could be worn afterwards as well as crape. If the mourner had no black dress of silk or cloth, she borrowed one.

Near us lived a family with many children. When the youngest child, a little boy of three, died, the mother and the two married daughters had no black dresses for the funeral. To wear anything but black would be a disgrace, they thought, and so they asked for and received mother's and Aunt Alice's and Aunt Kate's precious black silks, and the father and sons-in-law somehow got hold of long black "weepers" for their hats.

I'm afraid mother and my aunts did not very much want to lend their best dresses to these neighbors, for they talked gloomily about the necessary airing afterward. But a funeral was a funeral, and it would not have been held decent to deny anything that brought comfort at such a time. Mother herself did not believe in wearing mourning. She said it was no help for heartache. I remember only one woman in our church who went into what was called "deep mourning," and I remember her because the dress was so becoming. Mrs. Van Braemar was a delicately pretty widow, left well off, and both she and her daughter, lovely Miss Allie, came to church in softly flowing black dresses and long crape veils hanging from enchanting little black bonnets that were edged with dull black beads. There was a sort of Mary Queen of Scots effect about the picture they made, and their black kid gloves completed the Portrait of Darkness.

The World Wars ended the practice of wearing mourning. In the midst of universal death, the question of black clothes lost its significance. Grief went unaccompanied by outer signs. Mourning had never really had a foothold in rural life.

On the whole, fashion was followed at a good distance, far enough to hear that something was in style, but getting nearer to it only as it was about to change. Since dresses were constantly made over and hats retrimmed, local talent was sufficient; and a wardrobe trip to the city was not necessary oftener than once in the spring and once in the fall. Everyone spoke of "going to the city" as if Syracuse had no name, just as today suburb and country talk of "going to town."

When we were too little to be taken along, mother brought home our hats or coats, the coats usually on the large side for us to grow into. I remember the day she came back and showed us our new winter bonnets. They were velvet bonnets, exactly alike except that Ethel's was pearl grey with blue ribbons and mine was garnet with matching ribbons, and each had a white ruching next to our faces. We were very proud of them. Mother was often tempted to spend more on hats for us than either she or father thought necessary. Once when she was looking for summer hats, the clerk brought out a wide-brimmed leghorn. It had fluted edges and blue ribbons and blue flowers. The effect of the hat on Ethel's head persuaded mother to spend three dollars for it. Father didn't say anything much about the price. He thought the hat suited Ethel.

Our everyday dresses and underclothes were made at home by mother. She let Ethel and me choose turn-and-turn-about the color of our calico school dresses. Ethel always decided on turkey-red, a red of intense hue softened by a pattern of little black sprigs. Turkey-red was vivid and gay and expressed her personality. I chose either pink or blue, whichever looked prettiest at the village store. In school we wore aprons of checked blue gingham that covered most of the dress, since aprons were easier to wash and iron than dresses, although not much easier. We also had white aprons for best, shirred and tied in big bows on the shoulder. If there was to be a church tea at grandfather's in the afternoon, mother would take along our best white aprons. When we arrived there after school, she marched us into a bedroom, hurried off the gingham aprons, wayworn by four o'clock, and enveloped us in the clean starched white ones. We were little girls dressed for a party when we were produced before the company.

Our aunts' dresses inevitably became ours, to be made over in whatever way the original dress permitted. The colors usually belonged to the serviceable group. One of Aunt

Ellen's dresses that fell to me was a dull green, almost black, and trimmed with black silk. I didn't like it and I think mother didn't either, but she said it was a good dress for a rainy day. Aunt Sophy kept her wedding dress, the silk alpaca colored ashes-of-roses, for many years and it eventually became my best skirt in my senior year at college. Mother's wedding dress had met the usual fate much sooner; the soft grey wool was made over for Ethel and me when we were quite small girls. Those dresses were trimmed with red and grey plaid and had red silk cord laced across the front on pretty steel buttons—so we did not look too somber, and at the age of four I thought my new dress a thing of beauty.

Underclothes included fitted underwaists of muslin with buttons all round, to which drawers and petticoats were attached. Mother edged the drawers with a linen lace called torsion. She put rows of tiny tucks on the petticoats and used hamburg to finish them off. Hamburg was not yet the universal food, but a heavy German embroidery made in Hamburg and not expensive. It withstood hard rubbings and washings and could be transferred from one garment to another year by year and always looked pretty. Two petticoats were a minimum to wear. The worst made-overs we had to suffer were the petticoats contrived from grandfather's red flannel nightshirts. They were extra long and the tops wore out while the lower half was still sound—far too good to throw away. Grandfather kindly contributed them to become nice warm red flannel petticoats for Ethel and me. We wore them to school under a longer petticoat and prayed nobody would ever catch a glimpse of them.

Our second-best dresses were fine Anderson ginghams,

and our best summer dresses were white dotted Swiss muslin or India lawn. In winter the best dresses were of wool trimmed with silk. These best dresses for many years were the product of Miss Corny Means' art and care. She came for a week in the fall to sew us up for winter, and a week in the spring to get us ready for summer. With her she brought copies of *The Delineator* for the past six months and whatever paper patterns she had gathered in sewing round among her patrons. *The Delineator* was a fashion magazine, though its staid yellowish cover did not suggest this. It had drawings and patterns for everything, even ball gowns. So far as I know, Miss Corny was never called upon to make a ball gown, but had she been asked to attempt it, she would have done her best. The pages showed morning dresses and tea gowns and church costumes and capes and mantillas, all described in detail. There was a section on dresses for children and one for dolls, and over that I hung for hours, wishing that I could somehow conjure up dresses for my dolls that would make them the best-dressed dolls in the neighborhood. Miss Corny got her ideas, she said, from the book and never tried to copy the pictures exactly. Indeed, the finished dress often bore scant resemblance to anything seen in the book.

Miss Corny, all the aunts agreed, sewed perfectly. Her infinitely tiny stitches graced the hems in our dresses or fastened braid in wonderful swirls on mother's basque waists. To rip out Miss Corny's sewing was like deciding to destroy a masterpiece. Her clothes had no style, but then, the aunts did not particularly want style. They bought good materials, silk or wool, certain that Miss Corny would never waste a scrap, but figure carefully to make every inch count. She would lay the pattern on the cloth and arrange it in different ways to see which was the most economical, so that there was always cloth left for the time when the dress would be made over.

In addition to watching the sewing take shape in Miss Corny's hands, we had the pleasure of having Miss Corny herself with us for a whole week. She must have been about fifty when I first remember her. Her hair hung in silver curls to her shoulders, her eyes were the bluest of blue, and her soft cheeks looked rose petal. She wore a plain black dress and a little white apron, and while she sewed she told us long stories, told them in New England accents, gentle and sweet.

Miss Corny's own story was sorrowful. As a young girl she had been engaged to be married, and her lover had forsaken her just before the wedding day. She had been stricken at once with brain fever—surely a much more common disease then than now—and her brown hair had fallen out. It came in pure silver, and Miss Corny let it hang in curls about her face. She looked different from every other woman we knew, more interesting. How could any lover have forsaken dear Miss Corny?

She was one of four sisters, the "Means girls," and their father must have had a touch of poetry in his soul, for he had named his daughters Fidelia, Aureilia, Cornelia, and Angelia. Miss Fidelia had died before my memory. The other three sisters lived together in a little grey house. "Reily" had married an elderly man, who became so completely crippled by rheumatism that he could do nothing to earn money. They lived by Miss Corny's sewing and Miss Angely's garden and bees. Reily kept the house beautifully. There were fine old things in it that had been a part of what the sisters called "mother's weddin' settin'-out." A mulberry lusterware tea set testified to New England. His sisters-in-law always spoke of Reily's husband as "Mr. Clark," as if he were a visiting stranger. But there was no ill will in their attitude, and after Reily died, Miss Corny and Miss Angely took faithful care of "Mr. Clark" the rest of his life.

Year by year, the demand for Miss Corny's work grew less. New dressmakers appeared and made clothes that were dashing and up-to-date, and so gradually Miss Corny and Miss Angely grew poorer and poorer. Finally the little grey house and the garden and beehives had to be sold, and the sisters moved into a few rooms in the village where the landlady was a friend and kind to them. All the old friends for whom Miss Corny had sewed and to whom Miss Angely had sold honey in the honeycomb helped them as much as they could. Uncle Alfred took coal and wood and flour to them, and the womenfolks sent fruit and food. The precious possessions that had belonged to their mother were sold one by one to antique dealers. Then, before anything worse could happen to their pride and affection, Miss Corny and Miss Angely died within a day of each other.

Their funeral was largely attended; the Means girls had lived all their life in the community and were respected and loved. Uncle Alfred and Aunt Welt had gone in real sorrow, and at the close of the services, as people were leaving, the village lawyer came to Aunt Welt and asked her if she would not like to stay and hear the will read. When she got home Aunt Welt told us that she had read in English stories how after the funeral the family went into the library to hear the will read and how astonished and angry everyone always was with its contents. So she said she was pleased to be invited to sit in at the reading. Like the relatives in the English stories, she found it disappointing. The sisters had willed to each other what they had, and if anything remained after their deaths it was to go to a distant cousin whom they had never seen. The New England blood was thicker than water. But there was nothing left to be inherited.

Sickness and Health

WHEN WE WERE SICK, we stayed out of school. It was as simple as that. If there was a truant officer, he was never on duty and I never heard of any child who was urged to go to school against his will. Aside from measles, our sicknesses were mostly heavy colds which were treated by a variety of curative hot teas—ginger, spearmint, catnip, and sage. We liked ginger; though it smarted, it warmed away the shivers. Spearmint, like peppermint, was good; sage, even with sugar, left a bitter afterthought; and catnip we despised. Onion syrup was my favorite remedy and taken willingly. First mother cut half a dozen crisp onions in a bowl. These were covered heavily with sugar and set to draw on the mantel-shelf above the kitchen stove. Presently, although not so fast as I wished, a thick white syrup gathered on the onions, and I was given a tablespoonful of it to heal my throat and still my coughing. At intervals, whenever I was alone in the kitchen with the bowl, the dose was repeated. No threats, no coaxing—just the lure of onion-flavored sweetness. Usually I had the onion syrup all to myself, for Ethel disliked it.

But onion syrup and herb teas did not reach out to help plague-spots or prolonged illness. It must have been a reflection of the general sanitation of the times that warts were so plentiful among school children. Big ugly warts grew on dirty necks and near dirty ears and particularly on dirty hands. Hand washing was often made difficult in homes where soap and water were scarce, and at school there was no water except the pail of drinking water brought from Uncle Tim's well. An old tin wash basin stood next to the pail on the shelf in the cloakroom, but a good many hands went unwashed from morning to night.

We knew, as all children in the countryside knew, that warts came from handling toads. Toads had warts, big and little; it was a straight case of guilt by association. If you picked up a toad you might expect a rich crop of warts to follow. There was also a worse penalty attached. If you hurt a toad, the cows would give bloody milk that night and what would your father say then? I liked the golden eyes and gentleness of toads, but the risk was too great for intimacy.

Throughout the community too, warts were the peculiar sorrow of many, unpleasant to owners and onlookers alike. So those who had warts and those who didn't have them were greatly interested in discussing the best way to get rid of them. You could take a dry bean and rub the wart with it and then throw the bean down the well. By the time the bean had rotted in the water the wart would be gone. Or, better still and more efficacious, some said, you could find someone to talk off the wart. Remarkable cures seen or heard of backed up both methods.

Not just anybody could accomplish a cure by word of

mouth. The wart-talker had to possess some undisclosed power that gave his talking potency. Now, by great good fortune such a man lived not too far from our school in a decaying little grey house almost hidden among apple trees. Old Man Bevans claimed he knew how to deal with warts successfully by his own skill of tongue. He did not hang out a shingle; it was not necessary, for the wart-stricken beat a path to his door and he never charged for his services. He got his pay, I suspect, in talking and talking, for he lived alone. He was so crippled by rheumatism that his tall, thin figure was twisted, and he walked with a crooked stick, for all the world like the crooked man who went a crooked mile. Needless to say, we were afraid of him and whenever we saw him coming we gave him the road to himself. He would not have hurt a hair of our heads, but he did look witch-like, all a soiled grey color from his greasy grey hat and sparse grey locks to his tattered grey clothes and grey hands holding the stick.

Then, contrary to justice, for I hadn't touched a toad and I had washed my hands, a wart appeared on my little finger, not very big but an unmistakable wart. I was alarmed and ashamed and in doubt what to do. I didn't dare consult Old Man Bevans all by myself, and I couldn't get a bean down the mouth of the pump—so what else was there to do except to go through life disfigured by a wart that would double in size every third new moon? I prayed fervently that some easy way of getting rid of the thing might be revealed to me, but revelation was delayed until one day father noticed that something seemed to be on my finger. He took a close look at it and said, "That wart must come off." Come off—how? I was divided between relief and terror. Father took me out on the north steps and produced a little stick of something that looked like silver. He said it was lunar caustic and he rubbed it in and on the wart. Lunar caustic was stuff that didn't fool around on its working days. The wart smarted and turned black and I exhibited it at school to show how my father cured warts. In time the wart dropped off and I was clean and whole again. I did wish, though, that father had said he would take me over to see what Old Man Bevans could do with it. I had missed my only chance to see how magic worked.

Although there were two practicing doctors in the village, outside aid was frequently resorted to. This was the era of patent medicines and they were purchased at the drugstore or the grocery store, and however extravagant and unlikely their claims, they were believed in and used. Indeed, if the person taking the medicine died before the bottle was completely empty, some other member of the family swallowed the rest—just on the chance of warding off the disease the medicine controlled.

We know today that all sorts of people—bankers, gamblers, politicians, and actors—consult fortunetellers, have their horoscopes read, and rely on finding out their lucky or unlucky days. To each generation its own superstitions. The great advantage of magic, whether in words or bottles, is its certainty. No doctor could be half so sure of his diagnosis as the printed information that went with bottles and boxes from a store shelf.

But stranger than the cures or healing that patent medicines provided was the wonder-work of the Rag Woman. I never heard the Rag Woman's real name nor exactly where she lived—somewhere on the edge between city and country;

nor do I know how it happened that all at once so many people were talking about her and her astonishing powers. Some of our neighbors on Mud Mill Road began going to her. All who went were convinced that the Rag Woman had a gift of divination which guided her in recognizing the disease the sufferer brought to her and in knowing what should be done for it. As they described her, the Rag Woman was a plain ordinary woman to whom they could talk freely, and she lived in a plain ordinary house. She was by all accounts without medical education, but was able to create in her patients' minds the faith that they would get well. Probably she also possessed extrafinancial perception. Her treatment was entirely original. She tied a bandage around the place where the patients said the pain or discomfort was and ordered them to wear the bandage for a week or two and then report back to her. Report they did again and again. The Rag Woman examined the bandage, told what the trouble was and urged the patient to soak his feet in hot water daily or stop eating fruit or cover the aching spot with cold or hot cloths according to the indications of fever or chills. She charged a dollar a visit. If a long-distance believer was unable to go to her, he arranged his own bandage, wore it the required time and mailed it to her with a dollar bill. In return the Rag Woman wrote a letter of advice.

There were skeptics of course. One man in the village undertook to prove that fakery rather than faith was at work. He tied his bandage around the leg of a calf and later on presented it to the Rag Woman for analysis. She must have thought that all God's children are equal whether in house or barn, for she pronounced that the bandage showed the patient to be well on the road to health and he could expect complete recovery if he kept on coming. Reassuring for the calf.

Inevitably, as doctors scoffed and medical knowledge spread, the Rag Woman's help was less in demand. The strongest reason for this law of diminishing returns was that those with permanent illnesses grew worse and worse. Gradually only a trickle of patients remained. There was even talk of prosecuting her. But there was no basis for calling in the law. Those who sought her aid had come voluntarily, and she had not advertised nor given medicine. She died a wealthy woman, so it was said—with a fortune built on ignorance.

To my regret, mother never entrusted our health to the Rag Woman. If her own remedies failed, father came forward with quinine. Quinine had become literally a drug on the market and was sold freely without any relation to malaria. Father considered it suitable for coughs, sneezing, and running noses that lingered on and on. He kept a bottle on hand, and at bedtime he buried a good portion of the white powder in a teaspoonful of applesauce and told us to swallow it. The horrid bitterness of the quinine always managed to spread through the applesauce, and the taste of it lasted a long time. We didn't want applesauce for breakfast the morning after. When mother thought we really needed a doctor, old Doctor Strong came and charged fifty cents a call.

But none of the medicines compared in our minds with Mr. Skinner's lozenges. We looked upon them as a sure means of escaping father's quinine or Doctor Strong's green liquids flavored with wintergreen. Mr. Skinner was many things in our life. Though medicines were included among his wares, everything else that touched daily necessity was also included, and he was welcomed by the whole neighborhood. He was not to be regarded as a peddler. He might easily have been mistaken for one, with his horse and loaded wagon, but Mr. Skinner's horse was well fed. He was kept from running away, whenever his owner stopped at a house, by a horse anchor, a round heavy iron weight fastened to a chain that snapped on a ring by the bit. Another way we could tell that Mr. Skinner was not a real peddler was that he had blue eyes and wore a coonskin cap exactly like Daniel Boone's. Real peddlers were swarthy men who sometimes wore gold rings in their ears and always came to the back door.

Mr. Skinner, not being a peddler but a free-born American, was entitled to life, liberty, and the pursuit of profit as well as the privilege of entering the sitting room by the front door, and there he opened up an enormous black pack. It held essences and salves, and mother renewed her supplies of peppermint, paregoric, camphor, and lemon and vanilla extract. Sometimes she indulged her fondness for perfume by buying a little White Rose. White Rose was in favor with all the Moultons. It was ladylike and called no attention to itself across the room. A linen handkerchief scented with White Rose equipped the wearer for special social occasions. It was a genteel perfume. Mr. Skinner measured it out carefully in a little glass marked with ounces and fractions and held the glass up for mother to see that she was getting the full quantity she paid for.

Years later, after Mr. Skinner had ceased to travel the road, it became increasingly difficult to buy White Rose.

White Shoulders was plentiful, but had no portion in the retiring and refined White Rose. Since it was the only fragrance mother and Aunt Elvie wanted, I tried to find it for them and looked in vain in Chicago and New York and smaller cities. One summer in Boston I thought I would make another attempt. I went into the then old-fashioned store of Jordan Marsh and inquired without hope whether they carried the old-fashioned White Rose perfume. "Certainly, madam," came the answer. It surprised me so much that I explained how often I had tried in other cities to get White Rose. How did it happen that it was on sale in Boston?

The clerk looked at me distantly. "All the elderly ladies in Boston use White Rose," she said.

I carried two bottles of it home in triumph, but neither mother nor Aunt Elvie thought it smelled like Mr. Skinner's White Rose. It was pleasant, they said, only the scent had somehow changed with the years.

Essences disposed of, Mr. Skinner brought in from the wagon a second large pack and opened it. One side was like a preview of Woolworth-yet-to-come. We saw pins, needles, hatpins, safety pins, lace by the yard, shoestrings, and elastic rubber; handkerchiefs, plain and fancy; writing paper and envelopes and hair ribbons—everything good and well chosen.

On the other side of the pack were the medicines and lozenges. One of the medicines mother was always glad to buy. It came in a tin can with a red and yellow paper around it, labeled Lea's Ointment in large letters. Lea's Ointment preserved Ethel and me to grow up. Mother would put a little of it in a dish on the stove and let it get hot. Next she cut two good-sized squares, one of paper and one of cloth. Then she spread the ointment carefully on the paper and laid it ointment-side up on the cloth. The ointment side she plumped down on our shrinking chests, and paper and cloth were safety-pinned to our shirts. After the first reluctant touch of heat, it was rather comforting to feel the greasy paper next to our skins. Mr. Skinner recommended keeping plenty of Lea's Ointment on hand for children to ward off croup and soreness.

Lozenges are—*were,* for I fear they are in the past tense now—small, medicated tablets, each kind effective for pains and aches in different spots, coughing, stomach-ache, throwing up. There was no end to what a lozenge could do when it set to work. They came in colors, pink, blue, lavender, green, and white, and were as close to candy as any medicine could be. Sick or well, we enjoyed Mr. Skinner's lozenges.

Last of all to be taken out of the pack were the magazines. Mr. Skinner's sales talk won Aunt Elvie to subscribe to the *Ladies' Home Journal,* which became a part of our growing up and minded our manners and morals for us. One year Mr. Skinner thought mother and Aunt Elvie should give *Harper's* a trial. Mother enjoyed it, but Aunt Elvie preferred the *Journal.* She liked its accounts of little princes and princesses and the Unknown Wives of Well-Known Men. But Mr. Skinner's great contribution to our lives was *The Youth's Companion.* He persuaded mother to subscribe to it, and for twenty years it came faithfully each week, and a better paper for the young was never published. It was expensive as papers went then—a dollar and seventy-five cents a year. Each Wednesday Ethel and I walked a mile and a quarter to the village post office and watched the stage come dashing around the curve with the mail at five o'clock. Then there was a wait while the mail was being sorted, until at last the *Companion* was handed to us and we could hurry home. Wednesday night was reading-aloud night. Mother began at the front page and went straight through from the serial story to the poetry. The Pledge of Allegiance to the flag appeared first in *The Youth's Companion,* long before its recitation in public schools became a daily event throughout the United States. Mother thought it was beautiful and had us learn it. We read almost literally every word of each copy of the *Companion,* and then mother passed it on to the relatives.

Does every old person remembering the past think of some debt of gratitude he has owed to someone from his youth up, think of it, knowing that it is too late ever to say a word of thanks to the one he would like to reach? To Mr. Skinner, Ethel and I owed long hours of reading pleasure more valuable to us than even Lea's Ointment.

A Barn Is Built

GRANDFATHER was already an old man and had ceased to reign. Uncle Bill and Uncle Alfred had gradually assumed direction of affairs, and to the home place and the Thomas farm and the Talcot farm they had added the large and profitable Henry Loomis farm which joined their land south and east. So much land to be worked, so much help needed to work it, and for the womenfolks as much to do inside the house as the men did outside. All the land was under high cultivation, with crops to be cared for and stored till the time for selling or using them arrived. But the farm buildings were old and there was not room enough in them to hold the harvests and tools and stock. A new barn was required and the uncles resolved to build it.

It was to be one of the biggest in town—ninety feet long, very wide, and three stories in height, though the third story was merely scaffolding near the peak to hold extra straw or hay. The carpenters engaged came from Over

North, that distant land that we thought of as undiscovered country since it was a day's journey for horses to travel there and back. The two Bergen brothers hired for the work were pleasant, elderly men who brought with them several assistants, and all these men had to be fed and lodged at grandfather's. While the stone and mortar foundation walls were rising, lumber was drawn for siding; shingles for roofing and all necessities were provided, from the great beams that would carry the weight of the barn, down to the nails and doweling pins that would hold it together.

Barns did not leap into place then as prefabricated buildings manufactured in some far spot do now. In that time a barn had its birth on the farm it was intended to serve. The bents, or sections, were constructed and fitted together while lying flat on the ground; and every groove and pin was accounted for and ready, if the carpenters had done their work right, to slip into its appointed place. Nothing could be left to chance. The good barn carpenter did not become one simply by joining the union; he had to be a craftsman. To build a barn of the size the uncles wanted was a long summer's work.

The day of raising up the framework of the barn was important both for the tremendous exertion required and as a social event. A small army gathered. All the neighbors and their hired men came to help; relatives and more distant friends were there as a matter of duty, and always plenty of spectators arrived to enjoy effortlessly a scene exciting to watch and offering the possibility of dangerous accident if something went wrong. For days before the raising the aunts had been busy getting food ready in mountainous quantities.

When the morning arrived, tables were set out in a shady place in the yard and covered with pans of meat sandwiches and baked beans. Pies, cheese, cookies, and doughnuts stood near brown pitchers of switchel, and coffee in tall tin pots was brought on a run from the kitchen. With most of the men, coffee was the preferred drink, though switchel was a close rival. Switchel was a hayfield drink compounded of molasses, water, vinegar, and ginger. The men found it refreshing when they were sweating from heat and exertion, and the ginger was stimulating. It was a good drink for a hard job.

When the moment came for lifting the first bent from the ground, a line of men took their places before the heavy beams. Pike poles could not be used until after the bent was high enough up in the air so that the poles could be slid under it. Pike poles were long or short according to the height needed, with a sharp steel tip. The head carpenter was usually chosen as the leader to give the signals, for he knew best how all must pull together, and his keen eye could see in an instant any slackening in the line before the right height was reached. A last survey—then he waved his arms and shouted "He—oh—*Heave!*" With the cry of *Heave* every man strained to lift his part of the bent the required distance and hold it till other men could thrust the poles into it. There was a breathing space and then again all eyes on the leader: "He—oh—*Heave!*" and another yard gained. Every bent was raised in the same way and interlocked with those already up. By the time the last bent was in place, the skeleton of the barn was standing up for all to see. No other part of barn building was so hard or so full of risk as the raising. Shingling the roof, to be sure, might prove disastrous but some-how never did. I suppose that raising a barn with raw strength and pike poles was easier than hauling stones for the pyramids. Perhaps it was halfway between pyramids and prefabrication.

I hope my grandfather was pleased that his sons had the big barn adorned with a cupola, such as he had longed to put on the house in 1869 and could not afford. The barn cupola was a small house in itself, furnished with windows, and sitting astride the ridge. It would have made a lovely play-house if I could have got up there. Its purpose was ventilation. It also put a period to the barn.

The raising was thrilling from beginning to end for Ethel and me. Mother helped the aunts, father handled a pike pole, and Ethel and I watched and ran about in the wrong places and ate as much as we could. In the midst of waiting on the men, Aunt Elvie took time out to make Ethel still happier than she already was. Ethel had on a white muslin dress, and Aunt Elvie tied about her waist the Roman sash which Aunt Elvie herself almost never wore and which Ethel and I admired as too beautiful for anyone's dreaming of wearing. The Roman sash was of thick silk with fine stripes of rainbow color and bordered in robin's egg blue, the color now called aquamarine. As if the sash were not enough to fill Ethel's cup to overflowing, Aunt Elvie added her gold locket and chain, her most precious piece of jewelry. Arrayed in locket and sash, Ethel fluttered like a butterfly, lovely to see. The adornments were not very appropriate for the occa-sion, but weighed against a child's delight, appropriateness did not count.

In our community when a barn was finished and ready to begin its life work, it was customary to hold a dance for the benefit of whatever church the owner belonged to. If his church did not approve of dancing, the finishing of the barn passed unnoticed. Universalists danced, and as soon as the last nail had been driven there was a dance on the big barn floor at grandfather's. On that ninety-foot long floor the dancers had room aplenty to bow, circle, gallop, and swing. The musicians, never more than three for such occasions, sat in the empty hayloft and played until two o'clock in the morning. Refreshments of cake and ice cream were served and a tidy sum realized for the church.

I wonder now why barns were planned, almost deliberately it seems, to be inconvenient for men and animals. Stables for the cows were regularly located in the north and east part of the building, where all the winter winds struck coldest. Farmers took the cheerful view that the breath and body warmth of the cattle would keep them all warm. Horse stables were sheltered, supposedly, by having only one small window so that the poor creatures stood in purblind darkness in their stalls. The granary was as far from the stock as space could be found for it, while getting down hay from the loft required first a climb up a ladder and then a long carry. The entrance to the barn floor, where heavy loads of hay or straw had to be drawn for pitching off into the mows, was more likely than not to be up a steep grade. It took every ounce of strength the horses had to get the load up that grade and into the barn. I could not bear to see them strain and struggle faithfully to do what they should not have been asked to do. Then the horses and the empty rack had to be backed out and down the grade and driven to the field for another load.

In an indirect way the building of the barn at grandfather's led to the family quarrel. Family quarrels seem to have been a more common occurrence at that time than now; it may be because families today are likely to be widely scattered instead of being concentrated in the same neighborhood. Family quarrels, church quarrels, political quarrels, and fence-line quarrels all sprang up easily, often on grounds no more serious than which young lady in the choir should sing the solo or whose fence a patch of thistles belonged inside. The emotions roused usually ran deeper than the cause, and every once in a while the quarrel cut hearts and lives apart. The Moulton quarrel belonged to the never-ending kind.

The barn-building summer had been very hard on my aunts. Everything that was taxing in their daily life had been more than doubled by the extra work the carpenters and their helpers brought. The barn was scarcely in place when Aunt Welt fell ill. Her illness was the result of severe and unremitting toil from early childhood, and no one should have been astonished when the machinery gave out. The doctor called her sickness nervous prostration, a term in constant use then, but not heard today. For weeks she lay in a darkened room tortured by frightful headaches and too weak to lift a finger.

When at last she came downstairs, she was never again to be strong as she had once been and never again to be free from the torment of sick nerves. Aunt Elvie and Aunt Ellen too were worn out from keeping the household running and caring for Aunt Welt. There could be no lightening of the burden of farm work and a hired girl became a necessity.

Hired girls were generally employed in households where there was only one woman to do everything; the aunts had always managed by themselves. Most of the hired girls came from Over North. They were quite young and with very little education or training; and they had no means of earning money unless they worked out. It is hardly necessary to say that in our farming community a hired girl was not a servant or a maid. Only city folks talked about their maids, and only the long-standing rich had servants. It would have been contrary to the basic democracy of the countryside to assume that the hired help were inferior because they worked away from home. The hired girl was a member of the family and treated as such.

My aunts sent Over North for a girl to come, and with her coming life changed at grandfather's house for everybody. Unforeseeably and unbelievably, Uncle Bill at fifty fell in love with the girl, who was thirty years younger than he. Up to this time Uncle Bill had been a sober-minded citizen, settled and prosperous, so that his sudden romantic attachment took on the character of witchcraft. It was not surprising that the girl was willing to accept what luck offered her.

The aunts could not understand that no argument or entreaty could prevail against Uncle Bill's determination to marry his choice. He resented his sisters' opinions in furious anger and met their objections with outbursts of passion until violent words and cruel wishes subsided at length into bitter silence.

But what about the land and the big barn? Division of heart led straight to the division of property owned in common by Uncle Bill and Uncle Alfred. To divide land, livestock, tools, and ready money in a way that would be just and satisfactory to each would have been difficult even if there had been no cleavage of feeling. In the end, Uncle Bill took the Henry Loomis farm and Uncle Alfred, the Thomas and Talcot farms, and the neighbors could not agree as to who came off best in the division. Whatever Uncle Alfred thought about the arrangement, he never voiced any criticism.

What seems odd in the matter is that no claim was made by the womenfolks that they were entitled to a share of the property. Till middle age and beyond, they had worked as hard as their brothers. Without their unpaid labor the high prosperity of the family could not have been achieved. The hired help was well paid; reduced to its simplest and somewhat deceptive terms, the women got their board and clothes. The household was generously provided for, but the thrift and saving practiced in its management increased the money that could be spent in improving the farms already owned. The women were not willfully overlooked in the settlement. It was the custom of the period to disregard the money value of women's work.

After his marriage Aunt Welt never saw her twin brother again. Her long-past grief for her young soldier-lover had been without bitterness. The complete severing of the tie so dear and close from the brother she loved best was a scar too terrible ever to change. When grandfather died Uncle Alfred sent word to Uncle Bill to come to the funeral. But Uncle Bill did not come.

A Barn Is Built

The big barn stood on land that belonged to grandfather and he had willed the home place to his three unmarried daughters. Thereafter Uncle Alfred paid each one a good rental for the use of the farm and the buildings. Sadly enough, the big barn of which they were all so proud is now a storage place for boats in winter.

Miniatures

THE NEW ENGLAND Moulton cousins were in a sense off stage and did not play any part in our lives till we were grown up, though letters came often from them to the aunts and mother. The first sight we had of them was in our early childhood when they arrived, nine strong, on a week's visit at grandfather's. For a reason not explained to us children, somebody called Aunt Martha did not come, and there seemed to be much tight-lipped conversation about her when the women were by themselves. Aunt Martha, so far as we understood, belonged to Cousin Darius, whose name in New Hampshire was shortened to D'ri—easy to say and quite appropriate, so its owner told my aunts. It may not have surprised grandfather, but it troubled the household that Cousin Darius carried a bottle on his hip, and as soon as it was empty he saw to it that it was refilled at the village saloon. He passed the bottle generously to his New York cousins, who were fertile in finding excuses for not taking a drink just then. Darius himself was as unaffected by liquor as if it had been Aunt Elvie's lemonade.

The other cousins in private said that Darius was held to be very well-to-do, perhaps worth fifty thousand dollars. He had made his money by selling cattle up and down the country, knew everybody, and was always willing to stand treat or lend money. He had a shrewd mind, an amusing tongue, and an eye for various kinds of fleshpots. Everybody liked D'ri Moulton.

I learned about Darius and Aunt Martha after I grew up, when mother and I were on a long-urged visit to the New England relatives. We had spent some time with the Boston and Haverhill groups and had got at last to Plainfield in what the cousins called "up country." It was only five miles from Cousin Elmer's house where we were staying to Meriden where Darius and Aunt Martha lived. All the cousins had taken pains to tell us how unfortunate it was that D'ri was away from home just then and would not be back in time to see us. Mother was disappointed and I was too. I liked all the cousins and found them interesting and highly individualized, and Darius sounded even more so.

Cousin Emma said Aunt Martha was sick in what was probably her last illness, but we could call a few minutes to speak to her. So on a Sunday afternoon we drove to the tidy red brick house standing in a green river bottom outside Meriden. Aunt Martha's tall bed had been moved into the sitting room, and she lay like an ancient ghost in white nightcap and nightgown, propped among high white pillows. Her eyes rested on us without interest. Cousin Emma told her who we were, and mother expressed her sympathy for Aunt Martha's illness and her regret at not seeing Darius. Aunt Martha nodded and the call was over.

Back at Cousin Emma's we heard at last the story of

Darius and Martha, new to me and in greater detail than
mother had known it. I suppose the same thing might have
happened in other places than New England, and yet I am
not certain. The young Darius had been what Meriden called
a gay fellow, engaging in many weathercock attentions to
numerous delightful girls. His affections finally narrowed
down to two young ladies, one named Mary and the other,
Martha, but not sisters. Both came of good family. Martha
was an only child, and both were plainly in love with Darius.
The village was unable to decide who would be the chosen
one; they thought they detected a slight preference for Mary,
but they couldn't really tell. D'ri was just as likely to have
another girl in some other place.

Then Martha's parents died suddenly in an accident, leaving her alone with a handsome property. A few days after
the funeral the village was shocked and excited to learn that
Martha—*Martha*—had moved down from her home on the
hill into Darius' house and had taken up quarters there as
if she expected to stay forever. What was Martha thinking
of? Were they married? What would her father and mother
have said? What about Mary? The village was not equal to
answering the questions.

Mary faced the situation with a dignity that refused open
pity. Darius did not introduce Martha as his wife, and the
conviction spread that they were not married, but living in
sin that Martha had chosen of her own free will. No one
quite dared to remonstrate with Darius, and he continued
to come and go as usual and did not suffer at all from criticism about the strange way he was living. Martha did not
fare so well. She ceased to be invited anywhere or to have
any part in the pleasures of the community, those occasions

where opinions are expressed and judgments formed. Either by Darius' decision or her own, he never took Martha with him to public affairs or on neighborly calls, and his relatives were sadly put to it to know what to do. Martha was sometimes invited to family gatherings at Thanksgiving time, and the nephews and nieces had the kindness to call her Aunt Martha, but everyone felt awkward and uncomfortable lest something be discussed that would cause pain to her. As time went on, a sort of acceptance of the relationship as a fact of nature developed, but that did not alter Martha's standing.

One tale persisted and was vouched for by witnesses. All Darius' tastes leaned toward excitement. He loved driving a fast horse and would go racing through the streets of Meriden, admired as a dashing figure even though his speed was disapproved of. One day in the center of the village his horse took fright and started to run away. The carriage was overturned, and Darius was thrown out on the sidewalk at the very moment that Mary came along, lovely and irreproachable. Darius, uninjured and lying comfortably on the sidewalk, looked up at her and said, "Here I am, Mary, just where I've always been—at your feet."

Aunt Martha died a few months after mother and I returned home, and Darius kept house by himself for several years until his death. When I visited New Hampshire again, my cousin Carl, who had been the executor of his uncle Darius' will, completed the next-to-the-last chapter of the story for me. In going through Darius' papers he had found the marriage certificate of Darius and Martha. They had been married secretly before the death of Martha's parents. The last chapter of the story was lacking, for it could only be guessed. Why had he never acknowledged the marriage?

Why had Martha endured the shame of being believed immoral?

Carl thought that perhaps Uncle D'ri had married Martha on the impulse of a sudden gust of affection, or it might have been at Martha's pleadings. Darius was very kindhearted, Carl added.

"He does not sound too kindhearted to me," I said, "to let Martha bear the burden of doubt and suspicion all her life. What reason could he have had? He must have felt some affection for her to live with her so many years."

Carl said there might have been lots of reasons. "Maybe he was punishing Martha for getting possession of him when he really wanted Mary. And maybe Martha submitted to it because she was afraid of losing him altogether if she didn't."

"Do you think life with Darius compensated her for her world well lost for love?" I asked.

"I don't know. But there's a chunk of granite every now and then in the Moultons. It comes to light in different ways. You remember," Carl went on, "you didn't see Uncle D'ri when you and your mother were here. We told you he was away. Well, he was, but there was more to it than we wanted you to know. He was spending a month in the jail at Newberry."

"In jail!" I echoed. "What had he done?" After all, Hester Prynn and the Reverend Arthur Dimmesdale had been gone a long time.

"It was this way. Uncle D'ri liked young folks, and he got in the habit of driving over to Hanover and treating the Dartmouth boys. Pretty large groups by all accounts. Most of them were minors, and the state law is strict on that point. He was warned several times, but he'd always done as he pleased, and as a free-born American he didn't propose to be told what he should or shouldn't do. So he kept right on setting them up all round, and the boys kept coming until the college authorities decided it had gone on long enough and had to be stopped."

"I suppose," I could not help saying, "that he was too kindhearted not to want to share his pleasure in drinking with the boys."

"Might be. Anyway, Uncle D'ri was arrested and found guilty in court and the judge gave him his choice of a five-hundred-dollar fine or a month in jail. We were all upset about it except D'ri. He could have paid the fine without any trouble, and Aunt Martha, sick as she was, begged him to let her pay it for him. She was well fixed in her own right, you know, but he balked at the whole thing. He wouldn't contribute one cent to the State to support a law that wouldn't let a man buy a drink for his friends, and he wouldn't let anyone else pay for him. He would go to jail.

"That's where he was when you came. He and the sheriff were old friends, and Uncle D'ri moved his rocking chair to the jail, ordered his paper sent there, and sat out his sentence rocking in the jailyard and receiving callers—flocks of them. He had a very good time of it. It was hard on Aunt Martha, and the relatives didn't enjoy having him there, but everybody said it was just like D'ri Moulton."

So, like Thoreau—well, not exactly like Thoreau, but in his own fashion—Darius had upheld the American attitude toward law—as a matter of private conscience.

I must have looked doubtful, for Carl said, "In spite of all this, you would have liked Uncle Darius, and he *was* very kindhearted."

In the days before all the paths were made straight and all the rough edges smoothed off as affronts to group life, there was a chance for the unusual, the odd, or the eccentric to exist without anyone's feeling obliged to do something about it. The right of a man or woman to be different was unchallenged. The community thought, in fact, that those who broke the regular pattern of life improved things so far as food for thought and talk was concerned.

Mrs. Joyce contrived to be different, but she was not regarded as eccentric. She was a member of our church and a dear friend of my aunts. Her self-expression took a form that startled and amused people but somehow did not shock them. Mrs. Joyce had early resolved not to be bothered by the things that bothered most women. She had her iron grey hair cropped close like a man's—forever free of curling tongs, frizzes, and hairpins—and she wore on her head a man's soft black felt hat that fitted easily and lasted from season to season. Her outer wrap was a man's short coat, loose and comfortable, Mrs. Joyce said, after fussing with the now long, now wide, now tight coats made for women.

Short hair, a man's hat, a man's coat, and this in the eighteen-eighties and nineties. The famous Doctor Mary Walker who lived nearby in Oswego had gone farther than Mrs. Joyce and replaced womanly skirts with trousers. But everyone knew that Doctor Mary Walker had received permission from Congress to wear trousers because of her services on the battlefields of the Civil War. No other woman in the United States could appear in trousers on the public streets without running the risk of arrest. Mrs. Joyce was satisfied to wear the sweeping skirts of the period, which had a "brush braid" sewn on the inner edge of the hem.

This braid and the skirt too swept up the dust of stairs and floors and the dirt of sidewalks and streets. It is surprising that Mrs. Joyce did not carry her rebellion farther.

She took up diet instead and declared that supper was one meal too much after childhood. Her own supper was an apple and a glass of warm water. When she came to church suppers, she brought along a small tin pail into which she put whatever food she judged digestible and took it home to be eaten for her dinner next day. She always paid generously for her supper. Then she spent a pleasant evening arguing diets with those waiting restlessly to be seated at the table.

In spite of her mannish costume, and people got used to that, Mrs. Joyce was good-looking and we admired her. She had big grey eyes and finely cut features and her face was stamped unmistakably with intelligence. She liked to read law and had trained herself to draw up wills which proved sound and legal when brought into court. Aunt Welt and Aunt Elvie and Aunt Ellen had Mrs. Joyce make their wills. They felt much freer to ask her about the disposing of their property than if she had been a real lawyer.

She had one advantage over any other woman or man in town: Mrs. Joyce had gone to Europe three times—once especially to see the Passion Play at Oberammergau. After she came back from that experience, she paid a visit to the aunts, and mother and Ethel and I were there too, and listened to her descriptions of landscapes and cities and villages and peasants and the stupendous portrayal of the Crucifixion. She had seen the Old World before the gigantic breaking-up that lay ahead—a world that to the traveler's eye looked simple and beautiful and safe. It seemed to Ethel and me, and I am sure to mother, that to go to Europe and see what Mrs. Joyce had seen would be a happiness so great imagination could not stretch to it. We said to Mrs. Joyce that we would give anything if we could go to Europe, but it would never happen to us. I have always remembered how she answered us.

"Girls," she said, "the wonderful thing about life is that you never know what it is going to give you. I had a childhood of great poverty and when I married I had to work outdoors on the farm because we were too poor to hire a man. Sometimes we had only twenty-five cents to our name and took turns carrying it if we went anywhere. We had to have our grocery bills charged, small as they were, and then we had to struggle to pay them. If anyone had told me that I would ever go to Europe, I should have thought he was crazy.

"And yet—it constantly happens in life that things change unexpectedly. We didn't grow rich, but some of our land turned out to be profitable for sale, then a distant cousin I'd never seen died and left us some money—not a fortune, but a good deal for us. And that's the way life is. You think a thing can't happen to you, and then it does happen. You must always have faith in life."

I thought of Mrs. Joyce's cream-colored cottage shaded by a great mulberry tree and the good way her story had turned out, and I resolved that I would always have faith in life—at least as far as believing that some day Ethel and I would go to Europe.

Aunt Mary was Cousin Emery's wife and she managed, besides a large household of many children, hired men, and visiting relatives, the beehives that stood in the orchard. What kind of bees they were she neither knew nor cared. They were simply bees and their job was to produce honey. Bees were not then given any special treatment nor any delicacies furnished to help them go about their proper business. Reasonable bees could find all they needed close at hand. Basswood trees in number stood within a bee's length, and the fragrant blossoms in spring made the best honey in the world; in early summer there were clover fields and in late summer the musky-smelling white flowers of buckwheat. A sensible bee knew that all he had to do was to work for the winter nights that were coming.

Certainly Aunt Mary's bees were not ill-treated, and she took it unkindly when, on a summer day, the bees decided to swarm; that is, to make a dash for freedom and flee to a hollow tree—leaving the tight square wooden hive behind them forever. They gathered on the branch of a pear tree to hum it over before they started.

We were with Aunt Mary in her kitchen. She heard the suspicious sound, and pausing only long enough to grab two sheets from a closet shelf, she ran to the orchard, calling as she ran for all of us who were anywhere near to come and help.

Cousin Anna and Little Emery and Ethel and I each seized a pan and a tin spoon and got to the orchard as fast as we could. Aunt Mary had already spread the sheets under the pear tree.

"Now, children," she said, "beat on the pans as hard as you can, but stand far enough back so that if the bees go you won't get stung."

This was better than any orchestra practice. We beat on

the pans in varying rhythms and keys; we shouted at the bees and urged them to drop on the sheet as Aunt Mary said they would if we made noise enough. She said the beating on the pans confused them and they couldn't decide whether

to go or not. We were afraid of their being insufficiently confused and attacking us so we beat on our pans like drummers.

But Aunt Mary was right. Slowly and sadly the bees yielded to percussion and gave up the gay idea of freedom. They dropped down from the tree in a sort of trance-like bunch to the sheets below. Aunt Mary silenced our pans and carefully covered the bees. How she got them back into the hive I don't remember, but I think the hive was moved out near the bees, and finding themselves at home again they entered and settled down to work. Making music to help them with their decision was better than eating honey, though we loved that too, and we were glad we had saved the harvest for Aunt Mary. Her method of preventing the bees from flying off was in general use among beekeepers, But I am not sure it really had any effect on the bees. They simply changed their minds.

Moneylenders in a country community were usually disliked and feared. No banks existed outside of cities, and a farmer unschooled in the ways of banks and their financing would have found it impossible to go to strangers and explain how much he needed a loan to buy a new place or to help tide him over till the hay was sold or the tobacco crop paid for. His problem could only be settled by the town moneylender.

Borrower and lender met on unequal terms. The lender was sometimes contemptuous of a man who delivered himself into the hands of the possessor, and the borrower often felt a sullen resentment that his need drove him to ask, and if he received he must pay a rate of interest that ate up all he could save before a beginning could be made on the debt. Six per cent interest was legal, and eight per cent could be exacted without the borrower's recourse to law. It is not believable that anyone planning his life chose to become a moneylender. He discovered the talent and developed it in maturity.

In our town Sam MacPherson's name was synonymous

with mortgage holding. Nothing in his appearance suggested that he had enough money to pay toll on the road. He came along in a shabby old buggy pulled creepily by a rickety old horse, and he was of course always spoken of as "old" Sam MacPherson. His beard was white and his speech deliberate, and both speech and mannerisms were part of the picture of him that people had in their minds. Before he made a statement he prefaced it always with a hem or two. This gave the effect of careful scrutiny and prolonged the borrower's anxiety. It was commonly said that every time Sam MacPherson hemmed it cost a man five dollars. When it was suggested to him that someone he had invested in, so to speak, would never meet his payments, Sam was credited with a cheerful if menacing reply. "God make 'em able; I'll make 'em willing," said Sam.

He held mortgages from one end of the county to the other, and the mortgage could be a stranglehold on the farmer, no matter how hard he worked. A farm not far from us was mortgaged to Sam, and at the end of forty years when Sam was dead and the giver of the mortgage too, the debt was still unpaid. My Uncle John's farm was mortgaged, and all his struggles did not succeed in paying it off. It ran for twenty years, and when he died in a threshing accident, the burden was still there—left as a heavy inheritance. Yet Uncle John always said that if a man dealt honestly by Sam MacPherson he in turn dealt fairly and exerted no painful pressures. But in general, the pursuit of moneylending did not include affection among its rewards.

A stinted life, Sam's fellow-townsmen said, but it must have been one of interest and variety to him as he rode about. There were the farms to go to where he collected regular payments; he could consider new loans and new clients who came to him, hat in hand; and there was the sense of steadily growing power—all this must have offered matter for agreeable thought. And he had judgments to make and decisions—whether to be ruthless or relenting. Whatever it was outwardly, it was a satisfactory life to him.

He was such a familiar figure and apparently so indestructible that his death was like the failure of a bank. Who now would handle the mortgages and set the terms for payment? The town attended his funeral in large numbers. A few came because they had really liked the old man and said he had helped them in bad times. There were more perhaps who wanted reassurance that Sam had been permanently removed from their lives and would trouble them no longer.

His funeral text had a peculiar appropriateness. At that time a funeral text was chosen with great care, and at this distance the minister seems to have tried to make the text Sam MacPherson's epitaph:

"In my youth I went whither I would—but in my age another stretcheth forth his hand and leadeth me whither I would not go."

The way wealth is used or displayed depends on the nature and character of those who have it. If a man has large possessions he can choose to be a miser or a philanthropist. If his riches are only moderately greater than the average of his acquaintances, he can sometimes hit upon a way to indulge his vanity and suggest to others that he is more affluent than they guessed.

Mr. Orlin Hoople of our town had, it was said, somehow made money. He looked a little like an old-fashioned cartoon of the recently rich. He was short and stout and red-faced, and he wore a plaid vest crossed by a gold watch chain of the sort called a log chain from its size and weight. He had once kept the saloon in the village, and since saloons succeed even better in bad times than in good, Mr. Hoople's business had done well at all times. But the saloon had been sold, and had not produced money enough to account for Mr. Hoople's peculiar expenditures. The village thought he must have bought some oil stock in Pennsylvania or maybe some shares in a gold mine in Nevada. Oil stock and gold mine shares were being freely bought and sold everywhere if you had money, though in the country it mostly worked out that the stock and shares were sold with testimonials to farmers who later had cause for deep regret.

It was not so much that Mr. Hoople had money that excited the village; it was what he did with it. Father had not accepted the reports as true until he saw with his own eyes and could scarcely credit it even then.

The theater for Mr. Hoople's performance was either the grocery store or the saloon over which Mr. Hoople had once presided and where he felt more at home. He was a steady smoker of cigars—cigars of the best brand known in the village. Those who smoked the two-for-five-centers or made their own recognized the quality of Mr. Hoople's cigars by the fragrance of the smoke they threw off compared to the humbler kind. But the ceremony Mr. Hoople went through in lighting his cigar left them wide-eyed and speechless.

As father described it, Mr. Hoople first took out one of the expensive cigars and laid it on counter or bar. Then he detached from his watch chain the penknife carried by gentlemen for many purposes. The penknife cut off the closed end of the cigar neatly and it was ready to be lighted. Mr. Hoople felt unhurriedly in different pockets, but he favored his vest pocket as it took longer to reach into it and all this time suspense was mounting among those who had seen the outcome before and those who had been told what to expect. From the vest pocket Mr. Hoople extracted a one-dollar bill, holding it so that everyone could see what it was and its value. He rolled it tightly and smoothly, drew a match box from still another pocket, struck a match and set the rolled dollar bill to burning. Then came his great moment: he picked up the cigar and lighted it from the blazing bill. After that he smoked in a leisurely manner.

Mr. Hoople completed this gesture of having-so-much-money-he-didn't-know-what-to-do-with-it, and yet he must have sensed that somehow it all went flat. What he saw in men's faces was a mixture of disapproval and disgust. Not a man said, "I wish I was rich enough to do that." Only one man spoke, "Orlin, it takes too long to get a cigar lighted that way."

In a year or two the oil stock or the gold mine shares failed, and Mr. Hoople had no money to buy cigars and no one-dollar bills for any purpose. The town did not feel too sorry for him. As Uncle Charles said, being a damned fool was a bad disease, for there wasn't any cure for it.

When I was young courtship might start by a boy's escorting the young lady of his fancy home from church after young people's meeting on Sunday night. From there it moved by slow or rapid degrees to the hammock on the front porch in summer. Rain and winter were less propitious for affairs of the heart. After church walking and hammock sitting had made some progress, a young man, if fortunate enough to have a horse and carriage, either his own or the family's, could offer the girl a moonlight ride on quiet roads where conversation about themselves would not be interrupted or overheard. Their talk did not differ from that of the young-in-love of all times and places: their hopes, their discontents, their admiration for each other, and the glad surprise of finding that they liked and disliked the same people and even the same things to eat. To take a girl anywhere for a drink or a dance on Sunday night did not cross the young man's mind, and had he smoked a cigarette while driving, the girl would have felt insulted. The carriage and the lovers were due home not later than half past ten. In winter an afternoon sleighride was possible, but not in the evening unless the whole Sunday school class went together on a bobsleigh with a chaperon established at an observation point in the center.

Engagements were likely to be long; from two to four years was common. The young man was expected to have something substantial ahead—a home or a promising job—before he took a wife. It was not necessarily a more innocent world to grow up in; it was certainly a better protected one, and it lasted, not much changed, from the end of the Civil War to the beginning of the First World War. This was courtship at one level.

There were other levels. While she lived on the old farm, mother had a hired girl who rode out every Sunday with her young man. He was usually half drunk when he arrived and wholly so when they returned. But Carrie told mother she didn't mind at all because Isaac was so cunning when he was drunk. Carrie and Isaac decided to marry, and Carrie's red silk wedding dress was got ready. Since a "wasp waist" was the high point of beauty at that time, the wedding dress followed the suffocating lines of an hour glass. It is interesting and instructive to trace the various parts of the female figure that have been selected for emphasis by fashion over the years. The sixteen-inch waist reigned a long time.

But when Carrie was dressing for the wedding, she found it impossible, alone and unaided, to get herself inside the dress although she held her breath at the risk of her life. There was nothing she could do but to get mother and Aunt Sophy, who happened to be there, to come to her rescue. They ran to her at her shout and they agreed that they had better begin with the corset and work outward from that.

The corset of the time covered about a third of the body. It was made of cloth so strong and heavy that nothing could pierce it, and it was thickly reinforced by stays of whalebone and steel. It was truly a suit of armor that answered to Miniver Cheevy's thoughts about the mediaeval grace of iron clothing. Mother loosened the corset strings as far as they would go and fastened them around the bedpost; Carrie clasped the front hooks of the garment together and backed away from the post while mother and Aunt Sophy alternately pulled on the strings. Little by little, Carrie's waist melted and was distributed elsewhere—and mother used a buttonhook to pull the buttons on the front of the dress together. At length, gasping and grateful, Carrie stood bound in red silk and drove away with the cunning Isaac to be happy ever after.

Cousin Anna's wedding was different. Anna was Cousin Emery's daughter and lived in the brick house across the road from us. She was of almost ideal loveliness, the kind

of beauty that the word maiden suggests. Her voice was enchanting, and she had all the Victorian accomplishments.
She sewed perfectly; she painted flowers on china or ruined
mills in oils to hang on the sitting room and parlor walls;
she played the rosewood piano sweetly; and she was in spite
of all this of extreme intelligence.

Church weddings were unknown to us, and Anna's wedding was to be at home on a September morning. She was
nineteen years old and marrying a young Universalist minister who had fallen in love with her at first sight at a Sunday school convention in Buffalo.

Ethel and I had never been to a wedding and it almost
consoled us for losing Anna to know that we would see a
real bride and eat wedding cake. I had already glimpsed the
wedding cake when Aunt Welt was making it in the summer, and I remembered that she had said it must flavor
through by standing. By this time it would taste like a spice
drawer! The fruit cake was not to be the only exciting feature of the wedding dinner. Anna told us as a secret that
there would be olives. This was 1892 and we had neither
seen nor tasted olives.

A few days before the wedding Anna took us up to her
room and showed us her wedding clothes—all except the
wedding dress which hung shrouded in sheets on a nail in
the closet. It was, I suppose, a very simple wardrobe, but we
were enthusiastic over the wool "traveling dress"; and we
said the new gingham morning dress was beautiful; and all
her older dresses had been made over and looked as if they
had never been worn. Anna confided to us that she would
have liked to wear a veil, but Aunt Mary thought a veil was
too elaborate for a home wedding and Anna had yielded to

her mother's judgment. Besides, no bride in Cicero had ever worn a veil.

The September calendar poked along to the day, clear and sunny and mild. The ceremony was at eleven o'clock, and the relatives and neighbors arrived early. According to custom, the morning sunlight that blessed the day was carefully excluded. The window shades were drawn, the blinds were closed, and there were large lamps burning in every room. I wonder why that was done. I suppose it must have been to give the effect of evening, since evening weddings were all the fashion then; or Aunt Mary may have wished to prevent any passer-by on the road from taking a look at the ceremony. Whatever the reason, the shades of night fell fast upon the scene.

It cannot be only a trick of memory that makes that wedding group so shining as I think of it. The two bridesmaids, almost as beautiful as Anna, walked into the parlor to the music of the piano. They wore dresses of "seeded silk," one a faint blue and the other a pale pink. The "seeds" that gave the color were tiny flecks on the white background. Then Anna came in white seeded silk, her brown hair braided in a heavy coil, and fastened in it a single white rose. It was a pity that no picture was taken of the flower-like bride and bridesmaids, but it was unheard of to delay a wedding dinner while picture after picture was made, as at a modern wedding where the intergroupings of in-laws with the bride and groom reach mathematical permutations and combinations.

The dining room was so large that the long tables had to be reset only three times. But children were never indulged by being fed early. We could be faint from hunger at any social gathering, and no notice would be taken of it.

When Ethel and I were set down at the very late table along with whatever other young or less important relatives were still on the waiting list, we looked around for the olives. We might have guessed it. Everyone had been eager to make the olives' acquaintance, and they had been eaten up long before our turn came. But we had a good-sized piece of the wedding fruit cake, and when years later I ate my first olive I felt I hadn't missed much at the wedding.

Anna lived in New England the rest of her life and became more New Englandish than a birthright New Englander. Eventually she dedicated herself to the welfare of the Republican Party. The one desirable quality that might have been added to Anna's list of virtues and accomplishments was humor, in which she was entirely lacking. But I have always thought she was fortunate not to be troubled with it, for otherwise she could not so have worshipped any political party or found all the political sins in the United States lodged firmly among the Democrats. Humor can be a great drawback to absolute judgments. As Anna did not know she was born without it, her oratory on the Republican Party was unmodified by any doubts.

Best of all was her happy love story. She and Cousin James were devoted as few people are. Except for his own lively sense of humor he might have found her severe principles wearing at times. But that never happened and they loved each other to the end.

The Banquet

OF ALL THE VENTURES that our church attempted, the banquets stood alone in novelty and success. They began in my middle childhood and went on during the first quarter of the twentieth century. The idea of having a banquet came from Franc Loomis. She had paid her regular January visit to her Unitarian cousins in Syracuse, and while with them had attended a banquet at their church and had been impressed by its elaboration and formality. Franc was a sturdy believer that city folks could do nothing that country folks couldn't do equally well, and she came home resolved that our church should have a banquet that matched the one in town.

So far as they existed at all for the Ladies Aid, banquets belonged to kings and conquerors in the Bible or to politicians retiring from office in our own time. How could a country church, whose members had never got closer to a banquet than seeing a picture of it in the paper, arrange and carry through something sumptuous enough to deserve the name? Franc was sure they could, and as president of the Ladies Aid she called a meeting at her house to discuss the matter. The meeting was largely attended for it was known that a banquet was to be talked over and decided on. Father had gone with Ethel to the city that day, so mother took me to the meeting under strict orders to sit quiet and not say a word. The big parlor was filled when we got there, but a stool by Aunt Sophy's chair was empty and I sat down on it in the safety of Aunt Sophy's nearness.

Franc described the Unitarian banquet, the decorations, the unusual food, the interesting speeches, and then went directly to the question: Why shouldn't our church have a banquet just as good or better? What did they think?

"It would be an awful lot of work," said Mrs. Wilcox, "and right in the dead of winter when there'd prob'ly be a big storm that night."

"There's one thing, though," said Mrs. Millen. "There's never been a banquet here before and there wouldn't be any comparisons to hurt our feelings."

"What would we charge for it?" Mrs. McKinley asked. "If everything has got to be so grand and so much to eat, seems as if we ought to get fifty cents a ticket."

The regular church supper of baked beans, cabbage salad, pie, and coffee cost ten cents. If ham and cake were added, the price rose to twenty-five cents.

"I don't believe we could sell any tickets at fifty cents," Mrs. Crampton objected. "That would be a dollar if there were two in the family, and folks couldn't afford it."

"I don't think fifty cents is too much," Mrs. Herrick protested. "We'd have to have oysters and mebbe olives and that kind of thing and they cost a lot."

"How many tables could we figure on?" inquired Mrs. Black.

Franc said, "Well, I thought we could get nine tables in with twelve at each table—five on a side and one at each end. At fifty cents that would give us fifty-four dollars, but we'd have to give free tickets to the speakers, so we couldn't count on over fifty dollars."

"Fifty cents isn't enough," Mrs. King declared. "If folks are willing to pay fifty cents, they'll go farther and pay sixty. That's only ten cents more and it would make a lot of difference with the expenses."

Sixty cents fitted so well with the whole dazzling plan of a banquet that it was decided to charge the higher price and run the risk of having nobody come.

The menu, as worked out from suggestions, rejections, and adoptions, represented all that anyone knew or hoped to know about suitable food for a banquet.

The supper (supper came easier to say than banquet) would start at seven-thirty with oyster soup and wafers, the new thin white oblong crackers that Franc said were being used now instead of the little round salty ones. With the soup would go celery, and then roast chicken, mashed potato and gravy, cold ham, squash, canned peas (Mr. Loomis would donate the peas from his canning factory supply), and they must have raised biscuit—they called them rolls in the city—and jelly and pickled beets and pickled peaches or some kind of preserve, and they would have to have salad. The Unitarians in the city had had raw apples and celery and walnut meats cut up together and covered with a dressing. They served it on a lettuce leaf and it was called Waldorf Salad. Aunt Elvie said she didn't think the menfolks would care much for raw apples and celery, but anyway it wouldn't be very expensive. Then to finish they would have ice cream, cake, and coffee. Mrs. Deo could be hired to make the ice cream if they furnished the materials. There would be so much other cooking that day no one could fuss with ice cream.

They would have to count on two chickens to a table besides the ham. Who would agree to bring chicken? Franc asked. In the enthusiasm of the moment, eighteen chickens were pledged by reliable workers, and Aunt Elvie said Uncle Alfred would give them a bushel of potatoes—or two if they needed them.

Mrs. Ward pointed out that there should be a hostess to receive the guests, with perhaps two or three assistants. She said that as she had had greater social experience than most of those present, she would be very glad to act as hostess. They would wear their best dresses and she thought white gloves would be proper. An instant outcry came from Mrs. Stearns. Mrs. Ward could be a hostess and receive if she wanted to, but the glove business would spoil the whole thing. Farmers would have all they could do to get their chores done and get cleaned up and be at the church by half-past seven. If anyone stuck out a white glove at them, they would feel embarrassed and out of place. The Ladies Aid sided with Mrs. Stearns. Gloves were out, but Mrs. Ward could dress up as grandly as she pleased.

Josie Rogers said she would wash any dishes that had to be washed. (A footnote in my mind says it's always interesting to see how different duties in churches gravitate toward certain people. The Mrs. Wards of all churches arrange the flowers on the tables and move among the guests. The Josie

Rogerses invariably are found in the kitchen washing miles of dishes.) Josie was a very faithful church member. She had little money, but much good will. Her husband was a commercial traveler and twice upon a time was likely to get drunk. Josie accepted his shortcomings and didn't in the least mind recounting her struggles to keep him sober. She held up the banquet preparations that afternoon long enough to tell what had happened the night before. When John had arrived home he was still able to walk and talk, but he was plainly under the Influence. Josie said she looked at him up and down and said, "John Rogers, you've been drinking again."

"No, Josie, no, Josie," John said, "I haven't touched a drop."

"John Rogers, you can't lie to me," Josie had threatened.

"But I *do,* Josie, I *do,*" said John.

The banquet so far determined upon, all difficulties were brushed aside. Each table was to have a hostess, or two, if two women would like to take a table together, as mother and Aunt Elvie did. The hostesses would bring their best tablecloths and best dishes and good silver, and their parlor lamps to help light up the church. They couldn't do much dishwashing at the church, but at the table the hostess could have a clothes basket into which the soiled dishes and silver could be slid after each course. The tables were narrow so that the tablecloths would come down near enough to the floor to hide the baskets. Everyone would be so hungry by that time of night there wouldn't be any food much left on the plates to scrape off, and they could put a piece of oil cloth in the bottom of the basket to prevent leakages.

By degrees the banquet reached the program stage. The

committee could not be expected to proceed unguided in arranging the climax of the evening, and they might as well settle on the speakers now. Our own minister would introduce them and act as chairman, though Franc said we must refer to him as the toastmaster. Aunt Sophy thought it would be only polite to invite the Presbyterian and Methodist ministers to come and ask the blessing and give the benediction. Mrs. Auburn said we ought to ask the school principal, who boarded with her, to talk on education. Mrs. Plant said education was an awful dull subject, but she supposed it was important and we might as well hear about it.

Mrs. Andrews reminded the ladies that the supervisor should be included. "He'll prob'ly talk on what a good town this is and how he's working to look after our interests. But then, he's young. We better limit them all to ten minutes. They'll run over, but at least we can tell 'em ten."

"This is a farming community, and we ought to have a farmer talk," Mrs. Scott suggested. "Do you think Mr. Loomis would speak?"

Franc considered. "Well, you know how pa is. If he talks it'll be about how we need a rural free delivery of mail instead of farmers having to go to the village after it—or else he'll say that we ought to start spelling corn and colt with a *k* instead of a *c*. But I'll tell him you want him, and I'll see that he keeps under ten minutes."

"It's always seemed strange to me," Mrs. Soule began, "that women never get put on the speaker's list at anything important. They do all the hard work and never get a chance at the show-off jobs. I think we ought to ask Nina Whiting to recite something. Everybody enjoys hearing her, and it would be kind of new to have a woman on the program at the first banquet in town."

Everyone did indeed like to hear Nina Whiting recite. She was darkly handsome and graceful, but her great gift was her voice—a voice that had a harp-like resonance so extraordinary that what she said had a way of changing into music. She would lend brightness to any program.

"That's four, besides the ministers," Mrs. Davey counted. "Now, girls, I've thought of something. I'm not sure we can manage it, but if we can, it would be wonderful. I saw in the paper that Congress has adjourned for a recess. Seems somebody's died or something's happened and it's going to take 'em quite a while to get over it. The paper said Mike Driscoll is home. If we asked him to come out and speak for us, I believe he'd do it and that would be worth the whole banquet."

A smile suddenly lighted every face. Mike Driscoll had been our congressman for many years. All the women talked at once, "The men would rather hear him than all the other speakers put together."

Mrs. Pardee succeeded in making herself heard. "He always starts the same way: 'Onondaga County is the Garden of Eden.' We all kinda look for him to say that, but he can't very well say it in the middle of February."

"You wait and see. He'll get it in some way," mother was sure.

Franc nodded in complete accord. "That's the best idea of the whole afternoon. I'm going to the city tomorrow and I'll go to his office and ask him. Now is there anything else anyone wants to bring up before we close?"

Mrs. Travers got up. "There *is* something. I've always wanted to know, and mebbe this is as good a chance to find out as I'll ever have. Just what *is* the difference between Unitarians and Universalists?"

Franc hesitated not a second. "Well, I guess the only real

difference is that the Unitarians have always looked down a little on us Universalists as poor relations."

Unlikely as it had seemed beforehand to the few doubters, the arrangements for the banquet went forward with the greatest smoothness. Mrs. Lawrence thought it looked as if the Lord intended the Universalists to have a banquet. The Presbyterian and Methodist ministers said it was most kind to want their humble services on so unique an occasion; the home-talent speakers accepted with obvious pleasure the invitation to be part of the program, time limit and all; and Mike Driscoll promised that neither rain nor hail nor snow should keep him from coming.

There was a great deal to be done. The men of the church, complaining very little, considering, carried the long pews up to the gallery, except for some placed around the sides of the church to hold wraps and furnish seats for those who arrived early. Then the tables were brought in and chairs borrowed from the G.A.R. lodge rooms and the Grange.

But think a minute of what the women had wished on themselves: first, long linen tablecloths and napkins to be freshly washed and ironed; the silver to be "rubbed off," as Aunt Elvie said; and the big parlor lamps trimmed and filled to last the evening through. The tables were set the day before the banquet, because on that day the women would all be busy cooking. No one feared the silver would be stolen or the china broken by remaining unguarded in the church overnight. Everything was left in readiness, and the Ladies Aid braced themselves to attack the supper problem. Nothing could be substituted, nothing done the quick and easy way. Every dish had to be created from the foundation up, and every woman was bent on proving that for once in her life she could meet the most exacting standards. Mrs. King assumed the responsibility of making the coffee and the oyster soup. Two big coffee urns were brought over from the hotel and put in the back of the church. Forty cups of water to a pound of coffee was the right proportion, Mrs. King said. In the front entry behind a screen, Mrs. Auburn's oil stove would keep the soup hot in the hotel kettles, and Mrs. Klosheim, who lived next door to the church, guaranteed that her kitchen stove and oven would preserve the chickens and gravy from getting the least bit cold. There was no faltering, no turning back, and extra food was constantly being added. Mr. Loomis announced that as long as he was going to speak, he'd send down one of his best cheese. Cheese had not been planned on because the dessert wasn't pie, but everybody liked cheese and it could be passed with the salad, and that would be something new too.

The tickets sold so quickly that many who wanted to come had to be told there wasn't a single seat left. The February weather, never too much inclined to make life easy for anybody, came forth with clear skies and mild temperatures so that packing things in sleighs and getting them to the church wasn't as difficult as it might have been.

The menu cards were not finished until the last minute, but were an artistic triumph. Franc had wanted them to be like those at the Unitarian banquet, and it had proved to be more work than the makers had bargained for. Square white cards were bought, and to each one was fastened half an empty walnut shell. Tiny holes had been bored in the shell and a pink ribbon threaded through to tie it to the card. Father and Mr. Klosheim, each possessed of a spectacular handwriting, wrote the place, date, and occasion on the card, and under that "All in a →" with an arrow pointing to the nutshell. Inside the shell was a little folded paper on which the menu was written. The nutmeats were used for the Waldorf Salad so there was no waste. Ethel and I were allowed to help fold the menus, and that was as near as we got to the banquet.

Mother consoled us by saying that she would remember every single thing about it and tell us the next day, and so she did. The church, she said, had never looked so beautiful as when they drove toward it and the lamplight shone out through the big windows. Mrs. Ward had supplied herself and her assistants with red carnations to wear to distinguish them from the non-receptionists, and they looked very pretty in mother's opinion. She did not dwell much on the supper except to say that everything was very good and plenty of it and people ate a lot and there were no delays and nobody's best dress had anything spilled on it.

For mother the high point of the evening was the program. First of all, the Methodist minister asked the blessing. Instead of reminding the Lord of much that presumably He knew already, the minister thanked God because he had seen on the scroll by the pulpit that Universalists believed in the brotherhood of man, as all good Christians should, and it was in the spirit of brotherhood that they were gathered together that night in unity and peace. And might God bless the food to their use and the speeches to their profit and all of them to His service. It was a real good blessing, mother thought, and pleased everybody.

The school principal told the audience that he was grateful for a chance to say something about the school. The library needed new books and the children had outgrown many of the seats and the school building ought to be open for meetings and not just for five school days a week and then shut through the long summer vacation. But in spite of crowded classes and other drawbacks, there wasn't a better school in the county or finer children or more helpful parents and he'd be glad to have them all visit the school and see for themselves. Not so dull as Mrs. Plant had prophesied.

The young supervisor kept within the time set and was proud, he said, to be there as a town official. He hoped they were satisfied with his efforts and would overlook any mistakes he made, for he wanted to do as well by the town as they had done by him.

"You know, he sounded quite *humble*," mother said.

Mr. Loomis did exactly as Franc had predicted. His rosy old face shone, his white chin whiskers and scant white hair quivered when he shook his head to emphasize that farmers must demand Rural Free Delivery of their mail from the government. They were as much entitled to it as folks in cities and towns. Not that he had anything against city and town folks—he liked 'em—but farmers ought to have their rights. And if they would all start spelling corn and colt and such words with a *k* instead of that silly *c* it would make it easier to read the farm papers. He sat down laughing.

When Nina Whiting finished her recitation there was a sort of sigh all over the church. Mother said it made her think of people warming their hands at a bright fire and then having the fire die down and go out. She had been beautiful to listen to.

Then, a little breathlessly and with every eye on him, the toastmaster said, "I have the privilege of presenting to you— the Honorable Michael Driscoll."

In the midst of welcoming applause Mike Driscoll got slowly to his feet. He was a tall, rangy Irishman with a shock of white hair and the blue eyes of his race—eyes that looked out on the world in such kindness that he had never made an enemy and all who knew him were his friends. His story was the American story—born poor and working tirelessly in summer and walking over rugged hills in winter to get an education. He had chosen the law as his profession and had entered politics, not to make money, for Mike was little better off than the farmers who listened to him, but to serve the country he loved in gratitude for the opportunity it had given him in his poverty and need. Staunch, trustworthy, incorruptible—that was the way men thought of him.

He stood a minute smiling at the faces turned toward him.

"As I've told you many times, Onondaga County is the Garden of Eden. Tonight it is Paradise after the first snow-fall. I look around, and there is hardly a man or woman in the church whose hand I have not shaken and whose farm or store or shop I have not visited, and each face is the face of a valued friend.

"It's a good many years I've been serving you in Washington, and God willing, there will be a few years more, but not too many. The wings of Time are over me. The service has never been a burden. I have had always your affection and your faith to strengthen me. No man could ask more. You have known how I voted on every measure and why, and if you have disagreed with me you have given me the benefit of the doubt. That is a wonderful support for any man who must make the choice of judging what is right and best for the country.

"Now I am going to talk to you a little about some bills that are before the Congress and will be debated after the recess. They are important bills and concern us all."

Mother didn't try to tell us about the bills; she said we wouldn't be interested, though Mr. Driscoll had explained them clearly and weighed the good and bad in them so carefully that everyone understood how they ought to be dealt with. But she said she would never forget the close of his speech.

He had looked around him, a kind of gathering-them-all-in look, and smiled again.

"There's a last thing I want to say. It has always warmed my heart and lightened it to be among you, and I have had tonight that sweetest of all feelings—that when I come to you, I have come home."

Everyone was very sober when Mr. Driscoll sat down and mother noticed that the young supervisor stared at him like a man seeing a vision. Then Mrs. Poole went to the organ and they sang *America* quite solemnly. The Presbyterian minister raised his hand in benediction, but all he said was, "Bless the Lord, O my soul, and forget not all His benefits."

Elocution and Plain Talk

THE YEARS of our growing up coincided with the last years of the Age of Elocution. Elocution was not yet dead; indeed outwardly from 1885 to 1900 it seemed vigorous enough to lead its admirers and practitioners to believe that it was established among the arts forever. Its tones and accents had affected every kind of speechmaking from sermons to political oratory, and its gestures ("leading from the wrist"— what *did* that mean?) were employed to bring grace and "naturalness" to the words of anyone suddenly called upon to act as chairman. Not being a people given as a whole to talking with our hands, we had been in a measure set free by elocution to talk with our fingers, always taking care that the eyes followed the gesture, as that insured that the eyes of the audience would follow ours. Who could have dreamed that by the turn of the century elocution would end neither with a bang nor a whimper, but with a snort and a giggle? Yet I am glad I lived while elocution was still thought well of.

From the young to the grey-haired, everyone spoke pieces with very little urging. It was a great help at Methodist and Presbyterian church socials to be able to fall back on this well of talent as a means of entertainment, since card playing and dancing were not permitted. A number of recitations and a few pieces on the piano bridged the dullness between supper time and going home. Perhaps it was because our community, like most country communities, was so shut away from the theater that elocution flourished mightily, and it did sometimes happen that the speaker's beauty of voice or utterance rewarded the listener by carrying him away from the social altogether. But that did not happen very often.

Why was a "funny" piece never taken seriously? Why was it never admired as tragedy was, rarely given a prize? For one thing, comedy was not thought to require any special skill. Anybody could speak a funny piece, but to produce tears and horror among the company—that demanded more than ordinary powers. The average man or woman would probably have preferred to laugh rather than to weep, but the latter emotion argued greater depth of character. Comic pieces also were often in dialect and that hampered the performer to whom Irish, Negro, or Jewish spelling and idiom were unfamiliar. Many things thought comic were not really so, but rather showed the ignorance or shortcomings of groups that farmers and villagers were inclined to look down upon, and there was often an unhumorous touch of superiority in their laughter.

The Methodists would not have dreamed of allowing a play to be acted in their sanctuary, but once upon a time in May madness they announced an elocutionary contest at the church with a first and second prize. Any number could enter. I had just finished learning for my own pleasure Will Carleton's "Death Bridge of the Tay," a poem not far short of three yards long and concerned with a terrible train accident that had taken place in Scotland some years before. A great new bridge had just been completed across the Tay River and a train loaded with notables, officials, guests, sightseers, and humble folks was to make its first triumphant crossing. When the train was halfway out, the bridge gave way and the train dropped into the river below. All aboard were lost. The accident was dramatic enough to attract writers in much the same way as the sinking of the *Titanic,* disaster striking at what had seemed the highest moment of triumph and safety. Mr. Carleton told the tragic story well, and I asked mother if I might speak the piece at the Methodist Church.

Mother said, "Well, if you want to. I think the piece is too long, but I've noticed that people like to hear about somebody's getting killed."

So when the evening came, father, mother, Ethel, and I departed for the church. Ethel mourned that she had no piece ready; father said one piece in the family was enough. The village had packed itself into the church and father gave my name to the man who was checking the speakers. I wished with all my heart that I had not been so eager to show off my long piece, but I didn't dare say so after the man had written my name down on his paper.

A curious custom prevailed everywhere among amateur elocutionists. This was the time of long hair—the longer the better—and grown women did not appear in public except with their hair securely fastened in place by many stout hairpins. To have your hair down your back before people partook a little of being undressed. However, this rule did not apply to the performing arts. The hair hanging to the waist was part of the scenic background against which the elocutionist's tale was told. On this night I noticed Mary Andrews in particular. Mary was a pretty, young married woman, and she had chosen a piece about a mother driven insane by her drunken husband's cruelty and the loss of her child. She wandered about the stage shrieking and pleading and in the end was taken away to a madhouse. An uncomfortable piece to watch, but Mary went through it nobly. Her long light brown hair encompassed her so that she could retreat behind it or peer through it and stare wildly at the other candidates sitting in the front pew.

Other scenes of horror followed and formed a pattern into which the "Death Bridge" fitted exactly. Then the judges clustered together to confer and at length the chairman detached himself from the rest and came to the front with his paper. He cleared his throat as silence passed over the audience. I knew he was going to say poor Mad Mary had won the first prize, for nothing so curdling to the blood as her recitation had been heard that evening. To the astonishment of everybody, the first prize went to Mel Hamilton. Mel's full name was Melancthon after a classics-loving grandfather, but the chairman fortunately didn't know it. Mel was a tall boy who had spoken quietly about an old man recalling his youth. No outcries, no gestures, no movements back and forth. He looked surprised to receive the book held out to him, the judge complimented him and the audience applauded. Surely Mary would get the second prize. I was looking anxiously toward her when the chairman called my name. The "Death Bridge" had won the second prize. I am sure the audience thought that Mary should at least have had that, but I went forward and took the book the judge gave me and got back to my seat, miserably aware that no one thought I deserved it except Ethel. When we got home, father wrote my name in the book and the date, May 22, 1896.

But the laurels of elocution were not to be left withering. The summer of 1896 the Presbyterians had a young minister. Like the Universalists, they were likely to have young, unmarried students, from the nearby Presbyterian seminary at Auburn. But this young man was from Kansas. He had been ordained and had come east for experience. He had worked in the Kansas wheatfields and was so dark from the harvest suns that at first glance he looked foreign. But Mr. Mason was a man of good sense and all Aunt Alice's Class of Young Ladies admired him very much. It was Mr. Mason who persuaded the Presbyterian elders to hold another elocutionary contest. This was to be no ordinary one-night affair. It was to last *two* nights, open to the town, and was to be a very polished form of entertainment. The elders agreed with Mr. Mason's plans and word of it went abroad, so that in a short time everybody was talking about the double contest.

None of our group had decided whether we would enter the contest or, if we did, what selection we would choose. The date set was still a month away when one afternoon someone knocked at our front door. Ethel opened it and there stood Mr. Mason, dark and smiling, and carrying a bundle of books.

"I've come to arrange about your training for the elocutionary contest," he said. *Well.* There was no use in our saying we hadn't made up our minds to speak. Mr. Mason disposed of arguments and objections as lightly as if he were lifting sheaves of wheat, and before we had caught our breath, he had our full and true names set down in his little black book, our probable choice of subject (*his* choice!) recorded and the hours each week when he would come to train us. He must have gone through the neighborhood like a Kansas cyclone, for by the end of the afternoon he had settled schedules for our cousins Ray and Blaine, Burke Hamilton (Mel refused to take part again), Helen Millen, and Mabel Mitchell. No one except Mel escaped the net. We accepted our fate and set to work on our pieces. Learning the pieces was nothing; but the voice—the gesture . . .

Mr. Mason had fixed upon "Lasca" for me. I liked it quite well, but I could not meet Mr. Mason's demands that I convey how untamed Lasca was. He seized upon the lines:

> She was as wild as the breezes that blow;
> She was as bold as the billows that beat—

With unhampered breeze-like movements of my hands I was to indicate Lasca's complete freedom from restraint. The next line Mr. Mason beat out like a drum measure to suggest the billows striking the shore and the boldness of Lasca. Mr. Mason thought I could easily get the thought to the audience. I didn't think so.

Ethel and I heard each other practice and sat through the full training period and absorbed Mr. Mason's interpretations, though we did not always agree with them. In addition, father, who rather fancied himself as a drill master, would listen to us occasionally and give us his ideas on emphasis and expression. We resolved that on The Night we would recite our pieces as we thought best—taking courage from Lasca's boldness.

There had been no difficulty in finding speakers enough for a two-night program. We drew numbers which determined which night we were to appear, and for perfect fairness and honesty, the judges were to come from out of town. All this and more Mr. Mason had looked after. The Presbyterian Church was decorated with flowers and flags for as festive an occasion as it had ever witnessed. Ethel was wearing a dark blue cotton dress with a white yoke and in her belt she had tucked a bunch of deep red velvety nasturtiums. Whether they enjoyed her piece or not, the audience was sure to enjoy looking at her. My dress was a white muslin and I had a bouquet of heliotrope, sweet, but a dull color for evening. And so the contest began.

The selections would have been unbelievable to anyone who had not lived through the period. Those I remember best were the ones spoken by our own neighborhood group. Burke Hamilton had drawn the number one place on the first night and had the knee-shaking privilege of getting the contest off to a good start. He was a freckled, shy boy who had been unjustly condemned to deal with the "Death of Little Eva." In a hoarse voice he began, "Eva after this declined rapidly," and in the same queer voice, dropping lower and lower as Eva declined more and more, he almost whispered her out of the world. Mabel Mitchell fought a terrible fire on a cold bleak night, with a screaming mother freezing in the snow below while her child perished in the flames above in spite of the firemen's efforts. Ray came to grips with "The Pilot's Story," related by the pilot on a Mississippi steamboat. It concerned a beautiful young slave girl who

plunged to her death in the river when told by her master that he had sold her to a trader. My wild and bold Lasca died saving her lover from a cattle stampede—saved him, but was trampled to death in Texas down by the Rio Grande.

The death toll mounted with every speaker. Then came Ethel and the "Deathbed of Benedict Arnold"—three pages of printed prose full of poignant remorse and wild regrets and a burst of love for his country—all in a dying voice.

The White Ribbon-ers of the Women's Christian Temperance Union were strongly Presbyterian, and the evils of intemperance could not be passed over in any contest sponsored by them. Bernice Nash therefore recited "College Oil Cans." Two young college students bought two cans of oil daily for their study lamps. But the awful truth was that only one can held oil; the other was filled with strong drink. In a short time the two young men became drunkards and died in the throes of delirium, aptly and heartbreakingly rendered as a warning to any young man present. Not a single piece had a light moment except Blaine's. Because he was only ten years old and the youngest of the contestants, Mr. Mason had decided on "Little Orphant Annie" for him. The only flaw in Blaine's recital was that in one place he hesitated and repeated a line, but he did the poem so well that his forgetfulness did not seem important.

At the end of the second night there was keen speculation as to who would get the prizes, a ten-dollar gold piece, a five-dollar gold piece, and two dollars and fifty cents in everyday money—and an honorable mention for a runner-up. Twenty-five candidates to consider. Mr. Mason, who had managed getting us up and down the pulpit steps and had interspersed songs and organ music among the dead and dying, now congratulated the speakers on their fine work and the audience on the opportunity to listen to their gifted young friends. He promised that the words First *Annual* Contest meant that there would be another such event next year to which they were all invited. His speech closed as the judges signaled that they had reached a decision, and one of them came slowly down the aisle and went up into the pulpit. After a few general remarks on how brilliantly all the speakers had acquitted themselves and what a tribute to Reverend Mason's training the affair was, the judge pronounced sentence. The first prize went to Ethel, the second to the Oil Cans, the third to Cousin Ray, and the honorable mention to me. Then he called Blaine to come to the front, and we all thought the judges had invented some extra prize for him. Instead the judge informed him that he would have had a prize, probably the third, if he had not forgotten a line. Better luck next year!

The judge undoubtedly meant this postscript as a kindness and a consolation, but it seemed only humiliating to the child who had expected something different. He did not cry, but his face was puckered with disappointment when he went back to his seat. Aunt Kate was very much upset. It was generally felt and said that too many prizes went to one family, although it was agreed that Ethel had honestly won her gold piece.

In spite of Mr. Mason's announcement, there was never another elocutionary contest held in the town. Mr. Mason returned to Kansas and we saw him no more, and elocution drew its last deep breath.

Everyday speech among us was not self-conscious. It had a straight descent from New England and was scarcely tinged by foreign contacts. The use of slang as it came along fresh from the lips of the knowing was held to be bad because it probably had a bad meaning; but bad grammar in itself was either not recognized or thought of small importance compared to making yourself understood. What proved to be important later on was that the English idiom retained its essential form. A child might someday have to unlearn bad grammar, but he would not have to unlearn words and speechways alien to the English tongue. Yet words that we used and the way we said things were often curiously unlike what is said and heard today.

The changes made in words by shifting a letter from one position to another were usually in the interest of greater ease in saying them. All my aunts and uncles referred to the Adirondack Mountains as the "A-*dri*-ondacks" and were quite unaware that they had performed a transfer operation on the mountains' name. When the Spanish-speaking alfalfa clover began to be discussed and raised around here, Uncle Alfred accepted it as "al-*al*-fa"—and so it continued all his life. "Astosbestos" rolled out more rhythmically than simple "asbestos," and those who said it believed they had mastered a new and difficult word and were marked men among their fellows, for once upon a time "asbestos," with or without lengthening, was a very new word indeed.

All the Indian geographical names that ended in *i*, and they are many, were always pronounced with the sound of *y*. We said the "Big Missour*y*" without question. I have noticed a tendency in public speakers today, when they have occasion to lay hold of an *i* word, to treat it as if it ended in *a*. We hear "Missour*a*" and the like spoken confidently—and to the annoyance of the *y* sayers. Surely it is not wrong to improve one's speech, but this particular pronunciation has its pathetic side. It is obviously an attempt to avoid being classed with the hickories who said "Californy." We would no more have said "Missour*a*" than we would have said "Mississipp*a*."

The letter *a* on our tongues was neither the broad *a* of New England nor yet the flat *a* of the Middle West. Most of us growing up admired the broad *a* and would have liked to speak of our aunts with the same freedom that we pronounced the *a* in father. But we dared not attempt it. In moments of crisis we knew we would fall back to our medium *a* and be exposed as putting on airs when our native airs and *a*'s were not good enough for us.

Old forms of words and old uses stayed on. "Boughten" was constantly applied to store clothes at a time when most clothes were still homemade. We did not speak of coats, hats, or shoes as boughten; they were understood to be beyond the home stage of production. But boughten dresses were not much admired nor thought to be of as good quality as material bought by the yard. Bread too, if bought at the store, was never boughten. There was just one name to call the sour pasty stuff some housewives fed their families, and that was "baker's bread."

In the Moulton family "virtue" had no relation to or association with chastity. It meant always the special power or strength or value that something had. If a bottle of medicine or a plant had no virtue, that meant that it had ceased to have the particular quality that had made it of use. A maiden was never said to have lost her virtue; instead she lost her character.

"Beholden" was still known and heard in my youth. It is a choice old word, full of grace and gratitude from Shakespeare's England and its significance is as attractive as its sound. For to be beholden to someone was to acknowledge that you owed him obligation and affection. "Indebted" has no such meaning. How could it have when the harsh suggestion of debt is in it?

Words often were changed into similar ones without destroying their meaning, but with a twist toward the comic. We know now that jaundice is a disease to be taken seriously. In our town jaundice was "janders" and when janders turned a man yellow it was thought rather amusing. It was odd that janders never seemed to attack the well-to-do, the respectable, and the able. It fixed on the lowly and was suspected of being an indirect result of drinking and an ill-spent life.

Squash grew in everybody's garden, but "squash" was not what you did when you met a noxious bug on the path. You "squushed" it. You squushed bugs and flies and worms and mosquitoes if you could. And nothing ever squushed like squush.

There were many words that were held to be improper for a woman to use. One was "bull." A genteel lady of refined speech and feeling said "animal" if she had a bull in her thoughts. Many a farmer kept an "animal," and if you were unfamiliar with Victorian standards you might have been led astray into thinking that he had a bear or a wildcat caged on his farm. But the lady knew that he had a bull, and since she could not always refer to a bull in a roundabout way as the father of the herd, she said she hoped Mr. Hitchcock had his animal shut up.

"Belly" too was high on the blacklist. The children in our school were frequently taken with bad "stomachaches" and the pain was quite far south of the stomach, but we would have blushed to locate it more accurately. We were taught carefully that "belly" was a forbidden word and we grew up with a repugnance toward it that never left us. Yet "belly" has a better literary history than "stomach." The King James men did not feel obliged to picture Eve's serpent slithering along on its stomach, nor Jonah embedded in the stomach of the whale. They must have been coarse men.

There was a redundancy in at least one term. Children who went to school were called "school-scholars." There was no other kind of scholar in town, but "school-scholar" was so generally said that we never thought of it as queer. When a group of school-scholars came along the road in the morning we joined them, for we were school-scholars too. The term has a swinging sound, like the children's dinner pails as they walked or ran.

Extracted honey was unknown to us. From Miss Angelia Means we bought white clover comb honey in a square wooden box frame. This was called a "cap" of honey and you asked for as many caps as you wanted. I never dreamed that this term was unknown beyond our borders until I was away at school and once tried to buy a cap of honey. The storekeeper had no idea what I wanted. It was a home word.

"Lot" was a multifaceted word in constant use. "Lot" was destiny and "lot" was a field assigned to a special purpose or crop and "lot" was a portion of something or even the whole consignment. All these were noun uses and did not trouble us. But lot as a verb was quite different. Old Mrs. Ottman always "lotted" on going to the Sunday school picnic: she looked forward to it with high anticipation and pleasure. And Bill Johnson had "lotted" on Matilda Harris from boyhood, but, alas, Matilda did not "lot" on him. So "lot" as a verb could make the future look bright and "lot" could also mean to be deeply in love. "Love" was not a word to be lightly spoken and "lot" took its place.

"Wool" and "worsted" were undifferentiated in our vocabulary, with "worsted" more commonly used. We spoke of having a new "worsted" dress, not a "wool" one, and if not all woolen cloth was worsted we did not know it. And we said "woolen" rather than "wool" in reference to stockings and petticoats, perhaps because it balanced better than the brief "wool." But today "wool" has conquered and if we asked in a store to see a worsted dress, there would have to be an explanation.

Of all the expressions perfectly clear to us but without sense for an outsider "pull down" was the oddest. "Pull down" was applied to the act of taking down dresses or aprons from the nail or peg where they hung. "That's the third apron you've pulled down this week," mother would say in reproof. I have never heard the expression outside the Moulton family.

Decent women never used oaths and had any child taken the Lord's name in vain, soap and water would have been his instant portion. Of baser "barn talk" we heard nothing. Whatever the men might say among themselves, the lady-of-the-house (she was still called that) and the children were spared any foulness.

Like our mother, Ethel and I found new words fascinating and never let one pass unnoticed or untried. Ethel started reading newspapers as soon as she could read anything, and one day she said to father, "It says here that two battle lions have been sent to the relief of the town. What are battle lions?" Father took the paper and Ethel pointed to the word.

"That word is battalions," he said. "It's a body of troops in an army, not a new kind of lion."

Once when she was quite young he took her with him to the Farmers' Fair held at the Parker House. It included a dance and Ethel was invited to dance by an elderly young man—and was much impressed by him. It seems he was taking a short winter course at Cornell University. Ethel duly reported on him the next morning. "He must be very smart. He's studying orthography and gauging."

Father cast one of his looks at her. "Yes, it's a heavy course," he said. "Orthography is spelling and gauging is measuring the contents of a cask or barrel. That's what he's studying—spelling and how to measure barrels."

My own pronunciation of new words I kept to myself, quite satisfied with the way they sounded. In church on Sunday, we often sang "Rock of Ages, Cleft for Me." I did not bother to look in the hymnbook for the words. I learned by singing and my "Rock of Ages, Clever Me" was swallowed up in the general noise of the congregation, and what they sang sounded exactly like that. A hymn I liked even better was "Crown Him Lord of All," a shouting hymn, and the line I dwelt on was

> Bring forth the royal-doyal-dem
> And crown Him Lord of all!

The royal-doyal-dem that was to go on the King's head! I felt deprived of a treasure when it became merely a royal diadem.

Misunderstandings of sound that go uncorrected by not seeing the stumbling block in print are common with children who delight in words, and they scatter their improved versions, however far from the original they may be. One of the drawbacks of the Little Red Schoolhouse was that teachers passed on to us their own interpretations of the dictionary. It took us years to get rid of "des*pi*cable."

I should like to believe that language has improved. I cannot be sure it has, even in grammar. The vocabularies of ordinary people seem to me more limited and more given to clichés than those I grew up with, and speech consequently is slovenly and inaccurate because the necessary words are wanting. Old-fashioned talk had a directness and a vividness not often heard in common speech today. Homely words produced humor and drama and were a foundation on which could be raised eloquence and beauty.

Father

WELL IN THE FOREFRONT of our lives was the continuous discussion of politics. Few children in a countryside remote from the larger concerns of government can have heard so much as we did of political terms and political methods seeping down from the top to the local level. We knew what all the words meant: issues, delegate, chairman, committeeman, candidate, caucus, nomination, ballot, and election. The supervisor was the most important town official. Since father's heart was set on being supervisor or nothing, the process of getting himself nominated and elected was familiar to us and exciting.

There were nineteen towns in the county and nineteen wards in the city, and at that time the supervisors from both towns and wards met as a Board in Syracuse for six or eight weeks in the winter to debate business and settle affairs that affected the whole county. The town supervisors were always vigilant lest the city men get the upper hand in appropriations and tax rates, and the city supervisors were equally on guard against the towns. The Board was heavily Republican, but country versus city made it possible for a stray Democratic supervisor to attach himself to whichever side of the opposition promised the best deal for his ward.

In our thoroughly Republican town the nomination might or might not produce a fight. If only one candidate sought the office, all was simple to arrange and he could await the election returns in calmness. If several candidates came forward, competition could become severe. Anyone, of course, could declare himself a candidate unless his modesty preferred to have his friends tell the voters why Caesar deserved their love. The town's fourteen school districts elected delegates to the nominating caucus, the number varying from one to three, depending on the size of the district and the number of voters. The candidate visited each district and sounded out the principal men in it until he could be sure of three or four who promised to support him unflinchingly and to get themselves named as delegates to the caucus. The meeting for choosing delegates was held close to the date of the caucus so that time for meditation would not lead to a change of heart or a harder bargain. A voice vote was taken and if a man went back on his word, everybody knew it and could report it. The caucus was a minuscule convention and open to all party members to watch. If the strategy had been well worked out, the result was certain. The caucus too voted by voice, and a majority of the delegates from the school districts secured the nomination, which was then made unanimous.

All this planning and conniving and riding around and whispering in the dark suited father, and he won tidily over his rivals. If he was not loved, he was admired for what he had accomplished and for his insight into hard matters like taxes. The average farmer knew only too well what tax was demanded of him, for taxes, aside from school taxes, were laid solely on real property, that is, land; and a farm could not be hidden. But he had a very dim idea as to why taxes kept rising and where the money went. The taxes paid then seem tiny today and yet proportionate to the farmer's income they were burdensomely large. Father was elected for two successive terms—four years in all—to wrestle with the tax rate, get what appropriations he could for the road improvement, and in general defend the country folks against city encroachments.

He did well by the town and by himself too. For one thing, as a county supervisor he sold his entire potato crop to the county penitentiary for a good round sum. Nobody looked askance at the transaction. Like a government contract today, selling to the county was acceptable in the scheme of things. The prisoners had to have potatoes, and father's potatoes were good.

The penitentiary at this time was within the city. On one potato delivery father took me with him. The lumber wagon was piled high with filled sacks and father and I rode on the backless seat in front. When we reached the penitentiary, he left me in the wagon while he went inside the building to get men to unload the potatoes. The building looked very big, and there were bars across the windows and no trees or flowers at all. Presently some men came out. They were wearing suits with stripes running around the body, zebra-like. Father had told me that men in prison were dressed like this, but it was terrifying to see, and I wished that father would come back. The men were doubtless those under light sentences and trusted, and they set to work at once in a quiet, orderly fashion and were as well behaved as the hired men at home. Still I was glad when the last sack of potatoes was carried away and these stripe-suited men were no longer moving about the wagon. It is good that prison garments have been changed, at least in our state. The theory was that the striped clothes made escape less likely. But the stripes in themselves were a sign of disgrace constantly before the eyes of men who had little to encourage improvement in behavior or character.

It was while father was supervisor that the violent objections to having the penitentiary inside the city, in a place where prisoners could neither exercise nor work, reached a height that compelled the Board of Supervisors to do something about it. They agreed that the city was no place for the penitentiary, and they voted to build a new one somewhere outside Syracuse in a suitable situation. Father was a country member of the committee to select the site and get the building constructed. He found it an agreeable assignment. It required many journeys to highly improbable places which nonetheless had to be considered in order to deal fairly with each town, though not all the towns clamored for a penitentiary in their midst. Then too, the recently designed prisons in other parts of the state had to be inspected so that the Onondaga County plant should be thoroughly modern and include the latest ideas on prison sanitation and the health of the inmates—at the lowest possible cost.

The Commissioner of Police in New York City was no less a person than Theodore Roosevelt, his feet just planted on the ladder to fame. What could be more helpful to the committee, more likely to throw light on the dark places in their minds, than a trip to New York to interview Mr. Roosevelt? They could get his views on crime and prisons and do a little sight-seeing on the side. Father had never been to New York and neither had the voters who elected him, and he was proud to go in his official capacity.

The committee had a memorable week. Father never said much about what they learned or what they saw of New York's wonders. He came home so full of praise for Theodore Roosevelt that everything else was secondary. The magic of the Roosevelt personality had cast a spell over his country visitors that made them his men forever. He had taken pains to give them hours out of his crowded day; he had discussed prisons with them in ways they had never thought of; and he had suggested that making plans for helping the prisoners was as important as planning the new building. Above all, he had met them with such friendliness and had established such a sense of fellowship with them that they wished nothing more than to vote for him for any office he wanted. When Roosevelt became governor and later president, father felt it to be a confirmation of his own judgment and rejoiced exceedingly. No later deviation of Roosevelt from Republican ideology altered father's opinion. His hero-worship was untinged by criticism.

The penitentiary was eventually built at Jamesville, where the prisoners could work in the limestone quarries and plant gardens that would help their diet. For aught I know, the supervisors still, as in father's time, make a yearly pilgrimage there and eat bread baked in the prison ovens. Perhaps they, like father, take home a loaf to prove that the prisoners are pretty well fed.

When out of office father kept busy behind the scenes.

343

There was the handling of the political funds to think about. These funds were set aside by the party for the purpose of getting their candidates elected. If an election was likely to be close, a good deal of money would be apportioned to the town; if it was a sure thing, the purse strings were drawn tighter. No one inquired particularly where the contributions came from: the important thing was how much money the Republican party of the town received and how it was paid out. The price of a vote—to put it in the harshest terms —was one dollar. But of course it was not put in the harshest terms. The dollar some voters got was in theory merely the payment for their loss of a day's wages, since they spent the day in the village. The dollar usually ended up in the saloon.

The only voting place for the whole town was then in Cicero village, and the voters had to be carried there if they had no horses of their own. The men hired to draw voters were paid whatever the committee decided to give them. The job was regarded as easy money for faithful party workers. The town committee—father was usually on it—went to Syracuse a month before election for a talk with the boss and for the town's share of the election money. It would be pleasant to think that political bosses belonged solely to the bad old days of Tammany Hall and never to the green pastures and open-eyed daisies of upstate New York. But political bosses exist wherever elections take place. In Syracuse Mr. Hendricks was a Republican boss and so was Mr. Belden and there were others—besides Democratic bosses whose names were never mentioned. The bosses rarely wanted office for themselves; the true sense of power derived from the manipulation of men and votes. They knew the make-up of every town committee and called each man by his first name, but the committee called them Mr. Hendricks or Mr. Belden. Later when a committeeman was back home and relating the events of the day to his wife, the version might be, "Hendricks says to me, 'Bill, you have the right idea!' " In simple fact the bosses were managers, and if there was to be an election someone had to manage it.

The committee brought back the money, ranging from several hundred dollars to a trifling seventy-five—the sum determined by the boss's judgment of the outlook—and this was divided among the committee members. Whatever money was left after paying drivers and voters remained in the hands of any committeeman who had been economical in his distribution. It was frequently charged that some of the members kept too much in their own pockets, but unless the election went wrong the bosses did not ask questions. It was not easy to check, and faith was necessary when accounting was impossible.

The dollar-a-vote men were scattered all over the town, though the largest group lived by Oneida Lake and were known as fish pirates. The game laws were loosely enforced and these men got their living chiefly by catching fish and selling them in and out of season. No one thought much less of them for it. Fish by nature were made to be caught and eaten, and besides, the game warden was fond of giving fish parties for his friends. The pirates had big families, a few had poor little farms, and some "worked out" if a job came their way. Getting a dollar for their vote was like finding money on the sidewalk. Their consciences were clear, for the election was by ballot and when the moment came they could vote for anyone they pleased. But in general they gave an honest return for their dollar. They voted, they drank, they enjoyed the holiday, and they felt they had a part in governing the country.

My fondest political memory is of the visit of Judge Hiscock. He was a candidate for judge in one of the high courts of the state and was a little anxious over his chance of success. Republican strength lay in the country, but country voters paid scant attention to electing judges except the justice of the peace in their own town. They never expected to be haled into the superior courts and would have been as puzzled to name one of the judges there as to name the lieutenant governor. As a result of their disinterest, they regularly passed over the list of nominees for judge altogether. The Democratic voters in cities were better instructed on the importance of friendly courts and seldom failed to mark their ballots for the correct choice. So the Republican candidate for judge could lose by default while at the same election a Republican governor might triumph. This was the situation that worried Judge Hiscock and made him feel it was necessary to go out into the country and get acquainted. He planned to start with our town. Father admired him very much and either offered or was asked to go with him and introduce him to the farmers. They arranged to spend a day electioneering; the judge was to have dinner at our house; and if the town couldn't be covered and converted in one day he was to spend the night with us.

Then began preparations. I think mother dreaded the visit a little. The Hiscocks were a distinguished family, and mother felt shy about entertaining such company. Father decreed that fried chicken and apple pie would be the best dinner, and since mother could manage both excellently, father's mind was at peace. Mother got the spare bedroom ready with everything she could think of for the guest's convenience. The rag carpet was bright and new; through the white muslin curtains at the window was a view of meadow and orchard; the walnut bed was comfortable; and the marble-topped washstand held a decorated china bowl and a pitcher of water and was supplied with many towels. We thought it a beautiful room and loved its sloping ceiling that our heads almost touched. We hoped the judge would admire it as much as we did.

The day arrived and with it Judge Hiscock. He came into the yard driving a spirited team of dapple-grey horses. We could not have imagined that horses could be so handsome, so shining, so intelligent of eye—matching their beauty to the carriage and the driver. For Judge Hiscock was handsome too, beyond any man we had ever seen, though his had a different kind of good looks from most faces. We were not in the least afraid of him, and we stood with father in our best starched ginghams while the judge got out and fastened the horses. Father praised them, and Ethel found courage to ask their names. A horse without a name was awkward to talk about. The one nearest us, the judge said, was Zuleika. We had never heard of any horse with such a splendid name, and it was exactly right for the sleek creature it belonged to. The other horse was named, I think, Zenobia. Certainly Zenobia was the perfect name to go with Zuleika—so perfect in fact that I am half afraid invention has helped out memory. Zenobia was a familiar name to us. We knew all about her from our Fifth Reader and were in the habit of reciting "Zenobia's Defense," beginning "I am charged with pride and ambition. The charge is true and I glory in its truth." Zenobia was telling the Romans that she was the Queen of

Palmyra and aspired to be Queen of the East. There was no better name for any horse proud in its strength and aspiring to outdistance all others on the road.

Father and Judge Hiscock set out for their interviews and returned at noon for the fried chicken and apple pie. Mother's fears vanished. She was charmed by the judge's good looks, good manners, and good conversation. The judge declared fried chicken was one of his favorite foods, and there was no pie like an apple pie—and how delicious mother's pie was!

In the afternoon the electioneering continued. The farmers were delighted with the judge and his horses and promised that they would not forget to mark his name on the ballot and would remind slack voters to do likewise and not to stay at home if it rained. A rainy election day was always called a Democrat day since the Democrats in cities could go to the polls easily, while Republican farmers found the mud-deep roads discouraging to duty.

The outcome looked so assured to the judge that he decided to return home that night and not, as he said, put mother to any more trouble for him. But mother would have been very willing to be troubled to have him stay. Ethel and I thought it was too bad he wasn't going to see the nice room mother had fixed for him.

All went well for our candidate. He was elected and for many years truly graced the highest courts of New York State. We never forgot the cloudless pleasure Judge Hiscock's visit gave to us, and Zuleika and Zenobia were an inseparable part of it.

Votes for Women

As I LOOK BACK at the changes made in my lifetime to fit our laws to a changing world, the most remarkable of all in its far-reaching effects, so it seems to me, was embodied in the nineteenth amendment to the Constitution. This is the amendment which gave women the right to vote and ended a bloodless warfare fought without musketry or barricades. When the men of the United States granted the franchise to women, not as a gift, but as an act of justice, they were bearing witness to the long, slowly developing revolution that had taken place in their minds and in the minds of women. It is still astonishing that the law was enacted, for it was in opposition to habits, customs, fears, social theories, and the age-old belief in the natural inferiority of women.

I am struck too by the repetition in the attitude of those who see in every change a source of peril. The road followed has always been the same; first an enraged outcry against the measure proposed: next a stony resistance; then a snail-moving acceptance; and at last as the new becomes the old and a part of our way of thinking, those who did not live in the time of the struggle wonder why there was so much excitement over it.

The calm after the storm is the result of being able to see how the change has worked out—a quite different matter from the thunder and lightning of prophecy.

Out of our knowledge of the way elections were won and voters influenced, it came about that Ethel and I began to think women should have some share in politics besides listening and observing. The gap between mother's generation and ours was clearly shown in our increasing interest in votes for women. The Seneca Falls Suffrage Convention of 1848 had been held before mother was born, but the views expressed by those women and the demands they made had awakened no response that reached us in our childhood. The women we knew did not care about getting the vote. To them voting was as unimaginable as going to the moon; the idea could be mentioned, laughed at, and forgotten.

Much earlier there had been a famous suffragist in the town, but her work had not been done here. Down the road half a mile away from our house stood a classic white-pillared mansion where once Doctor Joslyn had lived. He had been one of the first physicians in Onondaga County, and his daughter Matilda was an eloquent speaker for Women's Rights. She had married and lived in Fayetteville and was long dead before we knew her name. Then when I was about ten, her niece, Mrs. Baxter, a friend of mother's age, entered our lives, and it was through her that Aunt Matilda Joslyn Gage became real to us. Mrs. Baxter was a gifted actress on the New York stage who spent her summers at her father's farm near us. She was a suffragist by inheritance, inclination, and experience, and she quoted Aunt Matilda's opinions to us and dwelt lovingly on her epitaph. Aunt Matilda had wished her convictions to be carried beyond the grave, and she had ordered carved upon her tombstone her summing-up of life's values for women:

> *There is a word sweeter*
> *Than Mother, Home, or Heaven—*
> *That word is Liberty*

It is easy to guess that Aunt Matilda's pleas for liberty had been met by references to woman's proper sphere. And her epitaph shocked all who read it. Aunt Matilda's husband did not choose to be buried beside her in the shadow of her Fourth of July Declaration. If a woman preferred a vote to heaven, well, Uncle Harry was definitely for heaven and he took no chances that the epitaph was off the record. But Aunt Matilda left no legacy of enthusiasm for her sentiments in our town and only Mrs. Baxter ever spoke of her.

Country women working in their own homes or helping their husbands on the farm did not see the need of the power and protection the vote could give as did women who worked in shops and factories. City women recognized what it would mean for them to have legal control of their children, their own earnings, and their share of family property. By themselves they could do little to achieve it. Education, some leisure, and self-sacrifice were required and no reform goes forward without finances.

As the end of the century approached, however, the talk of women's suffrage grew more frequent and more intelligent and had a sharper edge. Converts appeared constantly among the young and ardent, and men laughed a little less patronizingly. Mother said that as a matter of justice, women who paid taxes should vote, and that as a matter of common sense there was no reason to doubt that a woman would cast her vote with as much judgment as a man. To that point mother's years of looking on at politics had brought her, but there she stopped.

Besides those who thought votes for women too ridiculous to warrant attention, there were others who saw the matter as a threat to womanhood and a danger to the American home. (How ancient that sounds!) They honestly believed no good could come of it.

One sign of the times was that hoary jokes on "sufferage" were revived and repeated. The men's favorite was "Believe in women's sufferage? Of course I do. Let 'em suffer—we men have to!" In an argument this remark was considered both funny and final. The women countered in their turn: "If there's one job the men can do without getting us to do it for 'em, for heaven's sake let's let 'em keep the vote!"

Yet Aunt Matilda's faith kept spreading and at least the fringe of her mantle fell on Ethel. By the time Ethel was twenty she was committed to the cause and never wavered in her devotion to it. She could believe nothing halfway and to be a lukewarm suffragist she would have had to deny her nature. Her sense of responsibility was bolstered by her pride as a woman. Marriage left her views unchanged. One experience of hers, commonplace enough in the country, served to set a seal upon her mind.

She had not been long married, and she and Myron were living on a farm some three miles from the village. Myron was working in Syracuse; he had to leave early and did not get back till supper time. They had a hired man to take care of the horse and cow and look after things generally. This man was from the fish pirate group. His name was Jim Downey and, along with the heart of gold that goes with piracy, Jim had an unquenchable thirst. He was not stupid except when blind drunk; when far enough away from the saloon he was faithful, kind, and likable. He had grown up under the dollar-a-vote system and thought of it—if he thought at all—as an instance of the providential care extended to the less fortunate.

Election day was at hand and someone was coming in the morning to carry Jim to the village to vote. Voters like Jim were not re-delivered, and Myron warned Ethel that she had better go after Jim by four o'clock so that he could do the chores before dark. At four o'clock therefore Ethel harnessed the horse and started, resenting the errand, and expecting the worst of Jim's day of grace. She drove up and down the village street looking at the knots of men, but there was no sign of Jim. Finally she stopped and inquired of a man if he knew where Jim Downey was. The man shuffled a little and said, "I guess mebbe you better go back to the saloon. Jim was there when I left a few minutes ago."

Ethel turned round and drove up in front of the saloon and asked one of the men nearby to tell the saloonkeeper she wanted to speak to him. Mr. Murkey came out most agreeably to learn what the lady wanted.

Ethel said, "I want Jim Downey. I want you to send him out here and put him in the carriage if he's sober enough to ride."

Mr. Murkey said he would be happy to oblige her. Presently out came Jim supported by two companions and delighted to see Ethel and the horse so that he wouldn't have

to walk back to the farm. As soon as he was settled in the carriage, Jim said, "You know, Mis' Ames, I thought about that cow not three minutes before you got here. I was jus' gonna start back."

Ethel did not answer, but she told me that all the way home she kept getting madder and madder. Here was this ignorant drunken man who could sell his vote and squander the money on whiskey, while she, an intelligent woman, a taxpayer and wanting her country's good, had no part in the election except to transport him after he had registered a vote that had no relation to anything except his reward.

Jim stumbled through the chores and brought in the milk. "Mis' Ames," he said, lurching to the kitchen window, "will you come here and look down my throat?" Ethel went over to him, wondering what he could have done to himself, and with considerable distaste and not too closely, she stared down into the cavernous mouth and throat.

"Wha' do you see, Mis' Ames?" Jim asked anxiously.

"I don't see anything," said Ethel without sympathy.

"Mis' Ames, if you'd looked hard you'd see a little farm an' a team of horses an' three good cows—they've all gone down my throat. I've swallowed 'em all because I'm a mis'ble drunk. They ain't got no right to sell the stuff to us poor fellers!" Jim sobbed for his losses and the sins of saloonkeepers.

Ethel sent him supperless to bed. One of the mysteries was where Jim and his friends got their drinks on election day. The law forbade the sale of liquor until the polls had closed. Someone must have been thoughtful enough to provide beforehand against the drought.

Jim's brother Bart, whose pattern of life conformed to

Jim's, once made an effort toward redemption and acted out
a sort of morality play by himself. In a soberish interval he
confided his intention to his neighbors. They were gathered
by the lake when Bart, ragged, dirty, and unhappy, announced that he was going to stop drinking for good and
all—he was going to drown himself. Everybody laughed
as Bart started out into the lake and they heard him talking
to himself like a Voice from Heaven:

"Bart, you're nuthin' but a good-for-nuthin' drunk. You
never did anything for anybody—not a thing. You jus' get
drunk. Nobody cares whether you live or die. I'm gonna
drown you. Yessir, that's what you deserve and what you're
gonna get. I'm gonna drown you."

The men said that while he was talking he kept walking
farther and farther into the water until it was almost up to
his armpits. They began to be alarmed and to think that they
had better go and pull him out.

All of a sudden Bart stopped and faced about. He stood
still a minute and then said in the same loud voice, "Bart,
you poor ole cuss, I been thinking about your case. You ain't
much—like I told you; but you ain't so bad, and I'm gonna
give you another chance. Yessir, you're gonna have another
chance!" And with that, Bart waded back to shore.

The sequel to Bart's second chance was sad. Election was
over and Bart had celebrated by a particularly satisfactory
spree. Then he disappeared. No one knew where he had
gone, and Mr. Murkey and his patrons missed him and
wondered about him. In the spring some men working in
the swamp found him. He had sat down on a little mound
and leaned against a tree. The freezing swamp water and
the bitter cold had been too much for him. Or perhaps Bart
had decided that he didn't deserve another chance.

It was voters like Jim and Bart that lent substance to the demand for women's right to vote. It was drunkards such as they were that spurred the prohibition movement. They were men not lacking in goodness of heart but without the power to control a habit made easy by the sale of liquor everywhere. The work for women's suffrage and temperance went hand in hand—until suffrage was obtained and drinking moved out of the saloon into a more elegant atmosphere.

Even if suffrage had not at last won a victory, the women who worked for it would have found the effort worthwhile. Along with the work went an enlargement of mind as they learned of the laws concerning women that existed in other countries and in their own. The meekest American woman could be counted on to be rebellious over the fact that in one state in the Union a woman could not legally claim her engagement ring as her personal property. Their sympathies were stretched with their minds, and working together for a common purpose revealed to them that differing backgrounds need not preclude union of spirit.

Ethel went on fighting the good fight and refused to be classed with criminals and idiots as unworthy or incapable of voting. She argued and pleaded and marched in parades till her feet were swollen, and I followed her example as well as I could because I believed as she did. This was not a temporary obsession. We felt deeply and talked lengthily about the suffrage question in and out of season and must often have annoyed women who cared nothing about voting. Indeed, the women were likely to say, "Oh, don't begin on that again!"

Our cousin Grace, who agreed with our opinions in a mild way but disliked argument, thought our efforts to rouse the indifferent were carried too far. Yet when suffrage came, the women who had neither worked for it nor believed in it were the very first to run for office. They may have done so because they thought it safer for the town to have their assistance in governing instead of entrusting public affairs to radicals like the former suffragists.

But working for the vote was not all or even mostly discouragement and anger. The first women suffragists had to endure insult and abuse which the later sisterhood escaped. If some of the mockery from the sidelines in street or lecture hall was unpleasant, more of it was good-natured and merry.

Men were seldom disturbed by Ethel's oratory though they sometimes turned her arguments against her. When Myron was with an engineering party in the Northwest, a skunk began stealing Ethel's chickens. She set a trap and the skunk promptly got himself caught. Ethel did not dare to go near the trap and had no wish to dispose of the skunk personally. She went across the road and asked her neighbor Mr. Stone to come over and take care of the creature. Mr. Stone shook his head.

"Now, Ethel," he said, "you believe women should vote and have the same rights men have. That means you have a perfect right to kill your own skunk. That's real equality. You ought to get a plank in your platform that says you demand the vote and the privilege of killing any skunk that belongs to you."

But he went back with her and attended to the skunk, and I have no doubt that when the time came, Mr. Stone voted to give the franchise to Ethel. His suggestion was not incorporated in the suffragist platform.

Once in my early teaching it happened that no other teacher in the school cared about the vote problem. My history class faced the necessity of tracing the course of human rights down the ages and through the pages, and I called attention to rights that were sure to be gained in the future. Inevitably the subject of women's suffrage took over. The girls were a little doubtful but had the foundation for belief before them in the history book. The boys performed memory feats reciting what their fathers and uncles had said on the subject.

The day before the Christmas vacation a committee of boys came to my room with what was unmistakably a Christmas present carefully wrapped and tied. They ranged themselves in a circle around the desk. "Open it," they said. It was all too plain that things were not as solemn as the boys' faces were. I untied the ribbons and unwrapped the "Merry Christmas" paper and opened the box. Inside it was a pin, a gold-edged shield of white enamel and on it in gold lettering, "Votes for Women." I wore it all the term.

Last Caucus

EARLY IN THE NEW century, father had left home permanently and gone back to the old farm to live. He had once
told me that he had always wanted to be a gypsy and eat
under a tree. He did not become a gypsy; instead he took
up his residence in the parlor of the farmhouse. From it the
regulation parlor bedroom opened, and father kept house
in this suite and got his own meals or ate with the family
working the farm. In the years that followed, he suffered
two or three slight strokes which impaired his memory and
made his speech hesitant, though intelligible. The memory
of his successful supervisorship had never quite died out, and
father's interest in politics remained—dimmed, but still
there.

The financial affairs of the town continued to be snarled.
Farm prices went to new depths and taxes at the other end
of the seesaw rose higher. The various supervisors were not
to blame for the difficulties, and yet in the need of the public
to find someone at fault, the supervisors were judged un-

equal to the job of keeping taxes down where they had been in the golden days.

The minds of voters in a democracy often converge on men and measures so surprising that one can only be astonished at what is done and speculate on the motives that led to it. As election time approached, we heard with dismay that the Republicans were planning to nominate *father* for supervisor, the nomination almost certain to lead to election. What could they be thinking of, we wondered. All the town was aware that in his condition father could hardly manage his own affairs. What could the party gain through him and how dared they persuade him to undertake a responsibility for which anyone could see he was unfit? But the rumors persisted.

That fall too was to bring the last caucus of delegates chosen from the school districts. Except for three townships —ours was one of them—the state had gradually adopted a different process of nomination, and next year the new system would go into effect in the three towns that had clung to the ways of their great-grandfathers.

Ethel and I went to the caucus, hoping that at the last minute the local politicians had changed their minds or that father had not given in to their arguments. The meeting was held in the Odd Fellows Hall, and the big room was full. Undoubtedly many were there to see how this curious nomination would work out. It was also their last chance to attend an old-fashioned open caucus before the town moved into a new political world and with a leader so changed since his earlier service.

The delegates sat in a circle as always; the chairman presided as always; and the voice vote of the delegates went as smoothly as it had always done. Delegate after delegate stood up and named father as his choice until the nomination was made unanimous. Everything was just as it had always been —except father. He kept looking anxiously at the delegates as if he were trying to understand what it was all about.

When the voting closed, the crowd called for a speech. The poor candidate stumbled to his feet and hesitated. Then with a great effort the words came: "I thank you, gentlemen, I thank you very much," and he sat down. His daughters did not cry, though they wanted to. Our thoughts about the Republican Party were not pleasant.

The election answered the party's expectations and ours: father was elected and trouble began as soon as he took office. Supervisors then made out the tax rolls and dealt with all expenditures. Once it had been father's boast that nothing in the mathematics of taxes was too much for him, but in the twenty-six years since he had been in office a multitude of complicated taxes and services had come into existence, and father could not find his way through the columns of figures.

One of the things that ought to give us faith in life, as Mrs. Joyce had urged, is the arrival of blessings that cannot be anticipated. Bill Fundy was a heavy, rosy-faced man, plain of speech and manner, and had anyone ever called him a blessing, Bill would have taken it as a joke. He was the highway commissioner of the town and that was a very responsible job in our climate of snowy winters. It meant close association with the supervisor, for the men working on the roads were town employees and the machines used were town property whose care and replacement were serious matters. Bill Fundy was as kind as he was honest, and during the year father was supervisor, Bill carried the burden. He found the mistakes in father's figures and cheerfully corrected them; he explained what new laws accounted for unfamiliar items; and he did it all without the slightest impatience or any attitude of talking down to the old man.

I used to go to the farm on Saturday afternoons, and Bill Fundy was often there poring over the town books, carefully checking and adding and examining every detail so that there would be no errors in father's work. But as the months went by, father worried badly. He knew that the figures grew more tangled week by week, and he was not able to straighten them. One afternoon while Bill was working, and father and I had been keeping quiet so as not to bother him, father said suddenly, "Bill, I can't go on with this—I don't know how to do it—I can't do it right any more."

Bill laid down his pencil. I think he had been hoping for something of the sort and had wanted the suggestion to come from father himself.

He said in his kind voice, "Well, it really is pretty hard for you, isn't it? Everything so different. I've noticed how it worries you. It isn't good for you to get so excited about it."

"But what can I do?" father faltered. "What can I do, Bill? They put me in and I can't do the work."

"You can resign," Bill said offhandedly, as if resigning were the most natural thing in the world. "Just say you find it takes too much of your time and you aren't as young as you used to be and you want to be rid of the worry of it."

I added my encouragement to Bill's recommendation. Father looked from me to Bill and from Bill to me. At last he said, "Bill, will you tell 'em—to get someone else?"

"Of course I will," said Bill. "Don't you give it another thought. I'll tell the town board and they can appoint somebody and you won't have to do a thing."

It worked out as Bill said. For a little while, his anxiety removed, father seemed better. But from things he said it was clear that the hurt of failure did not leave his mind.

He died in the spring on Good Friday and was buried on Easter morning. The sky was dark and overhung with heavy clouds and snow lay deep everywhere. The saddest part about mourning for him was to know that father's life, once so highly accomplishing and successful, had fallen into unloving hands and in the end had been unhappy and unrewarding. Redeem Israel, O God, out of all his troubles.

It is time to stop. Out of the past the faces and the tales that belonged to them have risen in my mind and gone again. The Greeks held the belief that the dead when thought of could be summoned back to momentary consciousness and would press to the fatal river to get in touch once more with life—only to disappear in darkness. So it is with our summoning of time forever gone. The return is too brief to satisfy the heart. Is it strange that we should try so hard to make immortal our mortal loves?